THE
HUMANITIES
AS
SOCIOLOGY

MERRILL SOCIOLOGY SERIES

Under the editorship of

Richard L. Simpson

University of North Carolina, Chapel Hill

and

Paul E. Mott

THE
HUMANITIES
AS
SOCIOLOGY

An Introductory Reader

Edited by

Marcello Truzzi
New College

Charles E. Merrill Publishing Company
A Bell & Howell Company
Columbus, Ohio

For Elias Smith

Published by
Charles E. Merrill Publishing Company
A Bell & Howell Company
Columbus, Ohio 43216

ISBN: 0-675-09043-1

Library of Congress Catalog Card Number: 72-87426

1   2   3   4   5   6   7   8   /   78   77   76   75   74   73

Printed in the United States of America

CONTENTS

v

Introduction

The classification of sociology among the sciences versus its membership in the humanities has been hotly debated. Both sociology and the humanities center their attention on Man and his cultural products, and several philosophical positions (especially those stressing free will and indeterminism in the human order) would deny the possibility of any strictly positivistic analysis of Man as fruitful. For these reasons, many critics and a few sociologists would classify sociology as a member of the humanities.[1] Neither a solution to nor a critical analysis of this debate will be attempted here.[2] Rather, it is suggested that at least a part of this debate has resulted from the demands of some highly positivistically oriented sociologists, whose emphasis has been on the maximally empirical, that we ignore largely classical and "journalistic" attempts to describe and explain the social world. They argue that since these works — interesting though they might be as literature, etc. — do not meet the rigorous requirements of a scientific sociology, they may be ignored (except of course, as sources of empirical data themselves in the sociology of literature[3]). Thus, much of contemporary sociology has developed for the most part ignoring or rejecting literary and artistic endeavors to explain the social world, and with this rejection of such sources as presenting a valid picture of reality, there also has been a rejection of them as sources of insight. Nonetheless, many persons who have contemplated society have been more impressed by some of these humanistic insights than by the limited fruits thus far gained through the approach of extreme positivism, and this has led them to assert the superiority of the "older humanism" over the newer "scientific approach."

1

Such a debate between "narrow empiricism" and "classical human-ism" is unfortunate since it forces most sociologists—who usually see points of validity in both positions—into a false polarity. For, as some philosophers of science have argued, we may actually be dealing with two separate problems. The origination of insights and hypotheses about society is a problem in the *logic of discovery*, whereas the actual testing of such insights and hypotheses to deter-mine their truth value is a problem in the *logic of validation*. If, as Popper has claimed,[4] and is largely accepted by many contemporary philosophers of science, there is no simple logic of discovery, one can look anywhere for one's initial ideas about society, whether it be in the writings of historians or literary figures, the paintings or sculp-tures of visual artists, or even the mechanisms of a Ouija board. There are no clearly formulated rules for the most efficient develop-ment of creative insights—though many have attempted to study such penetrating cognitions[5]—and there is no reason to suppose that hypotheses about the human order might not best be found in what are usually not considered to be scientific sources. It is here that the humanities clearly can serve the interests of a truly scientific soci-ology.

Most of these humanistic writings, however, are not phrased with the intent of having their statements about Man submitted to a pro-cess of scientific validation. In fact, the writers of these works usually present their insights as if they had already been validated, depending upon the reader's empathetic acceptance of their reality. Such dog-matic presentation, however, is impossible for those of scientific mentality, and this, too, has probably led to some sociologists' es-trangement from what might have been potentially valuable sources of hypotheses. What is needed, therefore, is a clear statement of such insights in the form of hypotheses about social reality and not as dogmatic "arm chair" assertions.

The readings in this anthology represent attempts of sociologists to extract from such insightful works those items and propositions about Man which can be incorporated into a scientific and empirical process of validation and theory construction. It is hoped that by thus incor-porating a diversity of sources into our attempts at discovery, it will be possible to increase the likelihood of our ultimately obtaining a rigorously validated science of social relationships.

In an attempt to broaden the conceptual base of sociology to include the insights of the humanities, I am espousing a form of *humanistic sociology*. However, this term has included a mixture of orientations within social science. Edmund Mokrzycki has recently argued that there are two different forms of humanistic sociology present in the current literature using that name.[6] First, there are those who contrast *humanistic* with *technical* sociology. The former is seen as emphasizing what C. Wright Mills called *sociological imagination.* This form of sociological knowledge "shapes human attitudes and opinions, is a source of social orientations, helps comprehension of vital social issues, stimulates thinking and develops imagination," whereas the latter is "the base of social engineering, is used as an instrument of efficient social action, and provides recommendations for handling, or, as it is said derogatorily, manipulating human being."[7] The basic issue raised in this New Sociology[8] revolves around the question of the place of values in social science research.[9] This form of humanistic sociology is really centrally concerned with the problem of humanitarian versus nonhumanitarian *uses* of sociological knowledge.

This form of humanistic sociology is often confused with a second orientation which centers about the methodological issue of whether or not the *social* (what Florian Znaniecki called the *cultural*) *sciences* can successfully adopt the methods of the *natural sciences.*[10] These humanistic sociologists would argue that the sympathetic process of subjective understanding (what Max Weber called *verstehen*) that is possible in the examination of social phenomena but not for the natural phenomena of the physicist is central to the methods of the social sciences. There are varied positions taken by these humanistic sociologists. Some see the naturalistic approach to social data as impossible or distorting; others see it as merely limited in its fruitfulness. Some argue that subjective understanding is a necessary part of the conceptualization process for the sociologist or that it merely has heuristic value; whereas others argue that it is part of the validational process itself in the social sciences. But all of these humanistic sociologists argue for the need of subjective understanding as a basic part of the sociological method.

A third form of *humanistic sociology* is possible, however, and that is the position taken in the production of this collection. I would argue that the importance for sociology of the kind of "soft" knowledge and insights often present in the humanities does not depend upon such philosophic issues. The simple reality is that sociology is still an infant science in terms of its theoretical development.[11] As Robert Merton has argued: "perhaps sociology is not yet ready for its Einstein because it has not yet found its Kepler — to say nothing of Newton, Laplace, Gibbs, Maxwell, or Planck."[12]

Unlike the natural sciences, there is no true paradigm for investigating or seeing reality in sociology.[13] Thus, the sociologist is not theoretically directed towards the study of any special set of social phenomena as the next logical and needed step to advance the *major* direction of the discipline. Research problems are still largely defined by social rather than strictly theoretical considerations (including political and economic "pressures" but largely based on the folkways of the discipline which determine what is to be considered "mainstream" and what is to be "marginal" or "subterranean" research). In fact, I would be inclined to argue that one can find *some* existing "theory" to cover almost any research approach or hypothesis to be tested anywhere in sociology; problems and research interests are often found first and legitimated second, as most doctoral dissertations in sociology might demonstrate. Many, if not most, philosophers of science would argue that sociology contains no universal, law-like propositions (at least not yet), and that there is therefore no true theory in sociology at all (in the sense that theory exists in physics).

This state of affairs should make sociologists anxious to seek insight that might generate such law-like statements anywhere there might be a potential for it. In fact, our failure to generate such propositions internally should make us look more seriously at the progress of our neighbors in the humanities. This openness and receptivity to ideas, whatever their source, while fully recognizing the necessity to validate them through the objective and precise tools of science, is what is being argued for here. Finally, and more pessimistically, it should be noted that even if the propositions which the sociologist can extract from the humanities turn out to be no better than those we have generated internally, within sociology itself, these works will often enhance our subjective understanding of the social world. And even if such subjective understanding is neither necessary nor sufficient for explanation in social science, it does augment our total view of man. And the "soft knowledge" such subjective understanding gives us is certainly better than no "hard" knowledge at all.[14]

Thus, we are arguing for the practical uses of humanistic insight for the social sciences, however limited that might be. In searching for insights among the humanities, all its forms, including purely visual products such as painting and sculpture, can be seized upon for inspiration. Any reading of current art criticism quickly displays the possibilities of verbalizing insights about social life from nonverbal cultural products. However, any translation into sociological hypotheses is most simply and clearly done from an examination of literature. And it is with literature that the articles in this collection are primarily interested.

It is important to realize that we are concerned here not with what is usually termed the Sociology of Literature. Our interest is not primarily with the social causes or consequences of literature. Nor are we concerned strictly with the pedagogical values in having sociology students' reading literature in so far as that can, as Porterfield[15] has argued, (1) illuminate important sociological concepts, (2) enliven teaching through the crossing of departmental barriers, and (3) link sociological subject matter to the needs of the student. The authors of the following articles express some interest in these problems and functions, but our primary concern in this volume will be with litera- ture *as* sociology rather than with the sociology of literature or with the pedagogical use of literature for sociology.

The papers in this collection represent a first step in this direction. The papers developed quite independently of one another and are linked here only by this general theme. They are not presented with more than a generally chronological organization. Some of the papers represent essentially positivistic stances by their authors, others take quite different approaches. The shared element here is simply in be- lieving that the ideas of the various figures in the humanities which each examines say things that are and should be significant to sociolo- gists. And in so doing, it is implicitly argued that there should be more examination of thinkers in the humanities by sociologists who might gain something from their study.

While the primary emphasis here is on the uses of literature for the sociologist, it is also hoped that students of literature will find value in our explorations of their domain for its sociological insight and accu- racy. Many have bemoaned the separation of science and the humani- ties into what C.P. Snow called the Two Cultures. Partially through the presence of this collection, I hope that sociology can more fully carry out its role as the bridge between them.

NOTES

1. See, for example: "Sociology as a Humanistic Discipline," in Peter L. Berger, *Invitation to Sociology: A Humanistic Perspective* (New York: Doubleday Anchor Books, 1963), pp. 164-76.

2. For an excellent survey succinctly stating some of these problems, see: Richard Rudner, *Philosophy of Social Science* (Englewood Cliffs, New Jersey: Prentice-Hall, 1966), especially chapter 4, "On the Objectivity of Social Science," pp. 68-83. For two contrasting views, see: Peter Winch, *The Idea of Social Science* (New York: Humani- ties Press, 1958); and George Lundberg, *Foundations of Sociology* (New York: Mac- millan, 1939). For a recent statement of some of the issues, see: Daya Krishna, "On the Distinction Between the Natural Sciences, the Social Sciences, and the Humani- ties," *International Social Science Journal* 16 (1964): 513-23.

3. E.g., see: Leo Lowenthal, *Literature, Popular Culture, and Society* (Englewood Cliffs, New Jersey: Prentice-Hall, 1961).

4. Karl R. Popper, *The Logic of Scientific Discovery* (New York: Science Editions, Inc., 1961).

5. E.g., see: Calvin W. Taylor and Frank Barron, eds., *Scientific Creativity: Its Recognition and Development* (New York:Wiley, 1963). For an excellent demonstra- tion of the diverse sources and conditions of creation, see: Brewster Ghiselin, ed., *The Creative Process: A Symposium* (New York: New American Library, 1955).

6. Edmund Mokrzycki, "Two Concepts of Humanistic Sociology," *The Polish Sociological Bulletin* 20 (1969): 32-47.

7. *Ibid.*, p. 33.

8. Cf. Irving L. Horowitz, ed., *The New Sociology* (New York: Oxford University Press, 1964).

9. For a critique of this form of humanistic sociology, see: J.H. Robb, "The New Sociology: A Critique," *Australian and New Zealand Journal of Sociology* 4 (1968): 78-90.

10. This form of humanistic sociology would include such major sociologists as W. Dilthey, M. Weber, W. Sombart, R.M. MacIver, C.H. Cooley, F. Znaniecki, and P.R. Sorokin. Many contemporary symbolic interactionist and phenomenologically oriented social psychologists would fall into this camp. For a description of the beginnings of this perspective in sociology, see: Floyd N. House, "Die Verstehende Soziologie," chapter 35 in his *The Development of Sociology* (New York:McGraw Hill, 1936), pp. 393-402.

11. Cf. Norman W. Storer, "The Hard Sciences and the Soft," *Bulletin of the Medical Library Association* 55 (1967): 75-84.

12. Robert K. Merton, *On Theoretical Sociology* (New York: Free Press, 1967), p. 47.

13. For an excellent discussion of this matter, see: J.J. Smolicz, "Paradigms and Models: A Comparison of Intellectual Frameworks in Natural Sciences and Sociology," *Australian and New Zealand Journal of Sociology* 6 (1970): 100-119.

14. This position has been well argued by Abraham Maslow in his *The Psychology of Science* (Chicago: Henry Regnery Gateway Edition, 1969).

15. Austin L. Porterfield, "Some Uses of Literature in Teaching Sociology," *Sociology and Social Research* 41 (1957): 421-26.

ROBERT REDFIELD

1

Social Science Among the Humanities

Robert Redfield (1897-1958), primarily known as an anthropologist,[1] but one who received his graduate training in the sociology department at the University of Chicago,[2] was the dean of the social science division there between 1934 and 1946 and the Robert Maynard Hutchins distinguished service professor in 1953. Redfield is best known among sociologists as a student of social change. In this field he developed a theoretical continuum between *folk* and *urban* societies based upon differences in the relative size, isolation, and homogeneity of the communities which he studied that were at different points on this conceptual scale. However, towards the end of his life, he became increasingly interested in the relations between the social sciences and the humanities.

At the time of Redfield's writings, he was often labelled a "humanistic" sociologist because he concerned himself with the total reality of human experience and did not wish to limit sociology to a narrower analytic science in which the admitted need for objectivity and precision might lead one to be blind to existential realities. The following essay reflects his emphasis upon the need for openness to all the sources of insight available to the student of social life.

NOTES

1. Redfield's major works include: *Tepoztlán, a Mexican Village: A Study of Folk Life* (1930); *Chan Kom: A Maya Village* (with Villa Rojas in 1934); *The Folk Culture of Yucatan* (1941); *A Village That Chose Progress: Chan Kom Revisited* (1950); *The Primitive World and Its Transformations* (1957); *The Little Community: Viewpoints for the Study of a Human Whole* (1955); *Peasant Society and Culture: An Anthropological Approach to Civilization* (1956); and his collected papers which appeared as *Human Nature and the Study of Society* (1962) and *The Social Uses of Social Science* (1963)
2. Redfield received his Ph.D. in 1928, but a separate department of anthropology did not form at the University of Chicago until 1930.

SOCIAL SCIENCE AMONG THE HUMANITIES*

The social sciences occupy uneasy seats at the American feast of learning between the physical and biological sciences on their right and the humanities on their left. Sociology and political science hold the center, and do not often make formal connection with either group of neighbors. On the right, psychology is uncertain whether to emphasize its associations with biology or with social science, and geography makes a link between other studies of mankind and other earth-sciences. History and archaeology, often claimed by both groups between which we imagine them to sit, have their places immediately to the left of the other social sciences and connect them with the scholars of literature and the arts. And anthropology, a far-reaching claimant of territory of interest, will be found in one chair or another along the entire row. It sends representatives to the Social Science Research Council; it is seated with biologists and astronomers in the National Research Council; and it also has membership in the third of the three great academic federations, the American Council of Learned Societies, where it takes part in the work of the students of arts and literatures.

This distribution of seats does not produce a well-balanced conversational arrangement. On the whole social scientists in America have

---

*Reprinted from *Measure: A Critical Journal* 1, Winter 1950.:62-74, by permission of the publisher.

turned a rather cold shoulder to the scholars of the humanities who sit on their left hand, as the "natural" scientists on the whole have turned a not very warm shoulder on them. In part these attitudes express the hierarchy of status that exists among the disciplines. Like other differences of kind between human societies, those between disciplines tend to be regarded as superiority and inferiority. Certain sciences are "harder" than others, and so better. The "hardness" may have somehow to do with the intellectual difficulty of the discipline, or the mathematical character of the work. The prestige of economists as compared with some other social scientists appears to be so derived. But the "hardness" which goes with superior status also has something to do with the subject matter of the discipline: physical or biological subject matter is appropriate to a "harder" science. Anthropologists and psychologists, marginal biologists both, are joined together in one of the sections of the American Association for the Advancement of Science, and do well there; but the section or sections in which other social scientists are grouped have little importance and low status. As for the students of art and literature, they are of course unrepresented in the Association. The rough generalization which emerges is that nobody concerned with human beings, as such, is felt to belong to the company of scientists. Only anthropologists, of the social scientists, are admitted to Sigma Xi, presumably because they have something to do with skulls; their interest in the attitudes and sentiments of men may be overlooked. These facts suggest a sort of antipathy felt to exist between the subject matter, humanity, and the method, science.

In Germany the social sciences and the humanities are often thought of as belonging together and the word *Geisteswissenschaften* then includes them both. In England common origins of the humanistic studies and the social sciences in the study of the classical cultures are not forgotten. But in America the social scientists have for the most part urged only their likeness to the "natural" sciences. Whatever the physicists and chemists think of them, they think of themselves as similar to physicists and chemists. The claim of kinship, or even identity, is made by showing that the methods of the social scientists are the same as the methods of other scientists. It is declared that the social scientists describe — which is true; they have nothing to do with values — which is untrue. The social scientists have developed the use of questionnaires, tables, measurements and statistics. The building in which are housed the social sciences at the University of Chicago bears over its doorway a text from Lord Kelvin to the effect that knowledge that can't be measured is meager and unsatisfactory. A social scientist put that text there. It has sometimes appeared that in order to succeed the social sciences would have to become as much like physics as possible, and even that they were succeeding.

The comparison of the social sciences with the natural sciences exclusively, and with the natural sciences in terms of the similarity of method, goes on so frequently and is made so competently that there is no necessity to repeat it here. Two recent treatments of the theme, one by Lewis White Beck ("The 'Natural Science Ideal' in the Social Sciences," *The Scientific Monthly*, LXVIII [June, 1949], 386-94), and the other by Donald G. Marquis ("Scientific Methodology in Human Relations," *Proceedings of the American Philosophical Society*, LXXXXII, [No. 6, December, 1948], 411-16) show us that in their ways of formulating problems and solving them there are only differences in degree between the two kinds of sciences. Both writers are impressed with the similarity of the methods of the social sciences to those of the natural sciences, and both look forward confidently to a development of the social sciences in which the guiding example of the natural sciences will continue to be helpful.

Emulation of the natural sciences, and emphasis on formal method, brought about the differentiation of the social sciences from other kinds of thinking and investigating out of which they grew. The detachment of psychology from philosophy by way of the laboratory, and the development of the social survey into the more precise methods that sociologists now have for studying communities, are examples of this development. The striving to make knowledge systematic and comprehensive is a good thing. And that social scientists teach their students how to perform such controlled observation and rigorous analysis as are represented in sampling and other statistical techniques, in the construction of questionnaires and tests, in the marginal analysis used in economics, and in the construction of indices showing the position of individuals in social classes, is not to be deplored. Every form of knowledge may become as precise and systematic as the application of its methods to its matter makes possible.

On the other hand, as Professor Beck says while himself illustrating the truth of his remark, it is fashionable nowadays to underestimate the differences between the social sciences and the natural sciences. In America at least, the emphasis on formal method and the imitation of the physical and biological sciences has proceeded to a point where the fullest development of social science is hampered. The emphasis on formal method sometimes carries the social scientist into exercises in which something not very important is done very well. There sometimes appears in the use of statistical methods in psychology or anthropology or sociology an exercise of the intellect in which nothing very much is found out about human beings or societies. The knowledge is measured; yet it is somehow meager and unsatisfactory.

The identification with the natural sciences alone shelters the contemporary American social scientist from a stimulation from philosophy and the arts and literature which social science needs. Partly because of this the sense of problem in American social science has diminished. Because small matters can be precisely done, large matters are left unconsidered. American political science has departed so far from philosophy that now in many departments of the subject central problems as to justice, or as to the relations of the individual and the state, get little attention. Anthropology, a science currently enjoying success in many fields of enquiry, has almost nothing considered to say as to the nature of human nature. And psychology, as Sidney Olivier complained, having named itself the science of the soul, substituted the study of behavior—which is another thing.

The stimulation which the social sciences can gain from the humanities can come from the arts and literatures themselves, and through an understanding of some of the problems which interest philosophers and the more imaginative students of the creative productions of mankind. It is not argued here that the humanities have ways of studying mankind which social scientists should adopt. It is not denied that many academic students of Chaucer or of the French language emphasize the mastery of formal method to a degree that they too are shut away from the humanity of man and from consideration of the important questions about man. Pedantry and formalism are weaknesses of humanistic learning as of social science. What is here asserted is that the arts and literatures of the world are sources of understanding of man in society from which social scientists may enrich their insights and their sense of problem. It is also asserted that among the professional humanists are many whose work is so similar to that of many social scientists in spirit and purpose as to suggest that some deliberate cultivation of their common interests, now that the scientific character of the social sciences is well established, would enrich and improve the work of both. Let the social scientists turn and talk for a time to their neighbors on their left.

What shall they find to talk about? What have they in common?

The answer is simple. They have humanity in common. Humanity is the common subject matter of those who look at men as they are represented in books or in works of art, and of those who look at men as they appear in institutions and in directly visible action. It is the central and essential matter of interest to social scientist and humanist alike. As physics is concerned with energy and matter, and biology with organisms and life processes, so social science is concerned with the way men and women feel and act and think. Allowing for the fact that there is an aspect of humanity which may be understood when it is seen as a part of all animal life, it is the more important fact that the human qualities of our kind are so notably distinct as to provide a special terrain for systematic enquiry. In this field the humanist and the social scientist work together—in Montaigne's day there was no separation. If, in grouping the academic disciplines, emphasis were given today to subject matter rather than to method, the social sciences and the humanities would be one group, distinct from the other sciences. For the humanity of man is not the concern of physicists or biologists; it is the subject matter of these two other kinds of specialists, now too firmly kept apart.

Humanity is the central subject matter of social scientist and humanist as it is the central interest of mankind. As human beings, we care about the human nature of man; it is more valued than is our animal nature; here theological doctrine re-states the view of common sense. What matters to us all, what we live for, is sympathy, understanding, imagination, reason, tradition, aspiration, and personal and human associations. Without these we cannot really undertake to continue to exist, and in our hierarchies of values they are placed above the satisfactions to our physical and biological nature. These last-mentioned come first, in our demands, only because they must come first that better wants be satisfied; but all of us, from the Andaman Islands to New York City, know that companionship, a sense of participation in an effort felt worthwhile, and the confidence of those dear to us are more precious than the absolutely necessary food and shelter. In China, certainly a land where men are hard-pressed to find a livelihood, Confucius is reported to have replied to one who asked him what was necessary in the governing of a people that although food, force and faith (or the confidence of the people) were necessary, the first two, as responsibilities of the state, might, at the worst, be dispensed with. But faith in one another we must have to become or to remain a society of human beings.

Of the social sciences, anthropology maintain the greatest sense of the complete human being. In the small communities where he characteristically works alone, the anthropologist seeks to describe all the little society before him, to tell everything about its people. So he keeps a view of the whole man. In his discovery, or re-discovery, of culture, and in the recent excitement in considering the personalities of men and women, the anthropologist finds the work of humanists at hand, congenial and enlightening. The late President of the American Anthropological Association, Dr. Ruth Benedict, told her fellow anthropologists that "the very nature of the problems posed and discussed in the humanities is closer, chapter by chapter, to those in anthropology than are the investigations carried on in most of the social sciences." (Ruth Benedict, "Anthropology and the Humanities," *American Anthropologist*, N. S. L, No. 4, Part I [October-December, 1948], 585.) But as anthropology is a science "phrasing the study of man in terms of scientific generalizations instead of humanistic terms," she admitted her heresy while seeking to justify it.

There is much in current anthropology—the study of distributions of culture traits, for example—which is as remote from the humanistic study of man as is the marginal analysis of the economist. What we have today in the social sciences is a group of disciplines for the examination of special aspects of mankind, splinters of the whole broken off for their suitability for scientific treatment, and also a disposition, in many leaders of those sciences which treat of these specialties, to return again to humanity, to man as we meet him in daily life. The sociologist develops methods for the study of population, and certain practitioners become engrossed in the perfection of statistical methods to the point where they do not often think of human beings. Yet in considering population policy, the ways of human beings, as wholes, are again confronted and must again be comprehended. Psychologists, having developed schools and procedures that reduce mankind to little bits of behavior delimited by test or laboratory device, find themselves, through psychoanalysis, again confronting a view of human nature that is at least coherent and demanding of consideration. And economists from time to time become so discontented with the limitations of formal theoretical economics that they push past its limitations. They fall to investigating and describing the actual motives and conduct of men, and before they know it they become sociologists or philosophers. One thinks of Sumner, Veblen, and F. H. Knight.

It seems that in spite of the exactions of scientific method, to which they are properly committed, social scientists cannot escape the fact that they are fundamentally concerned with states of mind. Social scientists are closest to their subject matter when they are concerned with feelings, sentiments, opinions, standards, and ideals. They are in fact usually concerned with these, even when the language does not apparently have that meaning. An "economic policy" means only that somebody intends something, and a "political machine" is only figuratively a machine—it is people, with hopes, ambitions, intentions, understandings. Neither a family nor a religion can be learned about by counting people or by measuring a house or a temple; these two are states of mind, and the influence and relations of the states of mind of some people with respect to those of other people. By talking about "the origin of magic," or "the diffusion of matrilineal clans," even anthropologists managed to get some distance from a recognition of states of mind as their subject matter, as Dr. Benedict remarks. Under the influence of the scientific method that was adopted by students of humanity in the nineteenth century, humanity was cut into pieces of nature as much like plants and animals as they could be made. But as each fresh effort is made to understand humanity, "as it really is," the thing turns out to be made of states of mind.

And of these states of mind, the schemes of values of people are central and of most importance. The anthropologist who goes to a remote community there to find out about it and report to us, would not do what we expect of him if he brought back only a list of everything the people had, did or even thought. A human life is a sort of structure of sentiments and attitudes in which first things are put first, and other things are held in lesser worth. It is this scheme of values which we must come to understand if we are to understand a man or a tribe or a nation. As anthropologists have realized this, and have struggled with the problem of representing this structure of values, they have tried to find words for the relative order of values within the structure, and for the principal values which seem to give the lead to and to shape other aspects of life to their own nature. So we find anthropologists of today writing of "basic configurations," or of "themes of culture," or of "ethos and eidos," or of "the moral order." It is the choices that men make, the preferences they have, and the standards that they define explicitly or implicitly, which make up the central subject matter of social science. And these standards are moral, esthetic and intellectual.

But is not a concern with standards, moral, esthetic or intellectual, implied or expressed in every great novel, in the work of every great painter, and in the writings of great philosophers? So it is. However much the academic faculties of departments of humanistic learning may become engrossed with such lesser and formal matters as the choice of vocabulary in one writer as compared with another, or the more technical aspects of musicology, they have before them and must work with records of the search for excellence in some of the traditions of mankind. Both humanist and social scientist have access, through the study of materials both different and similar, to the systems of values that distinguish humanity.

To study states of mind, we need expressive documents. Whether we undertake the study of humanity as a student of the arts and of literature, or as a social scientist, we find or we make expressive documents. The materials of social science and of the humanities are essentially the same. A tool is expressive in that it shows the purpose of the user and perhaps something of the skill of the maker. In so far as it is a work of fine art it shows something still more significant: something of the standards of technical performance and perhaps of esthetic satisfaction. A personal letter is in many cases more richly expressive than a tool; and a curse, a chance remark, a word said in passion, a folktale and a novel — these are very expressive indeed. The answers written in a questionnaire do not express so much. In 1948 there was a revival of discussion as to just what is expressed by a man who replies to a poll asking him how he will vote at the presidential election. What the student of the lives of men, considered separately as individuals or collectively as social groups, must have, is expressive materials. If he seeks to describe these lives in systematic generalizations, it is his business, surely, to report formally and numerically whatever can be so reported. The anthropologist makes a census, or part of one, counts the houses and the people in them, and hopes to get enough cases of marriage so that he can give some figures as to the proportion of cases in which the couple settle with the wife's parents to those in which the home is made with the husband's parents or somewhere else. Yet if he does only these things he will miss most of what he came for. When he gets a member of the group he is studying to talk or to write freely and naturally about the things that matter to him most — his family, his ambitions, his faith and his doubts — then the anthropologist knows he has at hand the materials that are most necessary to his work.

These materials for the study of man in society by the social scientist are similar to and overlap the materials that are used by the humanistic scholar. Art expresses the standards of form, of beauty, and, in cases, the interests, political or religious, of the makers. And the materials of literature and philosophy are in part the same as those of sociology and in part are different but related. The materials for the study of Stoic philosophy are the writings of the Stoics, and the materials for the study of Navaho religion and thought are the texts of rituals, of life histories and of interviews, written down by investigators or by Navaho themselves. The fact that the humanistic scholar generally stays at some university and draws his materials out of the library while the social scientist interviews the Indian or the Chicago precinct committeeman is not an important difference in this connection. Both are reading the words in which other men have expressed their states of mind, their schemes of values.

The very differences between the humanities and the social sciences show us the areas of interest where those differences cease to be. We recognize that the humanities are more specially and emphatically concerned with the products of creative imagination, particularly as produced by individuals conscious of their effort, than are the social sciences. The more spontaneous productions of everyday life, the tools and the institutions that grow up of themselves, as it were, interest the sociologist, the anthropologist and often the political scientist and the economist, more than they are likely to interest the student of the arts or of philosophy. The interest in a work of art, with reference to its manner of composition and its standard of excellence, is not so characteristically present in the social scientist; and it is the philosopher rather than the social scientist who deals with systems of thought as developed by reflective individuals. Nevertheless, we find no clear line of demarcation here either, and in anthropology one may find a Ruth Bunzel studying the esthetic norms of individual Pueblo potters and Paul Radin studying the philosophy of Winnebago Indians; and economics may produce a Harold Innis who writes like a philosopher. As to institutions, on the whole social scientists have described their forms and their workings, and have accounted for their beginnings in terms of previous social conditions and in terms of the communication of ideas from one group to another. Perhaps they will become more interested than they have been in the way in which inventions and institutions arise in the minds of particular individuals and what conceptions of excellence have guided these productions. If they do so, their work will again become more like that of the humanistic scholars. The juvenile court is, among other things, a work of creative imagination, and might be studied as such, as the student of architecture studies the building in which such a court may be housed.

The existence of psychology, in part a social science, and the great current scientific interest in studying human personality, prevent one from asserting too strongly that it is the humanist who is concerned with man as an individual while social science regards him as a collectivity. Yet it is true that the humanities, academically recognized, are characteristically concerned with the productions of the few, while the social sciences are for the most part interested in the productions of the many. It is partly a difference between an interest in what is common to members of a society and an interest in what is made by a few of them, and perhaps enjoyed by only a few of them. It is partly a difference between an interest in any and every product of man's collective life, no matter how good or bad it seems to the investigator, and an interest in what is better. A responsibility for the development of appreciation, for the improvement of taste, is more apt to be felt by a student of art and literature, as a part of his work, than it is apt to be felt by an economist or a psychologist or an anthropologist. The social scientist studies markets, cannibalism, ward politics, taxi dance halls, nursery rhymes and the art-forms and social life of the juke-box set, but is not likely to be followed in these directions by professors of art, literature, or philosophy. On the other hand folklore exists as a study of popular productions occasionally under humanistic academic auspices, and psychologists' studies of symbolic behavior are studies of the creations of individuals. There is more than a little in common between one of Freud's cases, as he wrote them down for us to read, and Lowes' study of Coleridge's creative mind, *The Road to Xanadu*.

The relationship which the social sciences have with the other sciences is of course undiminished by what has here been written about a relationship in another direction. The former relationship exists in the scientific point of view and in the similarities of method, as to both obervation and analysis. The relationship with the humanities, as should appear from these pages, exists chiefly in the sharing of the same subject matter: humanity. This suggests one easy sentence in which one might perhaps summarize the two comparisons: Social science is a discipline with the methods of the natural sciences, and the subject matter of the humanities.

Like many other such easy sentences, this one is no better than an approximation. It requires qualification in both its parts. By no means all of the subject matter that social scientists take up for study is humanity. As has already been recognized here, much that is around or outside of humanity they find to be their business too: population statistics; the market as a function of supply and demand; military power and its influence; congenital reflexes.

And the assertion that social science has the method of the natural sciences requires modification also. Social science method is like physical science method in that it describes; it does not evaluate. Like physics and chemistry it strives for objectivity, system and comprehensiveness. It uses precise methods where it can, and where it can it experiments, and where it can it measures. But it differs in its method from the methods of all the physical and biological sciences for reasons that follow from the difference in its subject matter. In most of social science, human nature is itself a part of the method. One must use one's own humanity as a means to understanding. The physicist need not sympathize with his atoms, nor the biologist with his fruit flies, but the student of people and institutions must employ his natural sympathies in order to discover what the people think or feel and what the institution means. This is what C. F. von Weizsäcker has in mind when he says, in "The Experiment," that a philologist trying to understand the meaning an author puts into a text, or a historian seeking the intention of an acting man, enters "as an 'I' into the discourse with a 'Thou.' This kind of meeting with its object, physics does not know, because it does not encounter its object as a subject. This personal understanding is a mode of experience which is accessible to us in regard to our fellow man; but not in regard to the stone, the star and the atom."

The management of this human sympathy, this meeting of the object as subject, is a part of the art or scientific craft of the social scientist. Years ago Cooley gave it the name "sympathetic introspection." It is a part of the scientist's art, and, one may add, it is also in cases a personal difficulty or problem, for the social science field worker experiences in that part of his professional life an internal conflict between the yielding to human sympathy, as required by his method, and the standing apart, as science requires, so as to look objectively at that with which he sympathizes. This is not a problem for the physicist.

What is this "humanity" that both the social scientist and the student of art, literature or philosophy strive to understand? In what that is susceptible of systematic observation does humanity manifest itself, and what are the most inclusive words that can be used to denote its principal manifestations? No generally accepted answer to these questions can be put on behalf of the social sciences or of the humanities. For the latter an answer would perhaps be a naming of the forms of art and thought which recur in many or all times and places. If the answer to represent social science should be sought of a social anthropologist or sociologist it might be offered in something like the following words.

Humanity presents itself to our scientific notice as it appears in all men; as it appears in particular individual men; and as it appears in the conventional ways of life of particular continuing groups of men. Three terms are commonly used, nowadays, to point in the direction of these three different but interrelated manifestations of humanity; Human Nature, Personality, and Culture.

Of the three, human nature is the most general, for it is, in its content, universal. It may be asserted that all (normal) men and women have the same human nature (although it is not proved or universally admitted that this is the case). But it cannot be asserted that all men have the same personality, or that all groups have the same culture; although it is properly asserted that all men have personalities, and that all continuing groups of people who communicate with one another are characterized by culture. By human nature we mean that nature which everyone (after infancy) of our species has, if provided with the usual capacities, when he is brought up in a society characterized by culture. It is the nature we assume we shall meet in every man or woman, no matter where we meet him, or her. We assume, and rightly, that every human being has something of which he may be proud, and something of which he may be ashamed. Before we have even tried to communicate with him, we know that if we hit upon what he finds amusing or shocking he will be amused or shocked; that he will desire praise, and that he will give up present pleasures for some deferred good which he values highly. We cannot predict these qualities of the animals we meet (unless domesticated dogs, having been made just a little human, are a small exception), but we know we shall find these qualities and many others in the tribe as in the city, among peasants as among princes. This human nature is a thing built up on the basis of that original nature which we can never see quite clearly in mankind because it begins to change into human nature soon after birth.

This important and essentially characteristic aspect of the nature of mankind seems never to have been very carefully investigated by any one who looked much farther than inside himself. In recent times some of the psychologists have learned a good deal about the mechanisms whereby original nature gets made over into human nature, and the study of this process from the point of view of those concerned with relations between persons in the family and the neighborhood, and with the cultures of the groups within which the process occurs, has been enlightening. Some sociologists have collected material throwing light on the nature of human nature, and some have tried to study those exceptional members of our species, feral men, who grew up without acquiring human nature. But the content of human nature is not well understood.

Of course its existence is assumed by anyone who talks about human beings at all. It is a commonplace that philosophers and writers about social problems make assumptions about what human nature is like that vary greatly from one another, and the views of literary people on this subject are quite as various. One thinks of the different views of human nature suggested by Hobbes, Rousseau, Bentham, and Dostoievsky.

The anthropologist demonstrates the existence of human nature whenever he finds out what an exotic people are thinking and feeling. He can do this only by supposing that they have in common with him certain acquired propensities of attitude; these are human nature. To be able to find out what it is that a Zuni Indian is ashamed of one must first know what it is to be ashamed. Although anthropologists commonly make assertions to the effect that "human nature is infinitely malleable," or speak of "the refutation of human nature," as an achievement of their science, they in fact recognize its existence every day.

The sources as to the nature of human nature are the records of human living. They exist in ethnography and in history; they exist in biography and in psychiatric case records; and they exist in creative literature. No one is more deeply engaged in the examination and understanding of human nature than are the dramatist and the novelist. In learning about human nature, men of literature and men of social science share a common effort, a common interest. It may be doubted if the results so far achieved by the social scientists are more communicative of the truth about human nature than are the results achieved by the more personal and imaginative methods of the artist.

The common interest of social scientist and of creative artist exists similarly in the study of personality, the organization of human nature and of culture in any particular individual. Here also it is the man of literature and art who has the longest interest in the subject. A personality wholly invented, like Madame Bovary or Huckleberry Finn, provides a record of a human individual that tells us much about the nature of human personality, of its development in relation to other personalities, and to events. A biography may be so written, as that by Hervey Allen on Edgar Allen Poe or that by Marquis James on Andrew Jackson, as to show much of those relationships between original temperament, personal associations, the culture of the community, and the happenings of circumstance, as equally concern the students of personality who are social scientists.

It is perhaps in their common interest in what is called "culture" that the students of the humanities and many of the social scientists find their most obvious and fruitful field for co-operative endeavor. In considering this common interest of humanist and social scientist, one thinks of "culture" as the term has been developed in the comparative study of societies, in the sense which includes all the customs, institutions, and conventions whatsoever, "acquired by man as a member of society," in Tylor's familiar words. The conception is a sort of master-term that brings after it many of the more special concepts used by social sciences specializing in the study of families, markets, schools, law and so forth.

The difference between the meaning of the term "culture" as used by anthropologists, and the word as used by critics of art or literature, is not absolute; it is a difference of emphasis: anthropologist and humanistic scholar are talking about different phases of the same thing. As remarked in preceding pages, the student of the humanities looks especially at the thoughtful, deliberate, original and creative aspect of a people's life. So his meaning of the word "culture" brings it close to its original meaning of "cultivation." The social scientist looks usually at the spontaneous, common, average and less original aspects. His meaning of "culture" brings the word close to "folkways" or "customs." But the more original and deliberate phase of the antropologist's "culture" is essential to an understanding of cultural change, and especially to that development out of and beyond a simple or primitive culture which we call "civilization." In the development of folk culture into a self-conscious and reasonably guided improvement of man and society, the essential nature of civilization is to be found.

So it is that the humanistic scholar studies culture chiefly as it appears in literature and art. He knows it principally in the more civilized development of a people that have a literature, and so a history, and so also a consciousness of their esthetic and intellectual pursuits. He comes upon a culture from the top, so to speak. The anthropologist begins at the bottom, where the ordinary people work out their ways of life without benefit of books or Socrates. The student of art or literature is concerned with the finest flowers on a tree whose roots are investigated by anthropologists. But it is the same tree.

It is something of a misfortune that in the organization of academic learning the two lines of study have come to appear as unrelated. The man who studies Restoration drama does not seem to have much in common with the student of Navaho witchcraft or the student of boys' gangs. It is rarely possible to bring together in a single university department those archaeologists who dig up the Maya and those who dig up the Romans. Yet both in the first case, in which the procedures used are so very different, and in the second, where the field methods are much the same, there is really one common subject matter: the investigation of cultures, alway necessarily made manifest in expressive documents (an artifact being a kind of document).

Where might the humanistic and the social-scientific views of culture come together in more apparent and productive mutual stimulation? Such a joining together may be found in the application of science and scholarship to the study of the culture-civilizations of the Orient. There no long established academic tradition exists to separate the man who studies the books and the art, and the man who studies the village communities, the trade or the government. Or at least it may be said that so little study of the lives of the common people has yet been carried on that such work could well be developed in association with the study of the archaeology, history, art and literature of these Eastern Peoples. The Western anthropologist or sociologist or student of government who chooses China or India as his field of work will have to learn an Oriental language, to read it as well as to speak it, and he will find his work enriched as he comes to consider the history and the art and literature of the more reflective representatives of that same tradition which appears to him in village life.

Where a literate civilization, with people who reflect and organize thought, is built upon a local popular culture, there is plainly but one subject matter. There a new dimension of human living grows out of the local folk life. This is the "culture" of China, or of India, in both senses. It is the culture and it is the civilization. This culture-civilization can be studied in part through the customs and institutions of the many. It can be studied partly through the art and philosophical writings of the few. And in the study the connecting links will appear: in the effects of Confucian, Taoist, Buddhist or Brahmin teaching in the village; and in the development and modification of ancient folk tradition in the more reflective writing and the finer art. In the United States we have come in recent years to speak of "regional studies," by which we mean the organization of teaching and research in terms of part of the world characterized each by its way of life. Probably we mean not so much the study of a region as the study of a culture. Such a study might be completely humanistic, joining the way of study of the scientist with the way of study of those concerned with art and literature. We might say that for every such great culture there are two traditions, the Little Tradition of the village and the common people, and the Great Tradition of the reflective few. They are the two manifestations of humanity as humanity is locally and anciently organized in that part of the world. They have influenced each other, and one is a development out of the other. They can best be understood if they are studied together. To do this, social scientist and students of literature, art and philosophy will work together. Then the social scientists, without leaving their necessary connection with the other sciences, will turn from these neighbors on their right hand at the table of learning to converse with those humanistic neighbors who sit on their left.

J. O. HERTZLER

2

The Social Wisdom of the Primitives with Special Reference to their Proverbs

The validational process in sociology, as in all sciences, necessitates the statement of hypothesized relationships in clear and succinct form. This is largely due to the needs of operationalizing our body of theory to test it against empirical reality. Thus, there has been a distinct move away from the elaborate essay to propositional inventory in many quarters of sociology.[1]

In the following essay, J.O. Hertzler examines the large body of folk propositions about social behavior usually called proverbs. As has long been noted, the major difficulty with proverbial knowledge is that one can usually find a contradictory proverb in the folk literature as well (e.g., "Many hands make light work" versus "Too many cooks spoil the broth"). However, it is usually the case that both contradicting proverbs are insightful generalizations about actual forms of behavior. The key problem, for the sociologist as well as for folk who use the proverbs, is stating the conditions when one or the other version will be true. Exactly the same problem exists for most of the more formally stated propositions of social science, many of which also face daily contradictions. Despite such important problems, the succinct and lucid statement of generalization about the social order is a necessary (even if not sufficient) condition for the development of a social science.

NOTES

1. A major compilation of these is: B.R. Berelson and G. Steiner, *Human Behavior: An Inventory of Scientific Propositions* (New York, 1964).

THE SOCIAL WISDOM OF THE PRIMITIVES WITH SPECIAL REFERENCE TO THEIR PROVERBS*†

I

The indispensable prerequisites to any social thought are association and language. It is due to association that men, even the most primitive, become aware of the various aspects of human nature, and it is out of association that their attitudes and ideas grow, however vague and fantastic they may be, regarding social relationships generally, the requirements of group conduct, social and psycho-social processes, social institutions, and human life in general. Without language there can be no communication of any kind; nor are men capable of developing concepts of any kind.

To pick up social thought at the precise moment when man developed the combination of simple association and rude speech is impossible at this stage of the study of social evolution. We may in time know quite a bit about man at this point in his development. On the basis of his skeletal remains we now know something about him as an anatomical specimen, and with the aid of his rude artifacts we can piece together some aspects of his culture, but we have almost no inkling of his thought. The most rudimentary social thought now available is that of recent and contemporary primitive peoples—peoples who, while relatively rude, and simple, have a fairly substantial cul-

---

*Reprinted from *Social Forces* 11 (1933): 313-26, by permission of the publisher.
† This article has grown out of a perusal of Chapter II on "Earliest Social Thought" of *A History of Social Thought* by Professor E. S. Bogardus. In this chapter he demonstrated a true stroke of genius in examining the proverbs of primitive peoples as reflectors of their social thought. This chapter has led me to undertake a further examination which may be considered supplementary to the treatment of Bogardus.

ture, including established ideas, standarized relationships, a flexible language, and a full equipment of institutions.

The thought of primitive peoples is largely pre-scientific and pre-literate. Their ideas are not reached by deliberate reasoning nor by careful and conscious investigation. They are direct and intuitive, the products of minds that are alogical, uncritical and credulous on the whole, and that depend on common experience, observation, and imagination for explanations.[1] Being pre-literate, their thought, of necessity, is orally transmitted. It is thus in the main a matter of folk memory, and is cumulative and continuous.[2] Its outstanding forms are known collectively as folklore, and consist of myths, sayings, legends, maxims, sagas, fables, apothegms, proverbs, rhymes, riddles, tales, songs, and ballads. These are spoken of as "little pellets of practical wisdom or folk-experience."[3] Since these are orally conveyed they are in time given form and expression which makes them readily transmissible. They tend to be concise, trenchant, pungent, and graphic in statement.

These different forms of folklore do not all reflect social thought, however. In fact one of the outstanding characteristics of primitive thought is the relative scarcity of social thinking. This is partly due to the unrealistic, mystical manner of looking at things among primitives, and partly to the fact that the social conditions themselves are not particularly conductive to social thought, nor do these conditions demand much thinking about them. Primitive groups are mainly small, simple, kinship aggregations. Human relationships are fairly simple, as is life in general. There is no great demand for thinking on social structure, social organization, social reconstruction, the interdependence of groups, or any other social situations involving major groups or extensive group contacts.

Individual conduct is the primary consideration of a social nature in the simple group. Therefore, thought forms of primitives, in so far as they have social significance, deal with homely, more or less close personal or restricted social relationships and activities. They are concerned with individual attitudes and conduct among fellows in simple and oft-recurring social situations. The expression of these simple observations is almost without exception from the individual angle.

II

The language forms most clearly and abundantly expressing the social thought of primitive peoples are the proverbs. They are ubiquitous and almost universal among all races and peoples. The native American races, according to Kroeber, are the only exceptions, and some of these, notably the Omahas and Winnebagos, have epigrammatic sentences very like proverbs.[4] Going back to the remotest antiquity, we discover them embedded in the culture of Babylonia and Egypt; long before Confucius the Chinese had them. Non-literary savages almost everywhere have had their proverbs which they pass on from generation to generation.[5] In fact, primitive peoples often have a greater store of proverbial information than the more highly civilized peoples. Krappe states, ". . . . the Maori of New Zealand may help to make this clear. Their proverbial lore, all handed down orally, as goes without saying, is truly astounding and easily puts in the shade the sum total of ancient proverbs that have come down to us from the Mediterranean civilization."[6] Proverbs are a typical primitive product. Great stores of them, however, still survive among civilized peoples everywhere and are widely used by certain population elements.

Proverbs are typical, appropriate, highly popular, and well cherished expressional forms among pre-literate, illiterate, and partially literate peoples. Such peoples, devoid of writing, or unaccustomed to any very extensive use of writing, and yet being desirous of preserving the knowledge obtained from life and observation, both for themselves and posterity, found them satisfactory forms for storage and transmission. According to Krappe's definition "A proverb represents, in its essential form, some homely truth expressed in a concise and terse manner so as to recommend itself to a more or less extended circle."[7]

Proverbs represent the stage of unconscious organization of social thought as compared with the dialectical method in vogue from the Greeks to modern times and the very recent scientific method involving deliberate and if possible controlled fact-finding, exact observation, careful checking, and discreet generalization. Primitive or untutored men lived in a world of occurrences and experiences. Presently they observed or discovered what to them were certain facts or truths, pleasant and unpleasant, regarding these occurrences and experiences. They realized the importance of preserving the knowledge thus gained for use when similar circumstances should again arise, not only for their own use but also for posterity.[8] This best thought on some given point was passed on by word of mouth generation after generation, the meanwhile going through a perpetual selective process. If the idea was sound it was preserved, improved, condensed, and stated more tritely or dramatically, so that it readily sank into the memory and won a zest that no lengthy explanation or philosophy could give.[9] Thus they are the generalized experience of many generations of people, the specific statements of which, in quaint, compact, rhythmic, epigrammatic form, are the result of long correction, clarification, and polishing. "Truths and principles, thus pointedly and epigrammatically put, when forced upon the receptive intellect, would stick like barbed arrows long after the same . . . would have faded from memory."[10]

Proverbs, being drawn from the experiences and study of a people life, are among the most accurate index of that people's life and thought. They may not be true or represent truth, but they indicate what the poeple hold to as their rules and ideals of life and conduct.[11]

They are the safest index to the inner life of a people. With their aid we can construct a mental image of the conditions of existence, the manners, characteristics, morals, and *Weltanschauung* of the community which used them. They present us with the surest data upon which to base our knowledge of Volkspsychologie.[12]

They summarize, more or less, the everyday experience of a people — their thought in general, their intellectual status, their attitudes toward social situations and problems, their opinions and feelings, their group morality, their social ideas, their life goals, virtues and values — and do this better and more accurately than their religious or ethical system.[13] Among primitives proverbs form the foundation of their social philosophy. They are literally the voice of the multitude.

Proverbs are widely used as instructional aids. Having the endorsement of many different ages and generations they have peculiar authority as social control agents. In fact their principal aim is to influence people's wills and actions.[14] In ancient Egypt the Instructions of Kagemni and Ptah-hotep, the Teachings of Amen-em-apt, and the Maxims of Ani were orally taught the boys in the schools. The same use of proverbs was true of the Babylonians, the Chinese and various other ancient and mediaeval people. Among primitives everywhere proverbs are the choice coins in the treasury of the people's knowledge that are carefully passed on to the new generation by parents and elders both through daily conversation and admonition, and with the special emphasis of the initiation rites and secret societies.

Among primitives the most conservative attitude is maintained concerning their proverbs and other lore. In the repetition of proverbs or tales the smallest deviation from the original version will be noticed and corrected. This is probably due to the fact that the lore is felt to be vitally important, and since it is orally transmitted, they want no modification of it lest its significance and utility be lost. It goes without saying that proverbs not only reflect social life, but also play an exceedingly important role in the every day life of primitives. They are at the very center of primitive life and thought.[15]

There has long been a controversy as to whether proverbs originate with the people or come from wise men. Most of the evidence points to popular origin. While a given proverb may have been first coined by one individual, or while it may have been put in its final pithy, pungent form by some wise man, the idea expressed in it represents centuries of folk experience and discussion along a given line. Furthermore, their transmission and persistence lies with the rank and file and not the *litterateurs*. Strictly speaking, they spring from the masses and are a matter of group cogitation. They are the spontaneous product of human experience rather than the expression of the meditations of any individual sage. Even if they must be attributed to individuals, the individuals were socially conditioned; their mind content came from their culture, and only the specific statement reflects individual genius.[16]

Proverbs expressing very similar ideas are found among ancients and moderns, primitives and civilized peoples. Some of these similarities are due to diffusion; for proverbs like other valuable and useful culture elements are widely borrowed.[17] But among a given people, only those foreign proverbs are adopted that are in some measure congenial to their mind and mode of life; otherwise, they would wither and die.[18] In the main, however, the similar proverbs among different peoples must be attributed to the fact that a certain set of social conditions or situations, or a certain characteristic of human beings is dealt with which is very much the same the world over, and causes men to think, feel, or react more or less uniformly. The idea will be the same, but the peculiarities of the particular environment will give the proverb its local coloring; it will reflect the kind of life that the people live — their occupations and their way of thinking.[19]

The previously mentioned fact that proverbs flourish best among pre-literate, illiterate or partly literate peoples, is also borne out by the fact that they are a language form rapidly passing from usage in contemporary civilized cultures. Tyler, half a century ago, while granting that we and other civilized peoples were still using thousands of proverbs, maintained that among us the period of actual growth seemed to be at an end. He stated,

We can collect and use the old proverbs, but making new ones has become a feeble, spiritless imitation, like our attempts to invent new myths of new nursery rhymes.[20]

Albig quite recently has pointed out that current speech and literature provides but few quotations of or allusions to proverbs.[21] He found in several thousand pages of popular periodical material issued in July, 1930, only twenty-six proverbs, and of these seven were used to mildly ridicule them. Proverbs still flourish though in simpler societies where primary group conditions prevail, and in the primary relationships of our own modern life.

The increasing disuse of proverbs among the more civilized peoples is due to several factors. When a society becomes heterogeneous and complex, taking on the chacteristics of a secondary group, the social situations are of such a nature that they cannot be expressed in the manner of a typical proverb; they are not simple, nor are they similar for all individuals. A high degree of unanimity in social judgments does not exist among the people due to diverse cultural backgrounds. Furthermore, in a complex modern society, ideas are not orally transmitted to any great extent but are spread by means of the modern mechanical means of communication, which do not require the congregation of people, nor do they elicit response and discussion. Furthermore, as Albig mentions,[22] proverbs do not appear under conditions of rapid social change, and modern societies are especially characterized by such processes. Proverbs, in their very nature, apply best in more or less static societies where the situations and conditions they refer to remain fairly constant. Equally dogmatic but vastly more ephemeral language forms are used in changing societies.

Finally, we do not need proverbs any more. The rank and file of men are more highly educated than every before. They are led to think more for themselves; thinking is more direct, more scientific and realistic. We do not use nor do we often understand the roundabout, figurative way of stating a social fact or situation. In fact, today for us moderns there are distinct disadvantages in the extensive use of proverbs. They take away the necessity of individual generalization and explanation. They reduce the demand for accurate observation and analysis, and correct expression. Those who use proverbs extensively have their thought both guided and confined by them.

Among the higher strata of civilization proverbs, when used, reflect social customs and beliefs long past.[23] They are largely cultural survivals — holdovers from the days when life was simpler and more personal. When they are used today they apply only to the simple situations and problems.

III

The examination of proverbs that follows is strictly from the sociological point of view. We are not concerned with their anthropological or philological significance nor are we interested in their literary structure or the place they occupy in the formal study of folklore. We are devoting ourselves to them solely because they reflect the social life, social concepts, and social attitudes of primitive peoples.

In recent years anthropologists, folk-lorists and others interested in the forms of expression of primitives have collected and made available literally thousands of proverbs. By no means all of these have been available to the writer. Only a third to a half of approximately five thousand examined reflected social thought, and limitations of space have allowed the presentation of only a part of these. But those quoted, it is hoped, will convey to the reader the nature and spirit of primitive social thinking.

Classification of proverbs is difficult, as any one who has worked with them knows. Many may be classified under different heads. The arrangement below is an arbitrary one dictated by this particular sociologist's interpretation of the social content of the proverbs.

Observations of a social psychological nature abound in primitive proverbs. A recognition of the nature of habits, the processes of their formation, and their persistence frequently appears. The Ashanti, a West African people, say "A tree does not grow bent for thirty years that one should expect to straighten it in one."[24] Another runs, "When you follow behind your father you learn to walk like him." That old habits are not forgotten is expressed in the proverb found among certain Moroccan tribesman, "The dancer dies and does not forget the shaking of his shoulders."[25] The low-caste Hindu humorously puts the same idea as follows: "The thief has left off stealing, but not exchanging."[26] The Ba-Congo say, "Habit is a full-grown mountain, hard to get over or to pull down."[27] The parallel of our "You can't teach an old dog new tricks," is found in the Moroccan, "An old cat will not learn dancing," and an almost exact counterpart is the Yoruban, "An old dog cannot be taught."[28] Original tendencies more or less determine behavior also as certain of the Filipino tribes maintain: "Whichever side a tree leans there it falls,"[29] or "The zebra cannot do away with his stripes," as the Masai put it.[30]

The psychological and sociological implications of child training are thoroughly understood by the primitives. The plasticity of children is expressed by the Sechuana tribesman in the words, "Bend the twig while it is green."[31] The importance of the right kind of social environment for children is also put in the Sechuana proverb, "A young bird seldom crows except as it hears the old ones crow." To make instruction permanent start in youth. This the Moroccan tribesmen express in two proverbs: "Instruction in youth is like engraving in stones;" "Instruction in old age is like engraving in dung." The moroccans also maintain that improperly brought up children are due to the carelessness of parents. "The forest is only burnt by its own wood." The Ba-Congoese say, "Teach a child before it goes to the dance not after it has come back." The Vai of West Africa matintain that the parent must assume responsibility for the way his children turn out when they say, "If a man raises a snake he must tie it."[32] A more lengthy Hawaiian proverb points out the increasing persistence of bad habits as the individual grows older: "Tender are the little sins when the child is creeping; transient in childhood; obstinate in youth, hard to change in maturity; and fixed in old age."[33] The Ashanti have many wise observations regarding the care and training of children. "The child which is to turn out any good is not reared entirely on a beautiful mat." "When your child dances badly, tell him, saying 'Your dancing is not good; and do not say to him, (Little) soul just dance as you want to.' " "When a child does not hear the words of its father and mother, there is misfortune in that." "Out of nine mischievous tricks a child thinks to play on others, he suffers for five of them himself." "When a child says he wants to act as if he were already chief, let him do so; as to whether he will ever become one, that no one knows." "When the grown-up threatens to punish, but does not carry out his threat, the children do not fear him." Referring also to child habits, a Moroccan proverb states, "If he steals a needle, he will steal a cow." The Ibo of the lower Niger region in thinking of the importance of parental discipline in preparing each new generation for life say, "A son cannot first have a son before his father."[24] The Ba-Congo have several other most apt proverbs dealing with the parent-child relationship. When giving a reason for obedience to parents they say, "O space between two beds, obey the beds, you also will one day be a bed," and in admonishing a child not to get "to big" for his family they remark, "A fawn never forgets his own feeding ground."

The significance of experience is variously expressed. The Ashanti, emphasizing the importance of profiting by the experience of others and utilizing the cultural heritage, say, "When one stands on another's shoulders, then he sees over the market." The Arabs say, "Consult a man of experience, for he gives you what has cost him much and for which you give nothing."[35] They have another one which reads, "Experience is the looking-glass of the intellect." The Masai of Africa say, "We begin by being foolish and we become wise by experience," while the Ba-ila of northern Rhodesia admonish the young, "Get grown up and then you will know the things of the earth,"[36] and the Yorubas say, "A man may be born to a fortune, but wisdom only comes with length of days."

Various social pressures and stimuli that bear upon the individual are recognized. Fad or fashion at least as they affect externals is alluded to in the Arabic, "Eat whatsoever thou likest, but dress as others do." Group opinion and its mode of influence is reflected in the Ashanti proverbs, "When it is the unanimous wish of a people that you dress your hair in a certain way, you are compelled to do so." "When the united people want to kill you, then the chief kills you." The influence of associates upon the individual behavior is put in the following words by the Arab tribesmen: "Smoke is no less an evidence of fire than that a man's character is that of the characters of his associates;" the Vai of west Africa say, "One bad goat will spoil the herd."

Tradition and custom survive and are handed down. Thus the Ashanti say, "Ancient things remain in the ears," and also, "When you go into some village, the songs which the children sing, the old folks once sang and left behind to them." The Chaggas put the same thought in the words "The dead gazelle teaches the live gazelles."[37] The Maori of New Zealand commenting on the rightness of the ways inherited from the past say, "Great is the majority of the dead," or "It was not one alone who was awake in the dark ages."[38]

The idea of the "consciousness of kind" and "congregating with kind," has long been known and expressed in proverbial form. In *Ecclesiastes* it is stated, "All flesh consorteth according to kind, and a man will cleave to his like." Empedocles put it, "Like desires like." Since the days of Aristotle we have expressed it in the form of "Birds of a feather flock together." Another English version goes "Every bird flies with its own species; pigeons with pigeons, hawks with hawks." The French say, "Pour épouser un singe il faut être guenon." The Yoruban savage of the Guinea Coast tritely states the same idea: "A fool of Ika and an idiot of Iluka meet together to make friends," while the Sechuana tribesmen say "Vultures eat with their blood relations," or "Spotted leopards lick together."

The Sechuana are aware of the stimulus that comes from association: "Men surpass one another while they are working together," and the Yorubas say, "Working in competition quickens the hands." The use of what we call "defense mechanisms" is not unknown to the primitives. Thus the Ashanti declare "He who is guilty is the one who has much to say," reminding one of Shakespeare's "Methinks he doth protest too much." The Ashanti have another that expresses the same thought even more aptly: "When you do not know how to dance, then you say, 'The drum is not sounding sweetly.'" A group motive of much the same sort is expressed in the words "When an army suffers defeat a horn is not blown in its honor," which recalls Mark Twain's remark that of all the paintings of French battle scenes that he beheld in the Louvre not a single one depicted a French defeat.

IV

Various observations are made in primitive proverbs regarding the desirable and the undesirable personal relations. The natives of

Arabia have quite an array along this line: "Have patience with a friend rather than lose him forever;" "If you would keep your secret from your enemies keep it also from your friends;" "A friend is a second self and a third eye;" "He is a weak man who can make no friends, and still weaker is he who loses them;" "In social life be as friends, in business as strangers;" "The best friend is he who changeth not with the changes of time." Similarly the Moroccans say: "Your friend who is near is better than your brother who is far away;" "Little from the hand of a friend is much;" "The loss of goods is better than the loss of a friend;" "Face your friend, and turn your side to your enemy." On the other hand there is an old proverb current among the Japanese, "Lend money to a friend and he is a friend no more."[39]

Other shrewd observations regarding friendship are found. The Yorubas say, "Peace is the father of friendship." The Ba-Congo in making some shrewd observations regarding holding a friend say, "If you love a hunter, love his dog," or, appreciate what is dear to him. An equally shrewd one is, "A familiar call is only made between those who understand each other." They also say, "It (i.e. friendship) never uses a peppercorn as an eyedrop." The Bagandas of Uganda cryptically note, "You have many friends as long as you are prosperous," and also "I had numbers of friends before calamity befell me."[40]

The fact of social interdependence is appreciated by primitives. Thus, the Yorubas of Africa say, "He who injures another injures himself,"[41] while the Ashanti state, "One man's road does not go far without meeting anothers." Other pointed observations regarding human beings as psychic entities in groups follow. In Arabia it is said, "He who lives in a house of glass should not throw stones at people;" "He who makes enemies shall have many a restless night," and "Envy is a disease which does more harm to the envious than to the envied." The Sechuanan says, "Those who are fond of flattery are cheated out of their property," and "In the dark people hold to one anothers' cloaks," while the Bagandan observes "He who has not suffered does not know how to pity," and the Moroccan in indicating how one is to be liked by people says, "Sow wheat, don't sow thorns, all the people will like you and love you." The Ashanti, pointing out one of the effects of proximity say, "The enemy of the chief is he who has grown up with him from childhood."

The peculiar quirks of human nature are well understood by primitives. After noting some of them one is led to exclaim "Well people are like that." A short list of such, not always flattering, follows:

Arabia — They wooed her and she resisted, they neglected her and she fell in love.

Arabia — When the dogs are sated they make presents to each other of what remains.

Yoruba — A man of the town knows nothing about farming, or the seasons for planting, but the yams he buys must always be large.

Nandi — The Sun said, 'Whatever I do, the farmers curse me. If there is no rain, they say I burn their crops; if there is much rain, they complain that I do not shine.[42]

Filipino — A wise man's joke is believed by a fool.

Ashanti — As long as a chief leaves you alone, you say, "He and I are good friends."

Ashanti — One does not speak out one's mind in the presence of the chief, but behind his back one does.

Hawaii — The puffed mouth is full of wind.

Secbuana — The lout considers all other people louts.

Secbuana — Lions growl while they are eating (meaning that there are some people who will never enjoy anything).

Secbuana — Ears usually witness a matter without invitation.

Ba-ila — The prodigal cow threw away her own tail.

Morocco — The camel does not see his own hump, he sees only the humps of his brother.

Ba-Congo — When the dog has eaten the eggs his looks show it.

Ba-Congo — Don't set pigs to weed a farm of manioc nor cats to fry eels.

Ibo — The land is never void of counsellors.

Yoruba — He who marries a beauty marries trouble.

Baganda — A beautiful woman is the sister of many, (i.e., many want to be near her and share her favors).

Yoruba — He who has done something in secret, and sees people talking together, thinks they are talking of his action.

Yoruba — The glutton having eaten his fill, then calls his companions to come also.

Yoruba — A chicken having been delivered from death (from the hawk) by being shut up, complained because it was not allowed to feed openly on the dust heap.

The sly social opinion voiced by us in the words "When the cat's away the mice will play," has its primitive equivalents also. The Sechuana say, "The giant tortoise is asleep and the little ones graze where they like." The Banyoros of Central Africa put it, "When the master is absent the frogs climb up the house,"[43] and the Vai of West Africa say, "In the absence of the leopard the bush cat is King of the bush."

One finds interesting attitudes toward different types of people. Thus the Japanese comment, "When you find a truthful courtesan and a four-cornered egg, the new moon will appear a day before its time." Among the Arabs they say, "A harlot repented for one night. 'Is there no police officer,' she exclaimed, 'to take up harlots?' " The

Hindus in referring to an artful and lascivious woman who pretends to modesty and timidity say, "She wanders all night in the forest, and when morning comes is afraid of a crow." Our knowledge that some people are "all things to all men" is expressed by the Hindu in the words, "He tells the thief to steal and the honest man to keep watch." The Sechuanan in phrasing our "Fools rush in where angels fear to tread," puts it "We commoners rush in anywhere and plough over wide fields." The Omaha Indians in thinking of certain types say, "All persons dislike a borrower;" "No one mourns the thriftless," and "The path of the lazy leads to disgrace."[44] The Ba-Congo points out that, "He who pokes into the business of others is never without dirty feet;" "A doctor bald to the nape of his neck is not likely to cure anybody of baldness;" and that "Those who inherit fortunes are often more troublesome than those who make them." The Nandi observe, "The man who is always crying is not listened to," and the Yorubas declare that "Secrets should never be told to a tatler."

The noisy people may not necessarily be the wise ones. The Japanese say "The silent may be worth listening to," and also in referring to the loud talkers "While their tongues wag their brains sleep." The Arabians have one, "One coin in the money-box makes the more noise than when it is full," that is very similar to the inelegant but expressive mid-western proverb, "An empty wagon makes the most noise." Similarly the Mexicans say, "A howling cat is not a good hunter," while Arabians put it, "A crying cat catches nothing." Malicious speech and gossip is referred to by the Arabians in the proverbs, "The wound caused by the lancehead is curable, but that caused by the tongue cannot be cured," and "The tongue is the neck's enemy," while the Japanese say, "The tongue, but three inches long, can kill a man six feet high." In speaking of the inability to withdraw words once spoken, the Ashanti say, "When you place your tongue in pawn, you cannot redeem it," while the Samoans put the same thought thus, "Stones will rot but words never rot."[45] In emphasizing caution in speech the Nandi say, "Do not say the first thing that comes into your head," reminding one of our admonition to "Think twice before you speak." The Ba-Congo also state, "It is better to shout after the war than before it." In calling attention particularly to the evil chatter of women the Sechuanans say "Women's gossip breeds civil wars," and "A woman can set towns aquarelling."

The idea that compensation or retribution follow certain social acts is oft expressed. The Filipinos say, "You laugh today, I laugh tomorrow;" the Sechuana native states that "A crime eateth its own child;" while the Basutos of South Africa will say "The thief eats thunderbolts," meaning he will suffer vengeance from heaven, or

"The thief catches himself."[46] The Yorubas, voicing identically our idea of "Curses come home to roost," say, "Ashes fly back in the face of him who throws them." The Moroccan desert tribes, in addition to the rather widespread proverbs, "He who digs a pit for his brother will fall into it," and "As you sow you will reap," also have the following:

> He who has done something will have it done to him.
> Every sheep hangs by its own leg.
> He who sows good will reap peace.
> He who sows evil will harvest repentance.
> He who sows thorns must walk on them barefoot.

The Nandi, having observed that the innocent relations of the punished criminal also suffer, say, "If a dead tree falls, it carries with it a live one."

A great number of primitive proverbs and maxims are statements of simple social duties or obligations, and in them will frequently be found the expression of a typical social value. Interesting are the following:

Omaba Indian — Stolen food never satisfies hunger.
Filipino — Kindness is a great capital.
Arabia — To recompense good for good is a duty.
Arabia — The worst kind of recompense is to requite evil for good.
Morocco — What you desire for yourself you should desire for others.
Morocco — Beautify your tongue, you will obtain what you desire. (Good speech)
Yoruba — Who has patience has all things.
Filipino — He who despises counsel is on the way to misfortune.
Asbanti — When a king has good counsellors, then his reign is peaceful.
Filipino — Though my house is small, my heart is large. (Hospitality)
Morocco — If people are standing at the door of your house, don't shut your door for them. (Hospitality)
Morocco — None but a dog bites in his own house. (Disgrace of quarrelling with a guest.)
Ibo — One who does what he says is not a coward.
Baganda — Gentleness and not force arrives at truth.
Yoruba — Strife never begets a gentle child.
Yoruba — He who forgives ends the quarrel.
Yoruba — Covetousness is the father of disease.
Yoruba — Not to aid one in distress is to kill him in your heart.
Ba-Congo — Everybody to his own calling and nobody to any other.
Ba-Congo — Kindness wins men not pride.

Ba-Congo — Pride only goes the length one can spit.
Ba-Congo — Kindness is like trees in a farm, they lean towards each other.
Ba-Congo — It is best to let an offense repeat itself at least three times; the first offense may be an accident, the second a mistake, but the third is likely to be intentional.
Ba-Congo — O man, what you do not like do not to your fellows.
Ba-Congo — Mutual love is often better than natural brotherhood.
Ba-Congo — One must never pay back an offender in his own coin.
Ba-Congo — Other people's property ought not to make you envious.
Ba-Congo — If you see a jackal in your neighbor's garden drive it out, one may get into yours one day, and you would like the same done for you.
Ba-Congo — To take revenge is often to sacrifice oneself.
Ba-Congo — Don't trick others lest in tricking them you teach them the way to trick you.
Ba-Congo — A good deed never dies.
Ba-Congo — Help those who cannot help themselves.
Morocco — The niggard is niggardly with regard to himself, and the money of the generous will come back to him.
Arabia — Charity lies between two charities — one to yourself, the other to your needy fellow man.
Morocco — He is like a needle that clothes the people and is himself naked. (One who gives excessively)
Japan — To hate a man is like grinding a sword to cut yourself.
Arabia — He who treats you as he treats himself does you no injustice.
Morocco — A man who is pure and gentle is to the people like gold in the pocket.
Arabia — Extremes are a mistake — a middle course is best.
Winnebago Indian — Never overdo anything.[47]

Certain personal qualities and habits are emphasized.

Filipino — A lazy dog does not get even bones. (Industry)
Filipino — Working early is better than working hard. (Foresight)
Filipino — If you want to fool, pretend to be a fool. (Shrewdness)
Arabia — There is no good in a man who is not ashamed of men.
Arabia — He who respects not himself can have no respect for others.
Yoruba — He that forgives gains the victory.
Yoruba — Anger benefits no one.
Yoruba — He who has patience has all things.[48]
Vai — A man can leave his house, but he cannot leave his way. (His reputation sticks.)
Yoruba — Wherever a man goes to dwell his character goes with him.
Yoruba — A dog that is known to be very swift is the one chosen to catch the hare.
Basuto — Perseverance always triumphs.
Basuto — A good name makes one sleep well.

V

The importance of the wisdom and power of the great man or leader is generally recognized. The Yorubas maintain that "Ordinary people are as common as grass, but good people are dearer than the eye." The Moroccans have several proverbs on this point: "The herd of cattle should not be without a bull" (leader and ruler); "The lord of the people is he who is most useful to all people;" and "The supposition of the wise man is better than the certainty of the ignorant." The Ibo of the lower Niger, in pointing out the necessity of having a leader, say, "A canoe without a steerer can easily go astray." The natives of the south-east Solomon Islands, in referring to the importance of a chief, exclaim, "When a chief declaims the very ground is rent asunder."[49] The wisdom of being diplomatic with those in control is stated by the Yorubas in the words, "If a man powerful in authority should ill-treat you, smile at him."

The experience and steadiness of old men and the advisability of the young being modest among them is occasionally dwelt upon. The Ba-Congo say "Water drawn by old men quenches thirst" (old men are to be relied upon); and "A bridgepole (over a river) held by an old man (whilst you cross over) never shakes or turns over." On the other hand the Yorubas say, "The younger should not thrust themselves into the seat of the elders," and "The young cannot teach the elders traditions."

Marriage, family affairs, the desirability of children, mother-love, and family rank are the subjects of numerous proverbs. The Yorubas, using our idea of "Marry in haste and repent at leisure," say "Quick loving a woman means quick not loving a woman." The Omaha Indian girls are told, "A handsome face does not make a good husband." When contemplating marriage the Moroccan tribesmen warn, "The ancients said, marriage takes a night, thinking of it a year," or "Don't take a wife who has money, she will treat you with arrogance, and say to you, 'Fetch water (which is a woman's business)," or again, "Marriage without good faith is like a tea-pot without a tray." For the Arabic tribesmen marriage is a desirable state. They say, "The advantages of marriage are purity of life, children, pleasures of home, and the happines of exertion for the comfort of wife and children." Childless marriages are an extreme misfortune for the Moroccan who voices the thought in "A man without children is like a horse without a tether," or "A marriage without children does not last long for men." The Chaggas of the Kilmanjaro region, looking upon children as a blessing, in fact, as a form of immortality, repeat, "He who leaves a child lives eternally."[50]

The devotion to mothers is stated by the Ashanti particularly in two proverbs: "When your mother is poor, you do not leave her and go and make someone else your mother," and again, "Even if your mother is not a good woman, she is your mother nevertheless." The nature of mother-love is universally known. Among the Ba-ila it is expressed in the words, "What is ugly to other people is fair in the sight of the child's mother;" among the Moroccans it is said that "Every beetle is a gazelle in the eyes of its mother," and the Ba-Congo say, "Though a leopard gives birth to a palm-rat she does not eat it."

The relationship between a nation and its homes is expressed by the Ashanti in the words, "When a nation is about to come to ruin, the cause begins in the homes (of its people)." Family and rank get special consideration among many primitives. The Ashanti say "When a man of noble family is mad, people say he is only the worse for wine." On the other hand "Nobility should be borne as one eats fish (humbly) and not as one partakes of elephant flesh," (proudly, and boasting about it). Finally "An ancient name cannot be cooked and eaten; after all, money is the thing."

Wealth, poverty, the relationship between rich and poor, and the effects of poverty and wealth are the subject of some proverbs. The Ibo say "Wealth makes the soup taste nice," and also "Money is the source of right." Daily saving as a means of acquiring wealth is advised by the Vai in the proverb, "A little rain every day will make the rivers swell," and the Yorubas say, "By labor comes wealth." Of the wealthless state the Ashanti say, "Poverty is stupidity," "Poverty is madness." Again they say of its universality, "Poverty is like honey, it is not peculiar to one place alone." The poor are of little consequence and are given little consideration. In this connection the Ashanti say, "A poor man does not choose his sleeping place;" "The complaint a poor man brings is investigated briefly;" and "When a poor man makes a proverb, it does not spread abroad." The poor must do much bearing of their lot according to the Arabian tribesmen who say, "A poor man without patience is like a lamp without oil." The Moroccans say, "The speech of the owner of gold is exalted, and the speech of the poor man is rejected;" or, "If a poor man speaks the truth, they drive him away and in addition spit on him." The Ibo also say, "A rich man is seldom condemned, for the mouth which eats another man's property is benumbed."

"The poor man and the rich man do not play together," is the way the Ashanti express the social cleavage between rich and poor. The effect of riches or wealth is generally conceded to be bad. The Filipinos say, "He who is raised in ease is usually destitute," and in the opinion of the Arabians, "Riches are the fomenters of desire, the thirst after wealth is more vehement than after water," and "Covetousness is the punishment of the rich." The Chaggas, noting that riches create envy, say, "Your wealth is your destruction;" the desirability of a man with money is expressed by the Moroccans in the words, supposedly in the mouths of the women, "Oh, baldheaded man with money, give that head that I may kiss it." Veblen's idea of conspicuous display is foreshadowed in the Moroccan "As much clothing you dress in so much are you worth." Many will be encouraged to know that among the Arabian tribesmen for untold generations "The remedy against bad times is to be patient with them," and that "In business the middle way is best."

Finally things are not the same everywhere. The Arabians say, "The calamities of one nation turn to the benefit of another," and the Ashanti hold that "A matter which in one place is a subject of mirth in another place is a cause of tears." Change is everywhere noticeable. The Ashanti say, "In one chief's reign skins are treated by having the hairs singed off, in that of another the skins are spread in the sun." The Maori put it, "A chief dies, another takes his place," the Hawaiians, "Man is like a banana the day it bears first" (after the banana plant has borne fruit, it dies down and another takes its place), and the Masai, "Nobody can say he is settled anywhere forever; it is only the mountains which do not move from their places."

From this brief and partial survey it can be seen that while the proverbs of primitives are not sociological thought, strictly considered, and while they only rarely deal directly with social situations as such, they are rich in social wisdom, and reflect competently and concisely the social traditions, attitudes, and philosophies of the people using and perpetuating them.

NOTES

1. Cf. L. Levy—Brühl, *Primitive Mentality*. New York, 1925, 24-28, 433-47; A. A. Goldenweiser, *Early Civilization,* New York, 1922, 410-412; W. I. Thomas, *Sourcebook for Social Origins,* Chicago, 1909, 68-9.

2. Cf. W. Johnson, *Folk Memory,* Oxford, 1908, 18-20.

3. W. G. Sumner and A. G. Keller, *The Science of Society,* New Haven, 1927-8, 754.

4. A. L. Kroeber, *Anthropology,* New York, 1923, 196-197. I have also been informed by a graduate student, who has lived for years among the Cherokees of Oklahoma, that they have a rich store of proverbs that find abundant use in their daily speech.

5. Cf. article by J.A. Kelso in *Hastings' Encyclopedia Rel. & Ethics,* X, 413; E. Weekley, "Proverbs Considered" *Atlantic Monthly* 145 (April, 1930): 504.

6. A. H. Krappe, *The Science of Folklore,* New York, 1930, 143.

7. *Op. cit.,* 143.

8. Cf. C. F. Kent, *The Wise Men of Israel and their Proverbs,* New York, 1895, *Origin and Permanent Value of the Old Testament,* New York, 1919, 167.

9. Sumner and Keller, *op. cit.,* 2111.

10. Kent, *The Wise Men of Israel and their Proverbs,* 48.

11. Kelso, *op. cit.,* 412, 414.

12. A. Cohen, *Ancient Jewish Proverbs*, London, 1913, p. 13.

13. *Cf.* Sumner and Keller, *op. cit.*, 2068; D. E. Marvin, *Curiosities in Proverbs*, New York, 1916, 4; E. Westermarck, "On the Study of Popular Sayings," *Nature* 142 (Nov. 3, 1928): 702.

14. E. Westermarck, *Wit and Wisdom in Morocco*, New York, 1931, 63.

15. *Cf.* E. Westermarck, "On the Study of Popular Sayings," *Nature* 122. (Nov. 3, 1928): 702. See also his *Wit and Wisdom of Morocco*, 54-63.

16. W. I. Thomas, *op. cit.*, 162; Krappe, *op. cit.*, 146; Kelso, *op. cit.*, 412; Weekley, *op. cit.*, 506.

17. *Cf.* Kroeber, *op. cit.*, 196.

18. E. Westermarck, "On the Study of Popular Sayings," *Nature* 122; 702.

19. Z. C. Boyajian, "Wit and Wisdom from the Near East," *Contemporary Rev.* 122 (Dec. '22): 744.

20. E. B. Tyler, *Primitive Culture*, London, 1902, I, 90.

21. W. Albig, "Proverbs and Social Control," *Sociology and Social Research*, 15 (July-August 1931): 527-535.

22. *Ibid.*, 534.

23. Krappe, *op. cit.*, 149.

24. The ashanti proverbs here mentioned are taken from R. S. Rattray, *Ashanti Proverbs*, Oxford, 1916.

25. For the Moroccan proverbs see E. Westermarck, *Wit and Wisdom of Morocco*, New York, 1931.

26. J. Cassidy, "A Chapter on Indian Proverbs," *Westminister Rev.* 164 (Oct. '05): 445-9.

27. For the Ba-Congo proverbs see C. C. Claridge, *Wild Bush Tribes of Tropical Africa*, London, 1922, 248-259.

28. Yoruban proverbs from A. B. Ellis, *The Yoruba-Speaking Peoples of the Slave Coast of West Africa*, London, 1894, pp. 218-42.

29. See collections of Filipino proverbs by Jorge Bocobo in the *Independent* 98: 496, and also those in W. D. Wallis, *An Introduction to Anthropology*, 323-4.

30. A. C. Hollis, *The Masai*, Oxford, 1905, 238-51.

31. See S. T. Plaatje, *Sechuana Proverbs*, London, 1916.

32. The Vai proverbs are from G. W. Ellis, *Negro Culture in West Africa*, New York, 1914, 147-183.

33. L. S. Green and M. W. Beckwith, "Hawaiian Stories and Wise Sayings," *Publications of Folklore Foundation*, Vassar College, No. 3.

34. Taken from A. G. Leonard, *The Lower Niger and its Tribes*, London, 1906.

35. For Arabian proverbs see *National Proverbs: Arabia*, London, 1913, or J. Wortabet, *Arabian Wisdom*, London, 1907.

36. E. W. Smith and A. M. Dale, *The Ila-Speaking Peoples of Northern Rhodesia*, London, 1920, Vol. II. 311ff.

37. On the Chaggas see C. C. F. Dundas, *Kilmanjaro and its People*, London, 1924, 341-346.

38. P. Radin, *Primitive Man as a Philosopher*, New York, 1927, 166-7.

39. W. E. Griffes, *Proverbs of Japan*, New York, 1930.

40. On Baganda proverbs see J. Roscoe, *The Baganda*, London, 1911, 485-491.

41. J. A. Farrer, *Primitive Manners and Customs*, New York, 1879, Chapter II.

42. A. C. Hollis, *The Nandi*, Oxford, 1909, 124-132.

43. For Banyoro proverbs see A. L. Kitching, *On the Backwaters of the Nile*, London, 1912, 132-140.

44. W. D. Wallis, *An Introduction to Anthropology*, New York, 1926, 323.

45. G. Brown, "Proverbs of the Samoans," *Proc. Australian Association for the Advancement of Science*, 1913.

46. E. B. Tyler, *op. cit.*, Vol. I, 88.

47. Radin, *op. cit.*, 93.

48. Farrer, *op. cit.*

49. W. G. Ivens, *Milanesians of the South-east Solomon Islands*, London, 1927.

50. On the Chaggas see C. C. F. Dundas, *Kilmanjaro and its People*, London, 1924, 341-6.

GEORGE V. ZITO

3

The Sex-Role Differentiated Family in Shakespeare

William Shakespeare (1564-1616) is certainly the most widely known and most voluminously written about author in all of English literature. In addition to the thousands of books and articles analyzing and criticizing his works, there are hundreds of works dealing with his influences, his life, and even disputes over his authorship and existence. Analysis of his work by social scientists has not been neglected either, for there are scores of works dealing with his characters and his own personality[1] by psychologists and, especially, psychoanalysts. Sociologists, however, have given his work relatively little attention.[2] In the following essay, George V. Zito examines the social relations Shakespeare depicted in his plays and finds them to parallel remarkably contemporary insights into family structure.

NOTES

1. Possibly the most interesting of these for the sociologist is: Harold Grier McCurdy, *The Personality of Shakespeare: A Venture in Psychological Method* (New Haven, Conn.: Yale University Press, 1953).

2. One such study is: Emory S. Bogardus, "Social Distance in Shakespeare," *Sociology and Social Research* 18 (1933) : 67-73. A partial exception might also be: Theodore Caplow, "The Motives of Hamlet," chapter 8 in his *Two Against One: Coalitions in Triads* (Englewood Cliffs, New Jersey: Prentice-Hall, 1968), pp. 114-27.

THE SEX-ROLE DIFFERENTIATED FAMILY IN SHAKESPEARE * †

The concept of family structure predicated upon sex-differentiated instrumental and expressive-emotive roles was first posited by Robert F. Bales and Talcott Parsons (1955), an outgrowth of the Interaction Process Analysis studies of Bales (1950) and the theory of action considerations of Parsons, Bales, and Shils (1953). The 1955 study included a cross-cultural survey by Zelditch, which attempted to show that such a structure exists even in matriarchal societies. Essentially, the Parsons-Bales concept of family structure involves the father performing all instrumental, task-oriented activity within the family, while the mother is limited to primarily expressive-emotive activiies. This does not preclude the mother's performing daily routines of essentially instrumental functions, however; what it does say is that her primary function is emotive-integrative, unifying the family by furnishing emotional support to its members. Similarly, the father is not precluded from emotional involvement with his wife and children; but his primary function, in this model, is one of task or work orientation, including effective interfacing with the larger society.

The Parsons-Bales model was later challenged by Slater (1961), who presented experimental evidence which appears to challenge the efficacy of such a model when applied to the nuclear family. In particular, Slater cited studies which emphasized the expressive-emotive functions performed by fathers. Recently Theodore Caplow has summarized some of this evidence (1968, p. 86) supporting the Slater view.

The evidence cited by Slater and Caplow, however, leaves the matter unresolved. For example, although Kohn and Clausen (1956) had found a high incidence of schizophrenia associated with families composed of dominating mothers and emotionally non-participant fathers, with the mother performing all instrumental and expressive-emotive activities, it is not clear that such an epidemiology is destructive to the Parsons-Bales model; it may, indeed, support it. Similarly, the work of Lidz, Parker and Cornelison (1956), which emphasized the withdrawal of fathers from instrumental and expressive activity as a recurrent feature in the life history of female schizophrenics does not *in itself* challenge the model, although Caplow cites the work as supportive of Slater. Nor can one any longer derive satisfaction from Slater's footnote reference (p. 302) to the popularity of Benjamin

---

*This article was especially prepared for the present volume.

† I would like to acknowledge the constructive criticism of Ephraim H. Mizruchi in the preparation of this paper.

Spock's theory of child-rearing among middle-class families, with its call for "undifferentiated" parental roles. The success of Etzioni (1968) in employing the Bales paradigm of group processes and Parsonian structural-functional theory in the rehabilitation of mental patients appears to further mitigate Slater's earlier objections. Most recently Maris (1970) has claimed that the Bales paradigm is deducible from Homans's empirical generalizations, and Strodtbeck and Bezdec (1970) have again raised the question of sex-role identity enculturation via instrumental and expressive role dictates.

The sex-role differentiated family was one of those "obvious" sociological truisms "obfuscated" by Parsons, according to sociology's less insightful critics. The father works, and the mother nurtures the children. But if such a model of family structure is "obvious" to our critics, it is something less than obvious to the best minds our culture has produced. If we examine the plays of Shakespeare, for example, we find that the sex-role differentiated family is as problematic in his literature as it is in our own.

Of Shakespeare's thirty-six or thirty-seven plays (depending on whether we include *Henry VIII*), twenty contain daughter figures. Since so much of the recent social-psychological literature stresses the effect of father-role performance on daughter enculturation (cf. Caplow, p. 93), let us limit ourselves to these twenty plays, and see what insights may be gained.

SHAKESPEAREAN FAMILY STRUCTURE

A peculiarity of the dramaturgical format inherited by Shakespeare from the Italian theater is the relative absence of the mother figure. Fathers of daughters, when they appear in the Elizabethan-Jacobean theater, usually do not have wives; the daughters are almost always motherless and there is usually no mention whatever of a mother having ever existed. That this peculiarity is not limited to Shakespeare can be shown by considering other popular plays of the period, such as Kyd's *Spanish Tragedy*, Marlowe's *Tamburlaine* and his *Jew of Malta*, Beaumont's *The Maid's Tragedy* and Dekker's *Shoemaker's Holiday*. The format is widely employed, although few audiences are aware of its presence while witnessing a performance. We witness it today in innumerable "Medical Center" episodes of popular TV drama, with their subplots involving young female patients and their wifeless fathers.

In the earliest of the Shakespearean plays involving fathers and daughters, such as *Henry VI* and *Titus Andronicus*, the father is primarily an authority figure devoid of familial functions of any kind, other than performing the ritual surrender of the bride. In the middle period plays the father takes on increased familial duties of both an instrumental and emotive-integrative kind, particularly with respect to his daughters. In what may be Shakespeare's last play, *The Tempest*, his emotive-integrative aspects are strongly developed, although the daughter figure has suffered a loss in characterization oddly at variance with her increased verbal freedom, a result of the development of the Romance genre with its ideations of character types.

That Shakespeare was aware of the peculiar nature of the inherited motherless daughter format is shown by his attempt in 1596 to introduce the sex-role differentiated family in *Romeo and Juliet*. Prior to this play his daughter figures, such as Katherina and Bianca in *Taming of The Shrew*, Sylvia in *Two Gentlemen of Verona*, Hermia in *Midsummer Night's Dream*, etc., are all motherless. In *Romeo and Juliet* he gives us a fully sex-role differentiated family: Capulet, the father, is shown attending to the instrumental activity connected with his daughter's wedding, and Lady Capulet to the emotional and integrative activity; Capulet makes the required arrangement with Paris, sends his wife to his daughter to sound her feelings in the matter, acts as head of household in controlling servants, in quieting boorish guests, sees to the door uninvited guests, etc. His wife takes care of the emotional context of the activities, secludes herself twice with her daughter as her confidant, etc. When an altercation occurs between father and daughter, the mother interposes herself between them to mitigate the father's rage, but when the husband-wife coalition is threatened by the daughter's obstinacy the mother withdraws her support of the daughter to consolidate her own wifely role.

All these actions are consistent with the instrumental vs. expressive emotive polarization of parental roles by sex which are cardinal to the Parsons-Bales model of family structure.

Shakespeare's sudden incorporation of the mother figure in a play dealing with the daughter of a father was perhaps dictated by the demands of the inherited plot, which dealt with "two households, both alike in dignity, in fair Verona" (Prologue). The Montagues, rivals of the Capulets, are also provided with a mother figure. This would appear to mark a turning point in Elizabethan dramaturgy. But by the end of the play both mother figures have been rejected: Lady Montague has died and Lady Capulet is about to; even the mother-surrogate Nurse has been rejected by both Juliet and the audience for approving a second marriage for young Juliet while her first husband is still living. The adult women, in Elizabethan plays, are seldom given positive characterizations; Hamlet's mother Gertrude is as positive an adult female as one is likely to find in this literature, and even she, if not involved directly in her first husband's murder, is at least an adulteress and negatively polarized from the standpoint of the audience. Hamlet's father's ghost reminds us that the problem of the mother had best be left to heaven.

Shakespeare can be shown to have retained any variation he had himself introduced into inherited dramaturgical structures that proved to satisfy the demands of his audience. Thus, the three *amorosi* of the Italianate structure, once transformed into three English gallants and proven before an audience, was retained; we shall have more to say on this structure below. It is difficult to believe that, had the sex-role differentiated family worked before his audiences, he would not have retained it. But he did not. The year after *Romeo and Juliet*, in 1597, he gave his audience *The Merry Wives of Windsor*, a play in which both mother and father of Anne Page are presented. But there is no differentiation of parental roles in *The Merry Wives*: each parent instruments his own plan to snare Anne for the suitor of his choice, Mrs. Page prefering the Doctor and Mr. Page a local boy. No familial activity takes place, there is no husband-wife interaction or parent-child interaction, all of which had been present in *Romeo and Juliet*. Two years later he produced his third and final attempt at including a mother figure in a play which includes a father and his daughter: this is a fragmentary scene in *Henry V* where the silent Queen of France is present upon the stage for her husband-king's surrender of the bride, daughter Katherine. From 1599 on Shakespeare did not include mothers of daughters in his plays, reverting to his earlier format. It is true, however, that at the very end of his career, when he helped other playwrights arrange their works for the stage and contributed some acts or scenes of his own (as in *Pericles* and *The Winter's Tale*) mothers of daughters are present in the plot. At the very point in the text of *Pericles* where Shakespeare begins to write, however (Wright 1968, p. vii), he has the mother die upon giving birth to the daughter, eliminating her from the action of the play, although she reappears miraculously in the wholly contrived last moments of the final act. *The Winter's Tale* is a dramatization of Robert Greene's prose novel, *Pandosto*: here too Shakespeare employs the identical dramatic device he and his collaborator had devised for *Pericles*, eliminating the mother. In neither play is there any semblance of the sex-role differentiated family.

If Shakespeare found that the sex-role differentiated family did not work before his audience, and consequently eliminated it, as he appears to have done, then the reasons for such a failure appear unclear, at least initially. It is unlikely that the audiences found such a structure artificial, or unnatural. It is, after all, a purportedly dominant motif in the normative, if not factual, order of Western culture. On the other hand, the structure he initially and then finally employed, that of the motherless daughter of a father figure, can only be considered artificial and unnatural. Since this latter format does appear to have satisfied the expectations of his audiences, perhaps an understanding of this structure will help us to understand the failure of the sex-role differentiated family structure before an audience.

THE ITALIANATE STRUCTURE

The dramaturgical structure inherited by Shakespeare from the theater of the Italian Renaissance did not contain a mother figure. The mother figure appears to have been eliminated in the wild free-for-all aimed at the daughter's chastity by the three competing *amorosi*. The *amorosi* contend for the *amorosa* under the watchful eye of her father, himself an old bull who understands the game; there is as much sport in outwitting the old bull as in obtaining his daughter. The format is best known to American audiences through Mozart's opera, *Don Giovanni*. In the *maschio* of the Renaissance Italian male, the wishes of the female target are of little consequence: the game is a game played among males. This aspect of the game in itself helps explain the lack of a mother figure; but in addition it must be remembered that in latin cultures generally the mother figure is sacrosanct; to insult a man's mother was (and to a certain extent still is) the gravest insult one can offer a latin male. Thus the mother figure is eliminated from the *commedia della arte* theatrical format and from the Italianate theater of Elizabethan England. In the Italianate structure incorporated into *Two Gentlemen of Verona*, for example, Thurio, Valentine, and Proteus are the three *amorosi* competing for *amorosa* Sylvia under the watchful eye of her father, the Duke of Milan. The significant alteration in this format performed later by Shakespeare was his transformation of the three rivals into three friends, only one of whom is a suitor for the lady's hand; in *Romeo and Juliet*, for example, Romeo is the suitor, and with Mercutio and Benvolio completes the trio of gallants; in *Othello* Roderigo is the suitor and Cassio and Iago his companions; in *Much Ado About Nothing* the three are Claudio, Don Pedro, and Benedick, etc. The development of the three *amorosi* into three gallants worked before an English audience, and hence Shakespeare retained the innovation once he had made it. But his efforts to alter the Italianate structure to allow for the sex-role differentiated family did not, and he retained this portion of the inherited format intact. We can only surmise that although this format was foreign and imported bodily into England from a culture where sex-role definitions differed from those of the English, it nevertheless fullfilled certain expectations in the theater audiences of sixteenth-and seventeenth-century England.

FATHER-DAUGHTER CONFLICT

Conflict with respect to the daughter's choice of mate is involved in twelve of the twenty plays. Parent-child conflict of this variety is a persisting theme in disparate theaters. McGranahan and Wayne (1948) classified works of the German and the American popular theaters of 1928, and in their class E, *Patterns of Conflict in the Love Theme*, discerned eight principal variants. They then rank-ordered these variants by frequency of occurrence. If we score the twenty Shakespearean plays according to the McGranahan and Wayne criteria, the principal patterns of conflict in the love theme are as shown in table 1, with the German and American theater rankings obtained by McGranahan and Wayne shown for comparison.

TABLE 1. Patterns of conflict in the love theme of Shakespeare's father and daughter plays, employing the McGranahan and Wayne categories.

Rank	MW Rank	Category	No. plays	Percent
1	1	Youthful love vs. parents	8	40
2	2	True love vs. unwholesome love	3	15
3	4	Love vs. ideals, higher values	3	15
4	8	Miscellaneous	3	15
5	3	Love vs. temporary misunderstandings	1	5
6	6	Power conflicts for love	1	5
7	7	Love vs. outcast status	1	5
8	5	Idealists' love vs. social norms	0	0
		Total	20	100

It is seen in table 1 that *youthful love vs. parents* is the most frequent variant of the love theme in both these Shakespearean plays and the German and American plays of the early twentieth century. The most significant displacement in ranks is the elevation to third position of the *love vs. temporary misunderstandings* category, the familiar boy-meets-girl theme which ranked only fifth in Shakespeare's plays.

In the later theaters both parents are included in the principal love-conflict pattern; in the Shakespearean theater the father figure, as sole parent, assumes the parental side of the love-conflict motif. The Shakespearean format allows for a greater dramatic exposition, since the transfer of affection from father to husband, the sexual jealousy of the father, and the triumph of the young male may be explored with relative ease, heightening the love-conflict pattern which apparently is so popular with audiences. But it would be wrong to insist upon this feature as the sole reason for abandoning the sex-role differentiated family and reverting to the Italianate formula, for it must be borne in mind that the latter paid no attention whatever to the wishes of the daughter; in the Shakespearean version of the formula, the daughter's wishes assume an importance absent in the original formulation, and it is here that we are given our most significant indicator of the success of the formula before audiences unenculturated with *maschio* sex role dictates, and to the reason for Shakespeare's return to the format after having abandoned it temporarily in favor of the sex-role differentiated family.

DAUGHTER INDIVIDUATION

To appreciate the significance of the daughter as subject, rather than object as in the original formulation, one must consider the degree of individuation she is granted. One index of individuation is the level of verbal interaction she is permitted *as* daughter. In the earlier Shakespearean plays (*Henry VI*, etc.) daughters never speak directly to their fathers. As late as *Much Ado About Nothing* (1598) Beatrice reminds Hero that her role as daughter requires her to say "Father, as it please you" (II,1), although when it comes to her choice of mate she is to say "Father, as it please me." In earlier plays daughters, if they speak to their fathers at all, are limited to replies. Even Juliet and Hero are limited to desperation pleas when they speak to their fathers, a small but significant gain. In *The Taming of the Shrew* Katherina does rage at her father from time to time, although her sister Bianca, normatively obedient, never addresses her father in the course of the play. The only daughter to actually institute a conversation with her father is Miranda in *The Tempest*. In *Cymbeline* daughter Imogen argues with her father, but as an already married woman she is granted this privelege, as the text makes clear. Nondaughters of daughter age, on the other hand, are allowed to be highly voluble with uncles and other males of parental age (Beatrice, Viola, Rosalind, etc.). In table 2, column 5, we have indicated the presence or absence of verbal interaction afforded the daughter figure, without regard to the relative intensity. It will be seen that although Shakespeare developed increased mastery over his material with time, the level of individuation granted his daughter figures does not systematically increase, if we judge by verbal interaction alone. But we do see that it is most frequent in his great middle period, from *Romeo* through *Lear*; and it must be borne in mind that of the plays "completed by 1616," only *The Tempest* is wholly his own. What is most significant is that verbal interaction, beyond that signified by an N in the table, developed at all. Although two daughters are scored Y in the earliest period, these are problematic scorings: Lavinia addresses a formal speech to her father in the opening act, welcoming him back to Rome in a public ceremony: hardly interaction in the small groups meaning of the word; and Katherina's tirades are intended to give her a negative polarization: once "tamed," such activity ceases. But following this period there is a marked increase in verbal activity between fathers and daughters. And with very few exceptions (Cressida, Goneril, Regan) the audience is expected to sympathize with the daughter figure, especially when it comes to contention with her father regarding her choice of mate.

TABLE 2. Shakespearean Fathers & Daughters.

Play	Daughters	Fathers	Categories*				
			1	2	3	4	5
Completed by 1594							
Henry VI (1)	Margaret	Regnier	Y	N	N	6	N
Two Gent. Verona	Sylvia	Milan	N	N	Y	1	N
Titus Andron.	Lavinia	Titus	Y	N	Y	1	Y
Taming Shrew	Katherina	Minola	N	N	Y	1	Y
	Bianca	Minola	N	N			N
Completed by 1599							
Midsummer Night's	Hermia	Egeus	Y	N	Y	1	N
Henry IV (1)	L. Mortimer	Glendower	Y	N	N	8	Y
Merch. Venice	Jessica	Shylock	Y	N	Y	1	Y
	(Portia)	(Belmont)	N	N			—
Romeo & Juliet	Juliet	Capulet	Y	Y	Y	7	Y
Merry Wives Wind.	Anne Page	Page	N	Y	Y	1	N
Much Ado Nothing	Hero	Leonato	N	N	N	4	Y
As You Like It	Rosalind	Duke Senior	Y	N	N	4	Y
	Celia	D. Frederick	N	N			Y
Henry V	Katherine	King of France	N	Y	N	8	N
Completed by 1608							
Hamlet	Ophelia	Polonius	Y	N	Y	4	Y
Troil. & Cress.	Cressida	Calchas	Y	N	Y	2	N
Othello	Desdemona	Brabantio	Y	N	Y	2	Y
King Lear	Cordelia	Lear	Y	N	Y	1	Y
	Goneril	Lear			N	—	Y
	Regan	Lear			N	—	Y
Completed by 1616							
Pericles	(nameless)	Antiochus	Y	N	N	2	N
	Thaisa	Simonides		N	N		Y
	Marina	Pericles		Y	N		N
Cymbeline	Imogen	Cymbeline	Y	N	N	3	Y
Winters Tale	Perdita	Leontes	Y	Y	N	1	Y
The Tempest	Miranda	Prospero	Y	N	N	8	Y

* Key to categories: Y=yes, N=no.
  Categories:
    1: Anomie present in society of plays?
    2: Does daughter have mother in play?
    3: Is daughter in conflict with father re her choice of mate?
    4: Principal conflict pattern in love theme, using McGranahan and Wayne class.
    5: Verbal interaction between fathers and daughters in play?

ROLE EXPECTATIONS

A daughter's obligations to her father are stated by Desdemona and Cordelia in parallel texts of 10 lines each; life and education, obedience, love and honor while single, are cited. But upon marriage, preference is to the husband over the father. A father's obligations regarding his daughters are stated by Capulet: day and night, at work or at play, he is to strive to obtain a "good" husband for her. Minola, in *Shrew*, sees to it that his daughters are educated in music, etc., in order to become wives.

The inherited normative system which provides definitions for social interaction in these plays sees daughters as persons passed from fathers to husbands. Females are defined here by the males in their lives. Cut off from father and lover, Ophelia's existence becomes pointless, and she dies a suicide.

But as Van Meteren noted in 1575, England was "the paradise of married women." The married woman's attitude toward her husband are stated by Katherina, at the end of *The Taming of the Shrew* (V,2), and illustrated by her sister Bianca and The Widow: outright contempt, indifference to his needs or wants, and scorn of his maleness. Married women, in Shakespearean plays, are reprehensible monsters: it is Lady Capulet who cries out for Romeo's blood. Adult women, with few exceptions, tend to be scheming, diabolical figures such as Lady Macbeth, Goneril, and Regan. The adult woman role is a rejected one in these plays. The young woman role is, on the other hand, portrayed sympathetically.

In view of the inherited normative prescriptions illustrated by Cordelia and Desdemona, and presumed by all Shakespearean father figures, the sympathetic portrayal of the daughter figure in conflict with such norms must be viewed as satisfying the audience's identification with her, rather than the norms with which she contends. Coupled with the negative portrayal of the adult woman, this can only indicate the emergence of the young woman as someone of at least potentially greater individuation. It becomes apparent, then, that reversion to the Italianate format, since it allowed for the daughter figure to be seen apart from the mother figure as an individual in her own right in conflict with an inherited patriarchal normative order, admirably met the enlarged feminine expectations then manifesting themselves in Elizabethan England. It will be recalled that women ruled politically at the time, Mary Guise as Mary Stuart's deputy of Scotland, and Elizabeth in England, and John Knox bewailed the "monsterous regiment of women." Thus, a structure devised in conformity with the *maschio* expectations of the Italian male was admirable adapted to the emerging expectations of English females. It is no less significant that during the Jacobean period, as these expectations began to wane under an English king and the threat of a Puritan dictatorship, the daughter figure once again reverts to a stereotype as a dramatic convention.

McCurdy (1953) has tabulated the number of lines assigned each character in each play. He notes five plays in which the largest number of lines are assigned to female characters. These plays are listed in table 3.

TABLE 3. Plays about female characters, by line count.

All's Well That Ends Well	Helena	1600
Merchant of Venice	Portia	1596
Twelfth Night	Viola	1599
As You Like It	Rosalind	1599
Cymbeline	Imogen	1609

It will be seen that all are *young* women; there is no Shakespearean play "about" an adult woman. None of these young women have mothers in the plays, although three are daughters of fathers. With the exception of Imogen, an already married heroine when the play opens, these daughters all appear in plays written between 1596 and 1600.

It is significant that four of these five young women become transvestites in the course of their plays, for only as pseudo-males are they enabled to participate in their societies to the limits of their individual personal worth. Portia is, of course, the most striking example of this.

DISCUSSION

It would seem, on the basis of the above considerations, that under the conditions prevalent in England of the late sixteenth and early seventeenth centuries, popular audiences were particularly receptive to presentations of daughter figures, conveniently isolated from the influences of mothers, attempting to secure greater participation as individuals in their societies. The daughter is repeatedly shown to be in conflict with the existing, inherited normative order, of which her father often represents the principal dramaturgical focus. She is treated as an object and yet is given a positive polarization in her conflict, while her father as familial representative is given a negative polarization in her conflict, although he is treated as a subject.

We find increased significance in the fact that such daughter characterizations are most frequent in this literature immediately preceding the death of Elizabeth in 1603. If we compute the rate of production of Shakespeare's father-daughter plays, for example, we find this to be at a maximum between 1596 and 1599, during which period he composed no less than seven such plays, and only three of other genres. This is not only the same period in which the four transvestite daughters are introduced, however; it is also that period in which he attempted to introduce the sex-role differentiated family via *Romeo and Juliet* and worked away from this format to the version he had inherited. Although that version was imported from a latin culture where sex-role expectations differed from that of England, it was able to satisfy English audience role expectations because of the possibility of greater daughter individuation and the portrayal of the conflict between the normative and enlarged feminist expectations. But if such expectations were indeed enlarged, a consequence of increased political power by significant others of the female sex and heightened domestic power by married women, it is no less significant that institutional failures in the economic, religious, as well as the political sectors probably contributed equally to an already anomic situation.

Durkheim listed (1966, p. 255) as institutional failures contributing to the anomic state of a society, (1) the loss of the regulative power of religion, (2) government becoming the tool of economic life, (3) national efforts to acheive industrial prosperity. That all three factors played significant roles in the Elizabethan-Jacobean period requires little discussion here; the religious sector had become deregulative under Henry VIII, the enclosure movement had displaced populations, the loss of the Spanish Armada had placed England at the front of a new mercantilism, the importation of foreign ideas, products, and fashions had become widespread, etc. That the resulting anomic situation is reflected in these plays can readily be shown. If we score these plays for the presence or absence of anomie according to the criteria of table 4, for example, we find fifteen of the twenty societies portrayed satisfactorily fulfilling the requirements. (See table 2 for scoring.)

TABLE 4. Tests for anomie (cf. Durkheim, Merton).
1. Are church, state, and/or social institutions shown as ineffectual in regulating individual/collective behavior?
2. Do most characters express or exhibit alienation or anomia?
3. Are appetites enlarged, exceeding reasonable expectations of satisfaction?

The Puritan Commonwealth would attempt to reorganize the disordered state of English social organization; a heightened conservatism had already developed at the close of Elizabeth's reign.

Thus, the daughters are portrayed as participants within a deregulated societal context. This would seem to be consistent with their treatment in conflict with normative demands, which we noted earlier. Does this suggest that under conditions of anomie, we may expect an increase in feminist protest? and that coupled with such a phenomenon a decreased interest and emphasis on the sex-role differentiated family? The answer is by no means clear. Durkheim suggests that under conditions of anomie "all classes contend among themselves," and "the race for the unattainable goal (gives) no pleasure but that of the race itself," while "appetites, not being controlled by public opinion, become disoriented, no longer recognizing the limits proper to them" (p. 255). From this standpoint, women, as a class or caste in a society, can be expected to have increased expectations during periods of social deregulation. Does this help account for recurrent feminine protest? and does it, in turn, help account for social change?

CONCLUSION

Our treatment in the foregoing has been suggestive. The Sociology of Literature raises more problems than it is equipped to solve; sociological *solutions* require the application of rigorous research techniques on representative populations. But the Sociology of Literature, since it utilizes the productions of the greatest minds of our cultural systems, is capable of providing illumination and focus by its ability to inter-relate concepts in ways less available to a traditionalist sociology. By applying the methods and concepts of our available theoretical literature to significant literary works which involve sociological dimensions, we are permitted to see entire clusters and arrays which otherwise escape us, and which we ignore only at our peril.

It is clear that Shakespeare became aware of the limitations of the sex-role differentiated family in its appeal to a popular audience, and it is suggested that such a loss of appeal was due to the anomic situation then confronting English society, an anomie itself reflected in the plays. It is perhaps less clear that the referenced work of Slater, for example, took account of the state of deregulation in the populations sampled by his cited references, or those of Caplow; and it is perhaps more evident that the Parsons-Bales paradigm may be less representative of families during periods of great social change or deregulation. This consideration may be sufficient in itself to preclude dispensing with the paradigm as a useful analytical tool. Brofenbrenner is quoted by Caplow (93) that the "undifferentiated" parental coalition, which Slater footnoted as representative of Spock, may be the most dangerous: "The most dependent and least dependable adolescents describe families which are neither patriarchal nor matriarchal, but egalitarian." While a great deal of the available evidence appears to show correlations between dominating instrumental mothers (and fathers who have abdicated participation) and high rates of schizophrenia in female offspring, it remains unclear whether it is the domineering mother or abdicated father who is primarily diagnostic of the condition; perhaps it is merely the implied repudiation of the sex-role differentiated family structure by both parents. Shakespearean fathers, as surrogates of both parents, are called upon to perform both kinds of activities, the instrumental and the expressive-emotive. But they are also shown as being ineffectual, ultimately, in solving the problem of the daughter. For that purpose an adult woman figure is required who is less bloodthirsty than Lady Capulet, and less rejected than that we find in the Shakespearean literature, and in most of our own popular literature as well.

REFERENCES

Bales, Robert F. *Interaction Process Analysis*. Cambridge: Addison-Wesley, 1950.

Caplow, Theodore. *Two Against One: Coalitions in Triads*. Englewood Cliffs, N.J.: Prentice-Hall, 1968.

Durkheim, Emile. *Suicide*. Translated by John Spaulding and George Simpson. New York: Free Press, 1966.

Etzioni, Amatai. Dual Leadership in a Therapeutic Organization." *International Review of Applied Psychology* 17 (1968): 51-67.

Kohn, Melvin L., and John A. Clausen. "Parental Authority Behavior and Schizophrenia." *American Journal of Orthopsychiatry* 26 (1956): 297-313.

Lidz, Theodore, Beula Parker and Alice Cornelison. The Role of the Father in the Family Environment of the Schizophrenic Patient." *American Journal of Psychiatry* 113 (1956): 126-32.

McCurdy, Harold Grier. *The Personality of Shakespeare: A Venture in Psychological Method*. New Haven: Yale University Press, 1953.

McGranahan, D.V., and I. Wayne. "German and American Traits Reflected in Popular Drama." *Human Relations* 1 (1948): 429-55.

Maris, Ronald. "The Logical Adequacy of Homans' Social Theory." *American Sociological Review* 35 (1970): 1069-81.

Merton, Robert K. *Social Theory and Social Structure*. New York: Free Press, 1949.

Mizruchi, Ephraim H. *Success and Opportunity: A Study in Anomie*. Glencoe, Ill.: Free Press, 1964.

Parsons, Talcott, Robert F. Bales and Edward Shils. *Working Papers in the Theory of Action*. New York: Free Press, 1953.

Parsons, Talcott, and Robert F. Bales. *Family, Socialization, and Interaction Process*: Glencoe, Ill.: Free Press, 1955.

Slater, Philip. "Parental Role Differentiation." *American Journal of Sociology* 67 (1961): 269-311.

Strodtbeck, Fred, and William Bezdek. "Sex-Role Identity and Pragmatic Action." *American Sociological Review* 35 (1970): 491-502.

Wright, Louis B. "A Greek Romance for Shakespeare's Stage." In *The Folger Shakespeare, Pericles*. New York: Washington Square Press, 1968, p. vii.

MARVIN B. SCOTT

4

The Marquis de Sade and the Quest for the Nonabsurd

Comte Donatien Alphonse Francois de Sade, better known as the Marquis de Sade (1740-1814), the still controversial author whose licentious works were until recently unavailable to the general public, is today regarded by many as a profound thinker deserving of a high position in the ranks of French literature. Sade was the prodigious author of a dozen novels (each ranging from two to ten volumes), approximately sixty short stories, twenty plays, and many smaller works.[1] Much of his writing was done in prison and about one-quarter of his manuscripts were burned by the police. His life was punctuated by many violent sexual scandals which resulted in his spending a total of thirty years in prison where he spent the last thirteen years of his life.

Though his works were for years considered to be the ravings of a monstrous criminal mind, modern examinations of his writings by both literary critics and psychiatrists have argued that his work anticipated many elements in the philosophy of Nietzsche and in modern psychology.

NOTES

1. Sade's major works include: *Justine ou les Malheurs de la vertu (1791); La Philosophie dans le boudoir (1795); Aline et Valcour (1795); Juliette (1797);* and *Les 120 Journées de Sodome (1931-35).*

THE MARQUIS DE SADE AND THE QUEST FOR THE NONABSURD*

The absurd raises the problem of how one carves out meaning in a meaningless world. Thus a sociology of the absurd (see Lyman and Scott 1970) takes as its subject matter man's quest for the nonabsurd. While trying to understand how modern man achieves the nonabsurd, I happened to run across the writings of the Marquis de Sade. In the light of Sade's work, the following represents a preliminary orientation for understanding modern man's quest for the nonabsurd.

SADE AND THE ABSURD

The tireless heroine of Sade's novel, *Justine*, asks: "So pray tell me: what life shall be mine to lead?" To which Sade answers: "An absurd life."

To me the significance of Sade[1] rests upon his contributions to the analysis of the absurd. By the absurd I mean the subjective sense that one's established social worlds are hopelessly alien from one's conception of the good, the expected, and the "normal." The absurd may be experienced either as a sense that no effective and appropriate norms are available to produce meaning, and the result is a gnawing sense of confusion about the world and events; or it may be experienced as a sense of impotence, a sense that activities are matters of compulsion, and vehicles of coercive rather than individual expression.

The conditions that generate these two senses of the absurd can be gleaned from the world that Sade himself experienced. To begin with, the France of the late eighteenth century was a world of profound transition. The *Ancien Regime* was to give way to a new republic; and normative frameworks were to break down, ushering in an era of acute anomie—the feeling that one's experiences no longer fit with one's expectations.

*This article was especially prepared for the present volume. Copyright © 1970 by Marvin B. Scott.

Besides his experience in an anomicized world, Sade also spent half his adult life in a world equally pathological, and yet in every way the opposite of an anomic milieu. I refer to his years in "total institutions" (See Goffman 1961)—i.e., asylums and prisons—where he faced the deadening drudgery of routinized life. Rather than the feeling that one's experiences no longer fit with one's expectations (the condition of anomie), total institutions produce the feeling of a *too* predictable world—a condition Emile Durkheim called "fatalism."[2]

Sade thus experienced equally two opposite milieux: intense anomie and intense fatalism. His observations and writings are continually informed by this joint experience. From the absurdity of his own social existence, Sade formulated the fundamental human problem: How to achieve a sense of dignity and humanity; and at the same time, achieve a zestful, though continuously meaningful existence? To the extent that our age is characterized by the conditions of anomie and fatalism, and to the extent that the resulting human problem of our time is to achieve a sense of dignity, humanity, zest, and meaningfulness—to the extent that these are true, Sade's ideas are relevant for an understanding and analysis of the modern world.

On the basis of Sade's own experiences, then, the joint task of man—faced with absurdity—is to get outside of the deadening routine and to apprehend a sense of purposeful meaning. Efforts to resolve these two problems constitute the quest for the nonabsurd.

Sade provides a perspective to attain—and analyze—the nonabsurd. The key element of this perspective is, in a special sense of the term, *sadism.*

To clarify its meaning, sadism may be distinguished from two other notions often confounded with it, namely, *Schadenfreude* and algolagnia. *Schadenfreude* refers to the sense of joy or excitement one may receive when others have suffered some unhappiness. In the case of *Schadenfreude*, the person having the enjoyment is not responsible for the suffering of the other. The joy one might experience by watching a man slip on a banana peel is *Schadenfreude*, not sadism. Algolagnia refers to the sexual pleasure that one may receive by inflicting pain on others. Although the psychoanalytic literature often identifies algolagnia with sadism, it might be more properly thought of as a specialized type of sadism.

What, then, is sadism? In brief, it refers to "the pleasure felt from the observed modifications on the external world produced by the will of the observer" (Gorer 1962, p.156). Unlike *Schadenfreude*, the pleasures of sadism do not spring from the unhappiness of others, but from the knowledge that one is responsible. According to British anthropologist Geoffrey Gorer, what is central to sadism is the pleasure one receives by knowing that one's words or actions affect others strongly. "Sadism," Gorer suggests, "covers an enormous range of human activity, from creation of works of art to the blowing up of bridges, from making little girls happy by giving them sweets, to making them cry by slapping them" (Gorer 1962, p.156). Sadism is the pleasure a bank robber has when he looks at the horrified face of the teller as he says, "Stick 'em up!" Sadism is giving a great performance on the dramatic stage to the applause of an audience. In short, sadism involves any perceivable modification of the external world through one's own efforts.

If sadism connotes destruction and cruelty, it is because one is more likely to perceive a modification of the world by blowing up a bridge than by building it. And rape provides a reality missing in seduction.

Sade perceived the connection between absurdity on the one hand and assertiveness and violence on the other. The awareness of absurdity makes man free—literally, a libertine. But the price of freedom is the terror that comes with this awareness: the terror of fundamental ontological insecurity. As a result, the free man (or libertine) needs "violent emotions in order to feel the truth of his individual existence" (Beauvoir 1953, p. 63).

REBELLION AND THE NONABSURD

The "sadistic" orientation is, according to Sade, most natural to man's basic nature. Sade's image of man has a peculiarly contemporary ring. He sees man as a eudaemonic creature, as one who seeks stress, dissonance, and thrills. (For an examination of this conception of man, see May 1969; Klausner 1968.) Since it is his nature to be aroused, he will move in the direction of those activities that create an aroused state. And the activity most likely to produce arousal is *rebellion*: the flagrant violation of norms.

Because infractions trigger counter-reactions, the flagrant violation of norms is a sure way of perceivably modifying the world. The modifications produced by the rebellious act also include a restructuring of ordinary time and space. When absurdity is experienced, routine time and space is oppressive; to get outside of routine time and space becomes part of the quest for the nonabsurd. Rebellious acts collapse time into a single realizable event, and transform space into new settings rich with dramatic meaning. In brief, the *act* of rebellion itself is a way of achieving the nonabsurd.

Sade grants that what a man is—as a person, as a social animal—depends in part on the institutions in his social environment. But beneath this facade, he remains a rebel: man is a "stance-taking entity," whose spirit is beyond the control of all institutions.[3] Except under violence or torture, man never submits totally to his social institutions; or enclosed in a society where he may feel oppressed by morality and law, man somehow will seek freedom in the rebellious act.

As a society takes on the oppressive characteristics of total institutions, rebellion may take the form of idiosyncratic sexual behavior, exercised without restraint in the private sector of life. Sade is always sensitive to the distinction between private and public life. The public life of Sade's fictional characters is irrelevant to their happiness — which is located offstage in the private domain. In the private sphere man can practice secret roles and realize suppressed dreams. Sade, in his own life and in the fictional worlds he created, recognized the importance of having territorial control for the exercise of idiosyncratic sexual behavior.

In Sade's revolutionary program, one privately practices sexual irregularity until the private can be transformed into the public. With good reason, Sade's ideas have been called "obscene." But note that *ob/scene* means literally "offstage." Sade wants to take the offstage world and put it onstage. In Herbert Marcuse's phrase, Sade calls for an "erotization of the entire personality" (1955, p. 184). This is not measured by frequency of sexual relations; it means the spread of the private to a wide range of public societal relations. Sade, then, is concerned not only with freedom but with the *ecstasy* of freedom — which comes from transforming the private to the public, the offstage to the onstage.[4] In Sade's formulation, freedom equals obscenity.[5]

For Sade, then, sexual irregularity in private is but a rehearsal and a prelude of a new life, where the ecstasy of freedom will be expressed in the public arena. Until that day, sexual behavior remains the best defense against the oppressive social order. On this point, we may note an interesting convergence between Sade and Max Weber.

Weber (1922, pp. 236-42) recognized that the enemy of a bureaucratic, rationalized society is sexual behavior. He noted that "rationalization" and the methodical planning of life are seriously threatened by the peculiar irrationality of the sexual act. Wherever society becomes bureaucratized and rationalized — wherever it takes on the characteristics of total institutions — people will at a certain point resort to sexual activity as a defense against dehumanization. Sex is the last frontier where a person can exercise control and have a sense of mastery. The body can itself serve as a field to explore new meanings.

David Riesman (1961, p. 146), too, has pointed out that "sex provides a kind of defense against the threat of total apathy." The other-directed man looks to sex "for reassurance that he is alive."

The toneless, matter-of-fact sex of the other-directed man may solve the problem of apathy, but not absurdity. For Sade meaningful sexual behavior must always have something of a rebellious quality.

What is important is not the sex, but the rebellion. Sade clearly indicates that the act of rebellion is in itself the crucial thing that provides meaning. In rebelling one is producing dissonance in the world, and in upsetting the established moral order, the rebel invites counteractions. One need not rebel to ameliorate the world; the act of rebellion is in itself the crucial thing that provides meaning—as one gets the realization that he caused another to act. (For an application of this idea to an understanding of juvenile delinquency, see Matza 1964.)

Rebellion does not always begin as a consciously determinative act. Rather, it is often thrust upon individuals through the ineluctable workings of society. Since no complex society can be homogeneous, no universal morality is possible. All modern societies are composed of a plurality of groups. The laws, however, are always to be understood as being representative of some power-controlling group; and these laws are oppressive to many persons living under them. Some of these persons, in following their own conventional codes, may be singled out and labeled deviants or rebels. For Sade no actions are intrinsically deviant or rebellious. Deviance is merely a label that powerful groups can successfully pin on the less powerful.[6]

Once designated as a rebel, the individual literally *acts out the role of the rebel*.[7] Indeed, Sade sees the rebel as one who acts out stage spectacles in the setting of everyday life. The dramatic actor and the social actor become one in the rebel. The rebel—i.e., the person made conscious of his rebellion—acts out his fantasies to his own improvised script.[8]

For Sade the meeting place between theater and everyday life is in sexual behavior. Sade is aware of the historical connection between sexual behavior and dramatic ritual. In his own writings, Sade recommends that one engage in sex in terms of a ritual performance, that is, by the acting out of a sexual scene. The libertine—as Genet brilliantly depicts in *The Balcony*—plays at sex, and thus dramatizes it. Furthermore, in Sade's thinking, to dramatize *in* the world leads to the erotization *of* the world.

Sade was himself a playwright and actor, and this is of significance in understanding the relation among sadism, theater, and rebellion. As Gorer (1962, p. 184) notes:

By his skills, the playwright or actor commands the emotion of his audience, makes them laugh, or cry, shudder or exult, as he plays; he produces visible and audible changes in the people who are under his spell. But, in a crude and concrete way, this is precisely what a sadist wishes to do to his victims; in a great number of cases one might say that the sadist is acting out a play with an audience of one.

Clearly, the play's the thing. And rebels of all kinds are engaged in the construction of dramaturgy. For Sade, the full humanistic benefits of rebellion can be expressed only through an outrageous display of dramaturgical constructions. For the rebel, art does not imitate life. It becomes life. The rebel's very existence is theater. And when the rebel begins to regard clothes as costumes, facilities of all kinds as props, and streets as stages, he is capable of wreaking havoc in the social world—as his dramaturgical innovations break down the line between theater and taken-for-granted reality.[9] But in the process of destroying the world, he has made himself.

CONCLUSION

From a Sadean perspective, the proper subject matter of sociology is the rebellious act. If we wish to uncover the fundamental structures that undergird the social order, then we must turn to rebellious acts as our strategic research site. Through such acts the deep structures of society are brought to the surface. Thus to understand social order we turn to the study of disorder. Implied in this sociological perspective is that disorder should be the crucial focus of sociological investigation. The study of deviance and social disorganization should be viewed as always concealing solutions to the problem of order. Further, the study of deviance and disorganization can become tests of theories of order. The heightened observability that comes with deviance and disorganization can provide for us the maxims of conduct that make order possible.

One of the few sociologists who theorizes within this sociological framework is Harold Garfinkel. Garfinkel, (1967) following the phenomenology of Alfred Schutz, recognizes that social life everywhere is built upon a structure of meanings that is ordinarily shuffled back in consciousness. However, when a nasty surprise, a sudden interruption, or a striking violation of the ordinary occurs, the underlying meaning structure is thrust into the cognitive foreground. Garfinkel's version of ethnomethodology enjoins the sociologist to take an active role in disrupting the social world. Since sadism involves the modification of aspects of the world by one's own efforts, ethnomethodology may be regarded, in the special sense of the term used here, as a "sadistic" enterprise. (For a similar observation, see Gouldner 1970, pp. 394-95.)

Ethnomethodology shares one further assumption with Sade's sociology—and this is the most important point. Both are facets of a sociology of the absurd in that they share a common conception of the world as being absurd—without any intrinsic meaning. The human (or existential) implication of this is the theoretical commitment to maintain a lucid consciousness in the face of absurdity. To maintain this lucid consciousness, as Camus put it, the creator—the sociologist of the absurd—must describe the world with *nothing added* to it. "To describe: this is the ultimate ambition of absurd thinking" (quote from Camus taken from Hanna 1958, p. 37). Through description of experience the sociologist reaches out in a kind of personal awareness of others, and in this awareness indicates his common lot with mankind and in the process transcends his own absurdity.

NOTES

1. My concern is wholly with Sade's sociological significance. For a good sampling of Sade's significance in the fields of literature, philosophy and psychoanalysis, see Paulhan (1965) and Blanchot (1965). For an examination of Sade's contributions to the existentialist literature, see Beauvoir (1953); Camus (1956, pp. 36-46, *et passim*).

For a stimulating introduction to Sade's work, see Gorer (1962). For another excellent introduction that emphasizes the social milieu in which Sade lived and worked, see Bloch (n. d.).

2. In calling anomie and fatalism pathological social conditions, I am strictly following the orientation and conceptualization of Durkheim (1951).

3. On the basis of his study of total institutions, Goffman (1961, p. 320) concludes that man should be defined "as a stance-taking entity, a something that takes up a position somewhere between identification with the organization and opposition to it, and is ready at the slightest pressure to regain its balance by shifting its involvement in either direction."

4. For an interesting discussion on the relation between sexuality, political radicals and drama, see Schechner (1969, pp. 89-110).

5. Goffman (1963) notes that the symptoms of mental illness involve the violation of behavior in public places. This violation consists, in effect, in the carry over of private behavior into the public sphere. In these terms, the mentally ill are perceived as being not only insane, but also obscene.

6. The perspective that sees deviance as a result of a labeling process is nicely formulated by Becker (1963).

7. From the Sadean perspective we can find no better phrase to describe the rebel (criminal, or deviant) than that employed by Frank Tannenbaum (1938, pp. 19-20) in his theory of crime: the dramatization of evil.

8. This point is brilliantly explored by Sartre (1964).

9. For an application of these ideas to an understanding of student rebellion, see Scott and Lyman (1970).

REFERENCES

Becker, Howard S. *Outsiders*. Glencoe: Free Press, 1963.

Beauvoir, Simone de. "Must We Burn Sade?" In Paul Dinnage, ed. *The Marquis de Sade*. New York: Grove Press, 1953.

Blanchot, Maurice. "Sade." In Richard Seaver and Austryn Wainhouse, ed. and trans. *The Marquis de Sade*. New York: Grove Press, 1965.

Bloch, Iwan. *Marquis de Sade*. New York: Castle Books, n. d.

Camus, Albert. *The Rebel.* New York: Vintage Books, 1956.

Durkheim, Emile. *Suicide.* Glencoe: Free Press, 1951.

Garfinkel, Harold. *Studies in Ethnomethodology.* Englewood Cliffs: Prentice-Hall, 1967.

Goffman, Erving. *Asylums.* Garden City: Anchor, 1961.

———.*Behavior in Public Places.* Glencoe: Free Press, 1963.

Gorer, Geoffrey. *The Life and the Ideas of the Marquis de Sade.* London: Pantheon Books, 1962.

Gouldner, Alvin W. *The Coming Crisis of Western Sociology.* New York: Basic Books, 1970.

Hanna, Thomas. *The Thought and Art of Albert Camus.* Chicago: Henry Regnery Co., 1958.

Klausner, Samuel Z. *Why Man Takes Chances.* Garden City: Anchor Books, 1968.

Lyman, Stanford M. and Marvin B. Scott. *A Sociology of the Absurd.* New York: Appleton-Century-Crofts, 1970.

Marcuse, Herbert. *Eros and Civilization.* New York: Vintage Books, 1955.

Matza, David. *Delinquency and Drift.* New York: Wiley, 1964.

May, Rollo. *Love and Will.* New York: Norton and Co., 1969.

Paulhan, Jean. "The Marquis de Sade and His Accomplice." In Richard Seaver and Austryn Wainhouse, ed. and trans. *The Marquis de Sade.* New York: Grove Press, 1965.

Riesman, David, et al. *The Lonely Crowd.* New Haven: Yale Paperbacks, 1961.

Sartre, Jean-Paul. *Saint Genet.* New York: Mentor Books, 1964.

Schechner, Richard. "Speculations on Radicalism, Sexuality, and Performance." *Tulane Drama Review* 13 (Summer 1969): 89-110.

Scott, Marvin B. and Stanford M. Lyman. *The Revolt of the Students.* Columbus: Charles Merrill, 1970.

Tannenbaum, Frank. *Crime and the Community.* New York: Columbia University Press, 1938.

Weber, Max. *The Sociology of Religion.* Ephraim Fischoff, trans. Boston: Beacon, 1922.

FRANCIS E. MERRILL

5

Stendhal and the Self:
A Study in
the Sociology of Literature

Stendhal (a name probably borrowed from the Prussian town of Stendal) was the major of some seventy-one pseudonyms used by Marie Henri Beyle (1783-1842). He authored some thirty-three works, nineteen of which were published posthumously. His writings included works of criticism, travel, autobiography, fiction, a biography of Napoleon, and a treatise on love. He is best known for his fiction which included five novels (two of them unfinished) and two volumes of short stories.[1]

It has been said that most, if not all, of Stendhal's works are partly autobiographical in so far as all of them are concerned with the central enigma of self. As Merrill notes in the following essay, Stendhal anticipated many of the insights of the modern social psychology of self. The central figure in all of his celebrated novels is an "outsider," a person at odds with the society in which he lives and one who ultimately acts to disrupt it. In many ways, Stendhal was himself such a marginal man. Achieving relatively little literary success in his own lifetime, Stendhal felt that he was writing for posterity rather than for his contemporaries. He fully expected only posthumous appreciation of his total efforts.

NOTES

1. His novels included: *Armance* (1827), *Le Rouge et le noir* (1830), *La Chartreuse de Parme* (1839), *Lamiel* (1889), and *Lucien Leuwen* (1894). The short stories appeared as *Chroniques italiennes* (1839) and *Romans et nouvelles* (1854). For a sociological study of his literature, see: Geneviève Mouillaud, "The Sociology of Stendhal's Novels: Preliminary Research," *International Social Science Journal* 19 (1967): 581-98.

STENDHAL AND THE SELF: A STUDY IN THE SOCIOLOGY OF LITERATURE*

LITERATURE AND SOCIAL INTERACTION

"A novel," said Stendhal, "is like a bow; the violin which makes the sounds is the reader's soul." The novelist tries to communicate an emotional and imaginative experience to the reader, to which the latter reacts. From this interaction comes the "meaning" of the novel. The characters have no objective existence outside the pattern of words that comprises the novel. The important consideration is the impact of this pattern upon the "soul" of the reader. In a basic sense, therefore, reading is a form of symbolic interaction between writer and reader, in which the latter reacts like the violin to the bow.[1] Reading and writing are reciprocal forms of social interaction and hence constitute a subject for the sociologist.[2]

The most intensely "human" of all qualities, the ability to take the role of other persons and regard one's self as an object, has been intuitively grasped by a long line of psychologists and social psychologists from William James (not forgetting his brother Henry), through Cooley and Dewey, to Mead. In more recent decades the insights of these and other seminal thinkers have been subjected to experimental verification by persons using more refined research techniques.[3] This is not the place to review these investigations; the point is that literature, essentially "great" literature, is a major source of knowledge of the social self. "Artists," in short, "have . . . provided us with the richest mine of material in existence for the study of self-perception."[4]

Allport makes this relationship clear in his study of personality. "Through the ages," he remarks, ". . . this phenomenon of personal individuality has been depicted and explored by the humanities. The

*Reprinted from *The American Journal of Sociology 61 (1961)*: 446-53, by permission of the University of Chicago Press. Copyright 1961 by the University of Chicago.

more aesthetic philosophers and the more philosophical artists have always made it their special province of interest."[5] A novel is a picture of personality in depth, with the continuity that marks this dynamic entity and distinguishes one from another. In all too many cases the psychologist, in his study of personality, fails to realize or, more often, to measure this continuity. Hence he depicts personality as a series of virtually unrelated actions like—to use Allport's expressive phrase—those of a water-skate darting about on a pond. "Good literature," continues Allport, "never makes the mistake of confusing the personality of man with that of a water-skate." Hence personality is a theme for both the novelist and the scientist. Only by this collaboration can its full richness and depth be grasped.

Science is based upon the gathering of facts, their classification, and the recognition of their sequences and relationships. Literature involves the insights into human behavior of a man of genius. The two activities are of different orders, but they involve the same phenomena. Merely because literary insights do not ordinarily lend themselves to empirical verification is no reason to reject or ignore them. Literature is an important aspect of culture, which is clearly a legitimate object of scientific exploration. Literature uses language, which is the most social of all activities, employing the symbols of human communication. Man is uniquely a symbol-using and rational animal. "Man," said Pascal, "is only a reed. But he is a *thinking* reed."

There are, as Redfield has well said, several ways of making order of experience: among them are religion, philosophy, science, and art.[6] They are not mutually exclusive, even though their methods differ. The humanities add to our knowledge of behavior, especially that of a past society where men lived and died without benefit of attitude scales and research teams. "Literature," therefore, "is a paramount source of insight for the scientist who attempts to formulate the core values of a culture, to characterize its guiding tenets in brief compass."[7] The situation does not call for polemics—either pro-literature or pro-science. Each has its contribution to human (and humane) learning.[8] This essay is a modest plea for tolerance of the humanistic position, together with some notes on the insights of one author on the social self.

STENDHAL AND THE SELF

Stendhal, whose real name was Henri Beyle, is sometimes called the first of the "modern" novelists. He is unquestionably one of the greatest. In France his life and works have become the object of a cult whose fervor is surpassed only by the admirers of Balzac.[9] Stendhal was born in 1783 and took an active part in Napoleon's Italian and Russian campaigns in his youth. His military and political career came to an end with the fall of Napoleon, and he spent most of his adult years in "retirement" in Milan or Paris, writing continually. In his last years he held a minor consular post in Italy, from which he returned to Paris to die in 1842. He thus lived in a period of transition, social change, and intellectual ferment that has many of the characteristics of our own time. Perhaps this is why this writer, who predicted that he would hardly be read at all for fifty years and not widely for a hundred, is so enthusiastically accepted in France today. In an era of passion, humiliation, and self-doubt, he has a great deal to say to modern Frenchmen and, perhaps, to Americans.

Some years ago, the late André Gide was asked to name his favorite French novel.[10] The moralist and critic found himself in a difficult position. There was no question of his favorite novelist; Stendhal held that place beyond any question. A more difficult choice was that of his favorite novel: either *Le Rouge et le noir* or *La Chartreuse de Parme* deserved that honor. After considerable soul-searching, Gide chose *La Chartreuse*. For reasons that will soon appear, I choose *Le Rouge*. This novel is a study of the social self, perhaps the most subtle ever written. It is, as we have said, a "modern" novel, by which we mean, I suppose, a novel in which the self is constantly changing as the protagonist interacts with different persons and ideologies. The central character continually takes the role of the other toward himself and reacts accordingly.

Stendhal's intense preoccupation with his own self-image is apparent throughout his writings, both those which were frankly autobiographical and those in which the hero is a fictional projection of the person Stendhal would like to be. The most revealing of his autobiographical works is *La Vie de Henry Brulard*, in which he tells the story of his early years in Grenoble. In this amazing document he anticipated, among other things, the Oedipus complex. As a child, little Henry was passionately in love with his mother and, in later years, indicates that this affection was far from being merely platonic. He reports candidly that he wanted to cover his mother with kisses and wished her to have no clothes on. Madame Beyle loved her precocious son "passionately" and gave him kisses which the little fellow returned with such ardor that his mother was often obliged to leave him. He wished, he said, especially to kiss his mother on the bosom. It need hardly be added that, to complete the classic pattern, Beyle hated his father.[11]

But it was his clinical interest in himself that marks Stendhal as an unusual novelist, even in a nation that has produced such masters of self-analysis as Montaigne and Pascal. As he broods over his life at the age of fifty, he returns again and again to the crucial question of his own identity: "What have I been?" he asks himself; "What am I?" He sees himself as the product of his family milieu, his ancestors, and his times. He also sees himself as the object of his own self-attitudes, which he intuitively realizes are the result of a continuous process of role-taking. The heroes of his novels are likewise concerned with their own self-images, which might or might not be exact rendi-tions of the judgments of others toward them. It is no accident that Stendhal, the most self-conscious of men, should produce the most self-conscious of heroes.

THE RED AND THE BLACK

The central interest in this essay is *Le Rouge et le noir.* The time is 1830, the place France. Julien Sorel is the son of a peasant in the Franche-Comté, a province in the mountains of east-central France. At the tender age of nineteen Julien secures a position as tutor to the children of M. de Rênal, mayor of the little town of Verrières. Julien is planning to enter the Church ("the Black") because he believes that this is the only way a poor boy can rise to the top of his society. The days of revolutionary and military glory ("the Red") have passed with the fall of Napoleon, and the Church remains the chief vehicle of ver-tical mobility for him, even though he has no true vocation for it. During his stay with M. Rênal, Julien falls in love with the beautiful, tender, and motherly wife of the mayor, and she with him. When their relationship becomes widely suspected, he leaves Verrières to study for the priesthood in nearby Besançon.

By a fortunate combination of circumstances, Julien is soon rescued from this distasteful existence and is received as private secretary to the liberal and witty Marquis de la Mole, a great Parisian no-bleman and thus enters, at one bound, into the highest society of his day, although his position there is equivocal because of his peasant origin and his poverty. He is still an outsider, even though physically received into the upper nobility. At the same time, he falls in love with the brilliant, beautiful, and high-spirited Mathilde, the daughter of the Marquis. Julien regards this relationship as another challenge to him, and he seduces Mathilde (and she him) in a series of confron-tations that are among the most subtle in all fiction.

Mathilde becomes pregnant, and her father is naturally furious. Despite his chagrin, the Marquis decides to make the best of it, buys Julien a commission in a smart regiment, and settle some property on him and his daughter. At this point, a letter arrives from Madame de Rênal, written at the command of her holy confessor. The letter de-nounces Julien to the Marquis as a cold-blooded seducer and liber-tine. Beside himself with rage and frustrated ambition, Julien hurries back to Verrières. He finds Madame de Rênal in church and shoots, but does not kill, her. In his subsequent trial Julien refuses to defend himself, despite the entreaties of both Madame de Rênal and Mathilde. By so refusing he virtually commits suicide, and he is guillotined for premeditated attempted murder. Mathilde carries off his severed head and erects a chapel to his memory. Madame de Rênal dies of chagrin.

The story, baldly summarized above, has many facets. It is, first of all, a striking account of vertical mobility. The tragic saga of Julien Sorel is an account of the rise of a young man in Restoration France through a combination of good looks, exceptional intelligence, and the patronage of the rich and well born. The novels of Balzac, written at approximately the same period, also tell of poor boys from the provinces who storm the heights of the high society of the Faubourg Saint-Germain. *Le Rouge* is also a study of social institutions and their relationships, especially those of church and state in a reactionary society. For a while Julien cynically attaches himself to this venerable religious institution which, in conjunction with the nobility and the rising bourgeoisie, dominated the society of his day. The decade of the 1820's and 1830's saw the consolidation of the power of these institutions after the heady decades of the Napoleonic adventures.

Le Rouge is, above all, a love story, albeit one of the least "romantic" of all such stories. Love was a subject in which Stendhal maintained both a theoretical and a practical interest. His book on the subject (*De l'Amour*) is one of the most original and penetrating analyses of this tender sentiment that has ever been written. Love between the sexes is a direct and dramatic form of self-other relationship. The dialectic of love is the interaction of two persons, who are continually taking the other into account and responding in imagination to the resulting judgments. During this process the self-attitudes of the lover reflect his opinion of the attitudes of the other toward himself.[12] In a succession of subtle dialogues between Julien and Mathilde this self-other pattern is made abundantly clear.

"True" love is a matter of treating the other as an end in himself rather than as a means to an end. In this sense love is "that relationship between one person and another which is most conducive to the optimal development of both."[13] In the initial phases of his love affair with Madame de Rênal she was merely a means to Julien's ambition (self-feeling) and his fantastic pride. This ambivalence of affection and ambition was even more apparent in his relationship with Mathilde. His conception of himself was enhanced by his ability to bring this high-born beauty, literally, to his feet. He was never able to escape his ambivalent attitude throughout his affair with Mathilde, which is equivalent to saying that he never "really" loved her. After his attempted assassination of Madame de Rênal in the little church at Verrières, Julien realized that his love for her was truly unselfish. She ceased to be a means to his ambition and became an end in herself. He did not discover this fact until he lay in the grim shadow of the guillotine and it was too late.

THE DIALECTIC OF THE SELF

The dialectic of the self in *Le Rouge* has many aspects of the conception advanced a century later by George Herbert Mead. The latter saw the development of the self as a progression in which the person first takes the role of other individuals (mother, father, siblings, friends) toward himself. Later on he begins to take the role of the "generalized other" (i.e., that of society as a whole) toward himself and view himself in the light of these general precepts and behavior patterns. The generalized other is, in essence, sometimes the culture of the society and sometimes a segment thereof. In Mead's words, "the self reaches its full development by organizing these individual attitudes of others into the organized social or group attitudes, and by thus becoming an individual reflection of the general systematic pattern of social or group behavior in which it and the others are all involved."[14]

In *Le Rouge* Stendhal intuitively anticipated many of these ideas of the dialectical quality of the self. He was not, as he would have been the first to admit, a systematic thinker in the sense of evolving an organized system, much less of setting down a conceptual scheme such as the social self. Nevertheless, his insights were so acute that they foreshadowed many of the systematic ideas later developed by James, Cooley, Dewey, and Mead and subsequently verified empirically by others. I shall expand somewhat on Mead's dialectic by adding here a third interactive process, namely, that between the self and the "intermediate" other. The self of Julien Sorel will, therefore, be examined in terms of the direct other, the intermediate other, and the ideological (generalized) other.

THE SELF AND THE DIRECT OTHER

The most important contribution of the pragmatic school to our knowledge of the self is its insistence upon its objective quality. The self is seen as the object, rather than the subject, of self-attitudes. In this sense, Julien Sorel is continually regarding himself through the eyes of a variety of others — from Madame de Rênal and Mathilde de la Mole, who are very near and "direct"; through such intermediate individuals and groups as the people of Verrières, the young men in the seminary, and the aristocracy of the Faubourg Saint-Germain; to the abstract ideological elements of pride, ambition, and honor. His extreme self-consciousness is at once his glory and his undoing. His personality is marked by an extraordinary sensibility to the real or supposed judgments of others. "He was," comments Stendhal, "sick to death of all his own good qualities, of all the things he had once enthusiastically loved, and in this state of *inverted imagination* he attempted, in the light of his imagination, to interpret life. "This," concludes Stendhal gloomily, "is the error of a man of superior quality."[15]

Julien was, first of all, always taking the role of the other toward himself. Depending upon the circumstances, this other might be Madame de Rênal, Mathilde, the Marquis de la Mole, or his old friend and confessor, the good Abbé Pirard. In this dialectical interchange the author indicates how often Julien was mistaken in his self-judgments — thus emphasizing an important element in the analysis of the self that is not always sufficiently stressed. Many of his judgments of the attitudes of others are wholly or partially incorrect. Because of his inexperience, Julien was unaware of his good looks — although he was very much aware of his superior intelligence and, he hoped, his character. He therefore failed to realize how much his handsome appearance appealed to women; on the contrary, he usually regarded himself as a bungler. "It was," remarks Stendhal in this connection, "a fatal trait in his character to be acutely conscious of his mistakes" (p. 341).

In his confrontations with others Julien was, therefore, tremendously self-conscious. Even in his amorous transports he is aware that he is playing a role. "I'm playing an undignified part here" (p. 375), he thought unhappily. This feeling is first apparent in his liaison with Madame de Rênal, and it becomes even more evident in his affair with Mathilde, who is just as self-conscious as he. In this reflexive fashion Julien loves himself (not very often), is pleased with himself (sometimes), and more often despises himself. "He was frightfully contemptuous of himself" (p. 61). Whether trying to play the role of Don Juan in the boudoir of Madame de Rênal or Mathilde, to shine as a worldly courtier in the salons of the Faubourg Saint-Germain, or to act the dandy in the Bois de Boulogne, Julien constantly views himself through the eyes of others. In most cases he finds himself wanting, a quality that is often, to use Stendhal's phrase, the basic error of a person of "superior quality."

THE SELF AND THE INTERMEDIATE OTHER

By the "intermediate other" I mean persons or groups with whom one is not actually communicating (interacting) at the moment but whose real or supposed judgments nevertheless influence one's self-judgments. This concept is somewhat similar to the reference group, defined as "that group whose outlook is used by the actor as the frame of reference in the organization of his perceptual field."[16] The two concepts differ, however, in that the intermediate other or others are not necessarily united in groups, either cohesive or otherwise. The immediate others, indeed, may be disparate, and they may consist of isolated individuals with no sense of group unity. The person, furthermore, may or may not be conscious of his identification with the intermediate others. He may, indeed, be ambivalent toward this aspect of his environment and profess acute loathing for persons whose imputed judgments, nevertheless, play an important part in his self-feeling.

In the development of Julien's self there were a number of intermediate others whose attitudes he took into account. He was aware, for example, of the people of Verrières when he was considering his entry into the Mayor's home. When Julien's father raised this possibility, the boy's immediate concern was the figure he would cut in the community. He was not primarily concerned with his wages, living conditions, or work. His first question was about his *status*. "But whom," he demanded impatiently, "should I have my meals with?" (p. 39). In other words, what will be my role in the household of this leading figure? Will I be a servant and eat with the other servants in the kitchen? Or will I be treated as a member of the family and eat my meals with them? For, "rather than let myself be reduced to eating with the servants, I'd rather die" (p. 40).

When Julien goes to Paris and enters the town house of the Marquis de la Mole, he stands gaping in the courtyard of the great mansion. His sponsor, the good Abbé Pirard, admonishes him to look "sensible" if he does not want the Marquis' lackeys to make fun of him. "I defy them to do it," replied Julien, his self-possession rudely shattered (p. 253). When he begins to meet the men and women of the smart world, he becomes aware of his own shortcomings — his poverty, gaucherie, and peasant background. He constantly measures himself in the eyes of these intermediate others, and his self-attitudes waver between pride of his superior intellect and (later) his mastery over Mathilde, on the one hand, and a miserable self-deprecation, on the other. He was afraid of being shamed by these intermediate others, and his behavior was marked by an exaggerated arrogance to compensate for his galling self-judgments.

THE SELF AND THE IDEOLOGICAL OTHER

The ideological other in this context is similar to, but not identical with, the generalized other of Mead. The ideological other is the spirit of the times, the general patterns of belief that characterize a particular society at a given time. In Julien's case the ideological other was the *Zeitgeist* of France in the first three decades of the nineteenth century. This ideological imperative contained elements of the grandeur of Napoleon, the heroism of his revolutionary armies, the political adroitness of Talleyrand, and the seductiveness of Don Juan.

Julien was buffeted by these intellectual currents and saw himself first as one of these characters and then as another. Napoleon was dead, but his glory haunted the young man, even as it continued to haunt the aging Stendhal. As a young dragoon, the latter had served the Corsican in his Italian and Russian campaigns. Talleyrand was another cultural force whose talents for dissimulation, intrigue, and diplomacy comprised a different aspect of Julien's ideological other. The latter also aspired to be a great seducer of women, like Don Juan, a role in which he succeeded beyond his wildest dreams—in quality, if not in quantity. Two beautiful, well-born, and amorous women were his mistresses. As the book ends, they were both at his feet, as he languished in prison awaiting the guillotine.

In his affairs with women, Julien saw his love as a battle and himself as the hero. He tried to be a cynical man of the world, but his true goodness and sensibility did not allow him to play this role for very long. He feels that he "ought" to respond to Madame de Rênal's affection with some positive action. "This woman cannot despise me any longer," he mused, "in that case, I ought to respond to her beauty. I owe it to myself to become her lover" (p. 96). During his first rapturous night, his pride kept him from enjoying his experience, for he still regarded himself as a Don Juan, accustomed to subduing any woman at his whim. As a result, Julien "made incredibly determined efforts to spoil what was lovable in himelf" (p. 103). As he left Madame de Rênal's room in the dawn, he reflected: "Is being happy, is being loved no more than that?" (p. 104). Like one of Napoleon's troopers returning from the field of Marengo, Julien could think of nothing but his role. "Have I," he thought, "been wanting in anything I owe to myself? Have I played my part well?" (p. 104).

After his abortive attempt to assassinate Madame de Rênal, Julien spent several weeks in prison. During this time he thought of the different roles he had played during his life. He had never been able to lose the acute self-consciousness that so corroded his character. On the other hand, his self-pride was his chief sustaining force in his hour of adversity. "And what shall I have left," he reflected, "if I despise myself? I have been ambitious; I am not going to blame myself for that; *I acted then in accordance with the demands of the time*" (p. 509; italics mine). This self-conception led him to the prison cell; under other conditions, it might have led to a marshal's baton. In his own way Julien was a genius, or at least an exceptional man. In a corrupt society he was thwarted and struck down.

The ideological other was instrumental in forming Julien's ego ideal — that is, his conception of himself as he would like to be. This self-conception is a composite portrait, derived from taking the roles of a variety of others toward ourselves. Julien identified himself, first of all, with Napoleon, whose *Memoires* constituted virtually his sole reading matter during his most impressionable years. His ego-ideal also embodied certain elements of probity which he saw in his early friend, the old parish priest, Father Chélan. As he grew older and came in contact with the smart world of Paris society, he hoped to be a dandy, a duelist, and a drawing-room diplomat. Added to these elements was the driving force of ambition, whereby he hoped to be a "success" in his own eyes and those of the world. It was another measure of his innocence that the various elements in this ego-ideal were incompatible and could never be reconciled. Indeed, the cream of the tragic jest was that his basic goodness and integrity made it impossible for him to realize the mundane ambitions of his ego-ideal.

This essay has explored some of the relationships between literature and society in a single novel and a single facet of personality. The social self has been depicted as the object of different self-attitudes, derived from taking the role of the direct other, the diate other, and the ideological other; Julien Sorel is one of the characters in fiction that illustrates most clearly this interactionist conception of the self. The genius of Stendhal is distilled into this portrait of a young man who is both ambitious and sensitive. Julien was unable to realize the baser aspects of his ego-ideal, and he died because he could not reconcile the conflicting elements in his self-conception. The social self as seen by modern social psychologists is the product of the real or assumed judgments of others, and in several ways Stendhal anticipated this formulation. *The Red and the Black* is an account of the interaction between one man and the incompatible elements of his psychological world.

NOTES

1. Martin Turnell, *The Novel in France* (New York: Vintage Books, 1958), pp. 6-7.

2. Milton C. Albrecht, "The Relationship of Literature and Society," *American Journal of Sociology*, LIX (November, 1954), 425-36.

3. Martin H. Kuhn and Thomas S. McPartland, "An Empirical Investigation of Self-attitudes," *American Sociological Review*, XIX (February, 1954), 68-76; Carl J. Couch, "Self-attitudes and Degree of Agreement with Immediate Others," *American Journal of Sociology*, LXIII (March, 1958), 491-96; Ralph H. Turner, "Self and Other in Moral Judgment," *American Sociological Review*, XIX (June, 1954), 249-59.

4. Robert N. Wilson, *Man Made Plain* (Cleveland, Ohio: Howard Allen, Inc., 1958), p. 5.

5. Gordon W. Allport, *Personality* (New York: Henry Holt & Co., 1937), quoted in Wilson, *op. cit.*, p. 7.

6. Robert Redfield, "Social Science in Our Society," *Phylon*, XI (1950), 32.

7. Wilson, *op. cit.*, p. 12.

8. Robert Bierstedt, "Sociology and Humane Learning," *American Sociological Review*, XXV (February, (1960), 3-9.

9. The leading Stendhal scholar is the late Henri Martineau; see his *L'Œuvre de Stendhal* (Paris: Albin Michel, 1951); also his *Le Cœur de Stendhal* (2 vols.; Paris: Albin Michel, 1952-53).

10. This incident is recounted by Martin Turnell (*op. cit.*, p. vii).

11. Stendhal, *La Vie de Henry Brulard*, ed. Henri Martineau (Paris: Editions Emile-Paul Frères, n.d.).

12. Francis E. Merrill, "The Self and the Other: An Emerging Field of Social Problems,"*Social Problems*, IV (January, 1957), 200-207.

13. Nelson N. Foote, "Love," *Psychiatry*, XVI (August, 1953), 247.

14. Anselm Strauss (ed.) *The Social Psychology of George Herbert Mead* (Chicago: University of Chicago Press, 1956), p. 235. The words are Mead's.

15. Stendhal, *Scarlet and Black*, trans. Margaret R. B. Shaw (London: Penguin Books, 1959), pp. 368-69. The English translate the *rouge* in the title as "scarlet," rather than as "red." Subsequent page references refer to this edition. The italics above are Stendhal's.

16. Tamotsu Shibutani, "Reference Groups as Perspectives," *American Journal of Sociology*, LX (May, 1955), 565; see also Robert K. Merton and Alice S. Kitt, "Contributions to the Theory of Reference Group Behavior," in Robert K. Merton and Paul F. Lazarsfeld (eds.), *Continuities in Social Research* (Glencoe, Ill.: Free Press, 1950), pp. 53-59.

FRANCIS E. MERRILL

6

Balzac as Sociologist:
A Study in
the Sociology of Literature

Honoré de Balzac (1799-1850), the great French novelist
whose total writings fill some forty volumes, was certainly
among the most ambitious fiction writers the world has
known.[1] Attempting to link his novels and short stories into
a unity through having certain characters reappear from
work to work at different points in their lives, he produced a
remarkable literary panorama of his times. He called this
packaging of his many works *La Comédie Humaine,* and it
filled some twenty volumes and included over two thousand
outstanding characters.

All of Balzac's many novels concentrated upon
demonstrating the effects of external circumstances upon
individual lives, and his writings greatly concern themselves
with descriptions of the many small details of these external
conditions. Through such intensive and extensive
examination, Balzac attempted to fully describe and
interpret the age in which he lived.

NOTES

1. For works dealing with Balzac's writings and their implications, see: Philippe
Bertault, *Balzac and the Human Comedy* (New York: New York University Press,
1963); Herbert J. Hunt, *Balzac's Comédie Humaine* (London: Athlone Press, 1959);

and William H. Royce, *Balzac Bibliography*, 2 Volumes (Chicago: University of Chicago Press, 1930).

BALZAC AS SOCIOLOGIST: A STUDY IN THE SOCIOLOGY OF LITERATURE*

THE SOCIOLOGY OF LITERATURE

This essay is a study in the sociology of literature. It is, furthermore, a study of a particular form of literature—namely, the classical novel of the nineteenth century. It is, finally, a study of the novelist whom Henry James, as one professional to another, called "the greatest master of us all."[1] This man was Balzac, and we shall examine here one phase of his "packed and constituted, . . . palpable, *provable* world."[2] The essay will indicate one of the senses in which Balzac is perhaps the most "sociological" of all the great novelists.[3]

But first I wish to make clear, very briefly, the sense in which I am speaking of the "sociology of literature." I have examined the implications of this position elsewhere,[4] and shall merely repeat here that this approach considers literature as social interaction in imagination. The novelist places his characters in imaginary situations, where they react upon each other and themselves, Sociology is the study of human action in society."[5] The writer portrays various imaginary, altrayal of this interaction. As one scholar puts it, literature is "the conscious exploration through the imagination of the *possibilities* of human action society."[5] The writer portrays various imaginary, although possible forms of social interaction, and the reader participates in this process by taking the role(s) of the protagonists.

The relationships between literature and society have long been the concern of critics and novelists alike. De Bonald, Madame de Staël Sainte-Beuve, and Taine were among the first to examine this relationship. Novelists such as Stendhal, Flaubert, Zola, and (above all) Balzac found a close relationship between literature and society. The most self-conscious of all great American novelists, Henry James, further explored the role of the artist in this connection. "The only reason for the existence of the novel," said he, "is that it *does* attempt to represent life."[6] And again, "A novel is in its broadest definition a personal, a direct impression of life . . . "[7]

In recent years, sociologists with a literary orientation have further examined the relationships between literature and society. They have

*Reprinted from *Sociology and Social Research, 50 (1966): 148-59,* by permission of the publisher.

pointed out, for example, that the author is a member of a particular class of a particular society at a particular time. As such, he expresses the norms, values, and expectations of his milieu. These critics also point out that the reader is, in varying degrees, influenced by his exposure to the novel; in this sense, literature influences social interaction. Finally, the sociological critics have indicated that literature stabilizes the norms of the society by picturing behavior in normative terms by implicit approval of the "right" and (often) explicit condemnation of the "wrong."

The present essay does not seriously question these and related statements about the relationship(s) between literature and society. The emphasis here is rather upon another approach to literature, that of depicting social interaction in depth. Lowenthal states this position as follows: "The writer . . . develops believable characters and places them in situations involving interaction with others and with the society in which they live."[8] In this way, the writer conducts experiments in imagination that are clearly impossible for the sociologist. These literary experiments may not have the empirical quality of, say, an exercise in the small-group laboratory. The protagonists are not "real" people as defined by the Bureau of the Census. On another level, however, a Julien Sorel, an Anna Karenina, an Ivan Karamazov, or a Eugène de Rastignac may be more "real" than the data in a statistical table.

The novel is therefore a mine of information about social interaction. Most of this information has never been quarried, at least in any systematic fashion. *La Comédie Humaine* is the most extensive literary depiction of the group in interaction that has ever been made, with the possible exception of the works of Shakespeare. The critical literature on Balzac is both extensive and constantly growing. But to my knowledge very little has been done on the vast corpus of his work by anyone with a sociological orientation. A careful study of the interaction between the 2,400 characters of *La Comédie Humaine* might well produce some new insights into the nature and ramifications of this basic social process. The present writer does not pretend to the necessary erudition in the field of Balzacian criticism to do more than suggest some of the aspects of social interaction that are illustrated in his work. The present essay is, therefore, merely suggestive and selective.

BALZAC AND THE GROUP

Balzac was a great creator of these experiments in imagination. As such, he was perhaps the most truly "sociological" novelist of all time. This would appear to be the most banal of critical judgments,

inasmuch as Balzac has long been admired by both critics and ama-
teurs (in the French sense) as a great "literary sociologist." He was, it
is said, interested in "people." In view of his creation of more than
2,400 separate, viable characters, this is an understatement.[9] He was,
furthermore, recognized as a penetrating "social historian," and in his
grandiose project to write a literary history of his time, he came closer
than any other writer has done.[10] He was also a master of "sociological" description, both of persons and places, although it is debatable
whether in this role he was primarily a "realist" or a "visionary."[11]
Balzac was, however, a sociologist in the most precise modern
sense—namely, as a student of the group in interaction. In this capacity, he oriented his experiments in imagination about the group, a field
now accepted as the unique province of sociology.

The group may be defined as two or more persons who interact
over an appreciable period of time and share a common purpose in
this interaction. The tendency to come together in groups and act
with reference to them is perhaps the most important single characteristic of human beings. Other animals share some of these gregarious
qualities, but man is more influenced by the group than any other
species. The extreme plasticity of *homo sapiens* means that his behavior is continually subject to group definition and redefinition. In
the course of human history, man has acted primarily as a group animal, rather than as an isolated individual. In the latter capacity, he
never would have survived as a species.[12]

Balzac consistently portrayed man as a social (i.e., group) animal.
Social interaction for him always occurred in a group setting.[13] *La
Comédie Humaine* is a unified sociological whole, not merely because
of the recurrence of many of the characters from novel to novel, but
rather because the entire opus was conceived by the author as a picture of a society in interaction. This dependence of the individual
upon the group was one of Balzac's basic insights.[14] The present
essay will deal with the group in its face-to-face aspects, rather than
with the larger institutional patterns of church, state, and army.
Throughout his vast work, Balzac brought hundreds of groups to life
with a vividness that can almost be experienced with the senses. We
can virtually see, feel, touch, and (sometimes) smell them.

At first glance, Balzac's heroes seem to be the most individualistic
of men, as they single-handedly pit their energies against a hostile society. The prototype of the Balzacian hero is Eugène de Rastignac. In
Père Goriot, this young man is introduced to us after he has come to
Paris from the provinces to make his way in the world. He befriends
the old and wretched Goriot and, after the latter's death, is one of the
little band of mourners that follows him to his grave. After the fu-

neral, Rastignac climbs the heights of the cemetery of Père-Lachaise and gazes over the city below him. His glance is symbolically fixed at the part of Paris between the *Place Vendome* and the *Invalides* — i.e., the noble *Faubourg Saint-Germain,* the citadel of the high society to which he aspires. At this point, Rastignac launches his famous declaration of war against the world. *"A nous deux maintenant,"* he cries sturdily and thus seemingly epitomizes the spirit of rugged individualism — 1820 version.

Many critics assume that this is the last line of the novel. But it is only the next-to-the-last. The last line states matter-of-factly that "as a first challenge offered to society, Rastignac went to dine with Madame de Nucingen." In other words, our hero emphatically did not try to make his way in the world of *Restauration France* by sheer intelligence, hard work, and personal charm. He sought the assistance of a woman who could give him, if not high social status, at least wealth and beauty. To gain his immediate ends, Rastignac became, in effect, a gigolo.[15] He had previously availed himself of a remote family connection with the beautiful and aristocratic Madame de Beauséant, who first gave him entrée into the Faubourg Saint-Germain. In each case, he entered a *group* relationship with someone who could help him. He was likewise aided by the Baron de Nucingen, and this broad-minded banker later helped Rastignac make a fortune (*La Maison de Nucingen*). In this saga of status-striving, Rastignac ultimately married the daughter of his erstwhile mistress and, when we last see him, he has become a Minister of State.

The heroes and heroines of Balzac are always closely entangled in a complex web of interacting groups. These groups define the goals the heroes seek, as well as the means by which they gain them. The characters in *La Comédie Humaine* are never (or hardly ever) portrayed as isolated individuals, but instead as members of families, friendship groups, conspiratorial groups, criminal groups, professional groups, and other forms of human association. Their progress is pictured as a function of their successful group connections. Their failure is, conversely, a result of their lack of effective group ties. No matter how brilliant they may be (e.g., *Louis Lambert*), they are powerless alone. Some persons inadvertently lose their group ties, others break them deliberately, and still others never have them in the first place. In Balzac's world, the individual without group ties is doomed to frustration, unhappiness, and failure.

Balzac's literary experiments in imagination anticipated many of the empirical studies of the group that have taken shape a century after his death. In these studies, the motivations for forming groups are experimentally isolated as follows: (a) *Personal attraction.* People join groups because they like (or love) others and want to be with them. (b) *Group prestige.* People join groups because it is an honor to belong to them and their self-image is enhanced thereby. (c) *Task performance.* People join groups because they have certain goals that can be attained in no other way—i.e., they join with others to get a job done.[16] More than one factor is usually present in these conscious and unconscious motivations. The utilitarian (task performance) aspect occupies a central place in Balzac's universe, even though he was far from insensitive to the gentler motives.

SOME BALZACIAN GROUPS

The possibilities of group interaction were thus assiduously explored by Balzac. Some of these possibilities are bizarre and others verge on the fantastic. Balzac was, above all, a story-teller, and he sometimes let his inexhaustible gifts run away with him. But most of his literary experimentation was based upon ordinary life. The world that he carried in his head was the most complex in all literature and, after more than a century, it still possesses the "density" of the "real" world. The individuals and groups in *La Comédie Humaine* interact with an amazing verisimilitude, even to the latter-day reader. In his exploration of man as a group animal, Balzac was indeed a sociological novelist. By way of demonstrating this hypothesis, I shall briefly indicate some of the types of groups that he pictured in interaction.

1. The Unmarried Couple

The smallest, although not necessarily the simplest, group is the couple. In Balzac, the unmarried couple is an important social unit. Men and women are united by affection, self-interest, or both. Their union may be temporary, or it may last for years. The important consideration is that the couple constitutes, both in their own eyes and those of their intimate friends, a separate unit of society. In *Père Goriot,* as noted, Rastignac discovers that one way for a young man to get ahead is to have a rich mistress who will pay his bills, teach him the ways of the world, and introduce him to society. Another version of the unmarried couple is shown in *La Muse du Département,* in which the beautiful and talented Dinah de la Baudraye leaves her spouse and chateau in the provinces and comes to Paris to live with a journalist. She bears him two children, helps him with his work, and lives with him for several years. In *La Femme de Trente Ans,* Balzac tells what George Moore called the "classic" story of the older, married woman and the young and ambitious man. In *Béatrix,* Balzac portrays the same general situation, with an older and more experienced woman (Mlle des Touches) helping, advising and tutoring a young man (Calyste de Guénic). *Le Lys dans la Vallée* is, similarly, the story of a young man and an older woman. In the characters of Félix de Vandenesse and Madame de Mortsauf, Balzac added many autobiographical touches that are reminiscent of his own relationship with Madame de Berny, who was old enough to be his mother. In each of these relationships, the woman gives the young man the accumulated wisdom of her years (women often married at sixteen in those days) and receives in return the youthful ardor that she failed to find as a bride. All of Balzac's unmarried groups do not have these autumnal overtones, however, and many of them take other forms. In *Les Splendeurs et Misères des Courtisanes*, the orchidaceous and weak-willed Lucien de Rubempré lives with a succession of beautiful courtesans, who lavish their affections and their earnings upon him with equal prodigality. Coralie and Esther are prostitutes with hearts of gold, who ask nothing more of Lucien than his love. Irregular unions of this kind abound in Balzac, and his courtesans are often morally superior to some of the grand ladies of the Faubourg Saint-Germain.

2. The Married Couple

A second Balzacian group is the married couple. Relationships between the spouses may be happy, unhappy, or merely tepid. In *Les Illusions Perdues*, the David Séchards are a happy group; in *La Duchesse de Langeais*, and, indeed, in many aristocratic marriages, the reverse is true. Balzac's view of the conjugal relationship is not, on balance, an idyllic one. At the same time, however, he realized that the married couple is the cradle of the family. In *Le Cousin Pons* and several other novels of the Paris *bourgeoisie,* the Camusots are pictured as a couple held together by complementary needs. The wife provides the intelligence, aggressiveness, and vindictiveness that (according to Balzac) are so necessary for success, whereas the husband in this instance merely provides the rudimentary legal knowledge. Monsieur Camusot started as a legal functionary in the provinces and reached a high post in Paris, thanks to the above happy combination of qualities. *César Birotteau* is another picture of a bourgeois couple, in which the wife contributes the common sense (which her husband ignores in his quest for wealth and status) and César the technical knowledge. On a more exalted social level the young, beautiful, and intelligent Madame de l'Estorade in *Les Mémoires de deux Jeunes Mariées* infuses her lethargic provincial husband with her ambition, as a result of which he leaves the country, comes to Paris, and takes an active part in governing France. Without her gentle but determined support, he would have continued to vegetate quietly on his estates in Provence. In other sectors of *La Comédie Humaine*, married couples from other social statuses are shown in the same complementary relationship. In contemporary American society, the married couple is presumably brought together by romantic love and continues to interact as long as this affection lasts. In the France of the 1830s and 1840s however, other considerations were more important in the formation and continuance of this group. This does not mean that love was totally absent from Balzac's marriages or that all of his unions were those of convenience. It *does* mean, however, that, in many instances, the motives of the spouses were decidedly mixed. Ambition was often more important than love to these rising shopkeepers, merchants, aristocrats, and functionaries.

3. The Family

The family is not synonymous with the married couple, although the two are obviously related. The married couple is, by definition, composed of two persons, whereas the family includes the spouses, their children, grandchildren, and parents, plus an extensive fringe of aunts, uncles, and cousins. In Balzac's world, this group was the "extended," rather than the "nuclear," family of our day. In addition to its extensive personnel, the Balzacian family also included the real property; the investments (Balzac was always fascinated by the amount of money people had, how they got it, invested it, spent it, saved it, and bequeathed it); and the special norms, values, and traditions that evolved in each group during its long history. Families of the nobility usually have more of these tangible and intangible assets than those of the middle class, and the coats-of-arms of the aristocracy occupied a special place in Balzac's heart. But the various gradations of the *bourgeoisie* and even those of humbler origins had their own family norms as a result of functioning through time. Balzac's family is basically a "task-performance" group that stands ready to help its members in fulfilling their needs and reaching their goals. In *La Duchesse de Langeais*, the family holds a council of war to get their daughter out of trouble. In *Béatrix*, a noble Breton family conspires to break up the liaison of their son with an older woman—and a writer at that. Later in the same novel, another noble family conspires (with the help of their worldly Jesuit confessor) to save their erring son-in-law from the designs of the blond and perfidious (for Balzac, blonds were usually perfidious, brunettes virtuous) Béatrix. In *Eugénie Grandet,* the family functions as a combination mortgage and loan society and bank, with the merciless and avaricious Grandet acting as the president, chairman of the board, and janitor. Throughout *La Comédie Humaine*, the family usually maintains a united front to protect its members, however stupid, erring, or vicious they may be. The inter-action among members of the family as individuals and between the family as a unit and the rest of the world was fundamental to ordered society. In Balzac's words, the family is "a social cell," and it would, he believed, "always be the basis of society."

4. The Friendship Group

A fourth group that plays an important part in *La Comédie Humaine* is the friendship group. This type of group is often viewed in the soci-ological literature as one in which two or more persons participate solely or largely through mutual affection. In this sense, the friendship group becomes an end in itself, rather than a means to some ulterior end. This form of interaction is found in Balzac, but affection is often subordinated to the more mundane ends of task performance. The medical student in père Goriot, Horace Bianchon, maintains a disin-terested friendship for the increasingly worldly Rastignac, as the men grow old in *La Comédie Humaine*. But Rastignac is not above asking a favor of his friend, notably in the novel *l'Interdiction*. In *Les Illu-sions Perdues*, Balzac gives us a group of high-principled young art-ists (*La Cénacle*), who are genuinely attached to each other, but who at the same time are well aware that they can further each others' careers in the Balzacian jungle of the Paris artistic world. Other such groups are united by journalistic, political, or merely worldly inter-ests, and in this sense are task-performance groups in the literal sense. In *Le Cousin Pons*, on the other hand, we have an unalloyed friendship group consisting of two old and penniless musicians, Pons and Schmucke. In their unworldly way, each is so devoted to the other that he would give his life for his friend. This group is further cemented by the fact that each has certain traits the other lacks and each can thus complement the other against the philistine world. As in marriage, members of the friendship group possess qualities that complement each other. Each person has ambitions that he cannot attain through his own unaided efforts. The richest prizes of Balzac's world—power, wealth, love, status—elude the solitary individual. The realization of this crucial fact is the beginning of wisdom. The wise man joins with others and thereby helps himself.

5. The Conspiratorial Group

This type of group exists for the purpose of furthering some con-spiracy against society. The goal of the conspiratorial group is some-times merely an elaborate and unorthodox prank, sometimes more clearly antisocial activities. One of the most curious such groups is called simply "Les Treize" (the thirteen), and is composed of thirteen young men about Paris. Most of them are of aristocratic background, with similar interests, aspirations, and political convictions. This group appears in several of the novels, among them *Ferragus, La Duchesse de Langeais*, and *La Fille Aux Yeux d'Or.* The proximate group goals vary with the circumstances. In the latter novel, the principal goal is pleasure and the group mobilizes its forces toward seducing a mysterious and beautiful girl ("with the golden eyes") for one of its members. In *La Duchesse de Langeais*, the group organizes an amphibious operation, outfits a ship, and tries to kidnap a former mistress, who has taken refuge in a convent on a remote island in the Mediterranean. At still other times, the same group is concerned with shadowy political conspiracies. In each of these cases, the members act as a group and thereby multiply their power. In the novel, *La Rabouilleuse*, a group of young men in the provincial city of Issoudun unite under the leadership of a former officer in the Imperial Army. This group engages in elaborate practical jokes and depredations to relieve the boredom of provincial life. Balzac even carries his passion for conspiracy into socially beneficial, as well as antisocial, directions. In *L'Envers de l'Histoire Contemporaine*, a group of Christian men and women establish a charitable organization, which anonymously gathers and distributes funds to the worthy poor.

6. The Deviant Group

Another type of Balzacian group is the deviant or criminal group, whose goals are antisocial and whose members shrink at no crime in attaining them. The great Vautrin, who appears in *Père Goriot* and many other novels throughout *La Comédie Humaine*, is one of the most powerful criminal characters in all literature and as such symbolizes the anarchic forces always present in society. Balzac has strongly ambivalent feelings toward his creation, and admires his strength, intelligence and determination as much as he deplores his criminal activities. In the end of *La Comédie Humaine*, Balzac succeeds in reconciling his attitudes, for Vautrin ultimately rejects his criminal activities and, in a typically Balzacian *Volte-face,* becomes the chief of the secret police of Paris. Even in his salad days of crime, however, Vautrin is not a solitary figure. In virtually every operation, he is the leader of a group, with colleagues, accomplices, and minions. His operatives appear in the most unlikely places and under the most implausible disguises. They impersonate galley slaves and police spies, priests and prostitutes, ragpickers and concièrges, countesses and courtesans. In *Les Splendeurs et Misères des Courtisanes*, Vautrin himself impersonates a Spanish priest, and in the final climactic pages of this saga he enlists a motley army of operatives in a vain effort to save the life of his friend and protege, Lucien de Rubemprè. Vautrin is one of the strongest men in fiction, both physically and intellectually, but even this terrifying Lucifer is powerless by himself. He needs a group to exercise his full powers.

7. The Reference Group

The above Balzacian groups are all membership groups, in the sense that people physically "belong" to them and interact in a face-to-face capacity. Balzac also sensed the importance of what has been called the "reference group"—that is, the group to which the individual, consciously or unconsciously, "refers" his behavior, even though he does not actually belong to it. The reference group does not refer to a particular *type* of group, but rather to a certain *relationship* between the individual and the group. The reference group, indeed, has been defined as "that group whose outlook is used by the actor as a frame of reference in the organization of his perceptual field."[18] *La Comédie Humaine* is full of men and women who belong to one group and aspire to another. Rastignac, Lucien, and the rest of the *arriviste* heroes come from modest circumstances, but they conceive of themselves as belonging to the most exalted aristocratic groups in the *Faubourg Saint-Germain*. In this persistent search for status, Rastignac was successful and Lucien was not. The traveling salesman, Gaudissart, in the novel of the same name, belonged to the lowly company of *Commis voyageurs*, but he dreamed of owning the business, mingling with actors and artists, and entering the rich *bourgeoisie*. César Birotteau, who likewise gave his name to a novel, reached a pinnacle of commercial success in his perfume business on the *Place Vendôme*. But he too had delusions of consorting with counts and countesses, and this aspiration caused his ruin. In *Cousin Pons*, Madame Cibot, the concièrge, dreams of becoming a *rentier* and retiring to a little property in the country. In *Le Cabinet des Antiques*, the young magistrate is not content with the groups with which he must perforce consort in Alencon, but sets his sights for Paris, where he can rub elbows with the aristocracy. Reference-group behavior is especially characteristic of a dynamic society, where class lines are rapidly changing, and ambitious individuals can rise in the social scale. As he stated in his famous foreword to the *Comédie Humaine*, Balzac was the historian of such a society.

In this essay, I have outlined the concept of "social interaction in imagination" as one approach to the sociology of literature. As an illustration of this form of experimentation in depth, I have indicated the *group* nature of Balzac's *La Comédie Humaine*. The groups selected are merely representative of Balzac's approach, and the illustrations are not exhaustive. Social interaction in imagination, as so conceived, falls in the category of what Lazarsfeld calls "qualitative analysis"—namely, data that are more than illustration but less than definitive proof.[19] Literary material considered in this conceptual framework leads to an enhanced understanding of social interaction.[20] Individual and group are part of the same social process. In his vast experiment in imagination, Balzac sensed this relationship (perhaps) more clearly and (certainly) more extensively than any other novelist.

NOTES

1. Henry James, "The Lesson of Balzac," in *The Future of the Novel*, (New York: Vintage Books, 1956), 102.

2. *Ibid.*, 111. (His italics.)

3. The definitive biography of Balzac is: André Maurois, *Prométhée: Ou La Vie de Balzac*, Hachette, Paris, 1965.

4. Francis E. Merrill, "The Sociology of Literature," *Social Research*, to be published in 1966.

5. Hugh D. Duncan, *Language and Literature in Society* (Chicago: University of Chicago Press, 1953), 3. (His italics.)

6. Henry James, "The Art of Fiction," in *The Future of the Novel, op. cit.*, 5. (His italics.)

7. *Ibid.*, 13.

8. Leo Lowenthal, *Literature and the Image of Man* (Boston: The Beacon Press, 1957), 9.

9. Fernand Lotte, *Dictionnaire Biographique des Personnages Fictifs de la Comédie Humaine* (Paris: Corti, 1952).

10. Georges Pradalié, *Balzac Historien* (Paris: Presses Universitaires de France, 1955).

11. Cf. Maurice Bardèche, *Une Lecture de Balzac* (Paris: Les Sept Couleurs, 1964).

12. Ralph Linton, *The Tree of Culture* (New York: Alfred A. Knopf. Inc., 1955), 30.

13. Arnold Hauser, *The Social History of Art* (New York: Vintage Books, 1958), Vol. 4, p. 45.

14. In striking contrast to Stendhal, who was essentially a "psychologist," rather than a "sociologist" in the Balzacian sense. Francis E. Merrill, "Stendhal and the Self: A Study in the Sociology of Literature," *American Journal of Sociology,* (Paris) 66 (March, 1961), 446-53. [Ed. note: Reprinted in this volume.]

15. Felicien Marceau, *Balzac et Son Monde* (Paris: Gallimard, 1955), Chap. 14, "Le Thème du Groupe."

16. Kurt W. Back, "Influence Through Social Communication," *Journal of Abnormal and Social Psychology*, 46: (January, 1951), 9-23.

17. Cf. André Wurmser, *La Comédie Inhumaine* (Paris: Gallimard, 1964). This is a massive Marxist study of Balzac's life and thought.

18. Tamotsu Shibutani, "Reference Groups as Perspectives," *American Journal of Sociology*, 60 (May, 1955), 565.

19. Allen H. Barton and Paul F. Lazarsfeld, "Some Functions of Qualitative Analysis in Social Research," quoted in Seymour M. Lipset and Neil J. Smelser (eds.), *Sociology: The Progress of a Decade* (Englewood Cliffs, New Jersey: Prentice-Hall, Inc., 1961), 95.

20. Lewis A. Coser (ed.), *Sociology Through Literature* (Englewood Cliffs, New Jersey: Prentice-Hall, Inc., 1963), Introduction.

MARCELLO TRUZZI

7

Sherlock Holmes:
Applied Social Psychologist

Sir Arthur Conan Doyle (1859-1930), best remembered as
the creator of the fictional detective Sherlock Holmes,
would have preferred to be remembered for his many other
works, especially his historical writings and his defense of
spiritualism.[1] He even attempted to discontinue Holmes's
adventures by having him nobly killed in "The Final
Problem" which Doyle published in 1893, but he found the
great demand of the public for their hero enough incentive
to bring Holmes back to life in 1904 to continue the saga.[2]
The image of Holmes as epitomizing the application of
rationality and scientific method to human behavior is
certainly a major factor in the detective's ability to capture
the world's imagination. The following article examines the
value and application of Holmes's method in social
psychology.

NOTES

1. Doyle's major works aside from the Holmes stories include: *The Captain of the
"Polestar"* (1887); *The Mystery of the Cloomber* (1888); *Micah Clark* (1889); *The
White Company* (1891); *Rodney Stone* (1896); *Sir Nigel* (1906); *The Lost World*
(1912); *The British Campaigns in Europe* (1928); *The Great Boer War* (1900); and

History of Spiritualism (1926). Re Doyle's role as a spiritualist, a sympathetic account can be found in: Sherman Yellen, "Sir Arthur Conan Doyle: Sherlock Holmes in Spiritland," *International Journal of Parapsychology* 7 (1965): 33-57.
2. For a consideration of Holmes's more general perspective in relation to scientific method, see: Karl Kejci-Graf, "Sherlock Holmes, Scientist, Including Some Unpopular Opinions," *The Sherlock Holmes Journal* 8, no. 3 (Winter 1967): 72-78.

SHERLOCK HOLMES:
APPLIED SOCIAL PSYCHOLOGIST*

THE REALITY AND RELEVANCE OF SHERLOCK HOLMES

In her remarkable survey of the history of the detective novel, Alma Elizabeth Murch has noted that:

There are in literature certain characters who have come to possess a separate and unmistakable identity, whose names and personal qualities are familiar to thousands who may not have read any of the works in which they appear. Among these characters must be included Sherlock Holmes, who has acquired in the minds of countless readers of all nationalities the status of an actual human being, accepted by many in the early years of the twentieth century as a living contemporary, and still surviving fifty years later with all the glamour of an established and unassailable tradition, the most convincing, the most brilliant, the most congenial and well-loved of all detectives of fiction. (Murch 1958, p. 167)

In all of English literature, it has been said that the only other three fictional names equally familiar to the "man in the street" might be those of Romeo, Shylock, and Robinson Crusoe (Pearson 1943, p. 86).

Although the Holmes saga consists of only sixty narratives[1] by Sir Arthur Conan Doyle,[2] which first appeared between 1887 and 1927,[3] the foothold Sherlock Holmes gained upon the popular imagination has seldom been equalled. The depth of his impact is nowhere better demonstrated than by "the belief, held for years by thousands, that he was an actual living human being—a circumstance that constitutes one of the most unusual chapters in literary history" (Haycraft 1941, pp. 57-58). Thus, in addition to countless letters from troubled would-be clients addressed to "Mr. Sherlock Holmes, 221-B Baker Street, London" (a non-existent address, too) and many sent to him care of Scotland Yard, the announcement of Holmes's retirement to a bee-farm in a 1904 story brought two offers from would-be employees (one as a housekeeper, the other as bee-keeper). Doyle received sev-

---

*This article was especially prepared for this volume. Copyright 1971 by Marcello Truzzi.

eral letters from ladies who had been contemplating possible marriages with Holmes (Lamond 1931, pp. 54-55) and there was even a gentleman (one Stephen Sharp) who believed himself to be Holmes, and he made several attempts to visit Doyle from 1905 onwards (reported by Nordon 1967, p. 205).

Aside from those who naively believed the Holmes legend, however, and much more sociologically significant, has been the fact that the "legend of Holmes's reality has been swelled by other enthusiastic if more sophisticated readers who know well enough that their hero has never lived in flesh and blood, but who like to keep up the pretense that he did" (Haycraft 1941, p. 58). More has probably been written *about* Holmes's character than any other creation in fiction, and it is remarkable that it is Holmes and not Sir Arthur Conan Doyle who has been the focus of so much attention. Thus, Holmes has been the subject for biographies,[4] encyclopedic works,[5] critical studies,[6] and numerous organizations honoring and studying the Holmes character exist all around the world.[7] Several movements have even been started to get a statue of Holmes erected near his alleged home on Baker Street.[8] As Christopher Morley has often been quoted as saying: "Never, never has so much been written by so many for so few."

Apart from the delightful games of the Sherlockians and their playful mythologies, however, the character of Sherlock Holmes and his exploits touches a deeper reality, for, as has been noted, "this legend fulfills a need beyond the realms of literature" (Nordon 1967, p. 205). Though, as Pearson (1943, p. 86) has observed, Holmes symbolizes the sportsman and hunter, a modern Galahad hot upon the scent of a bloody trail, the character of Holmes even more clearly epitomizes the attempted application of man's highest faculty—his rationality—in the solution of the problematic situations of everyday life. Most of the plots of the stories came from real life events found by Doyle among the newspaper stories of the 1890s (Nordon 1967, p. 236), and remarkably few of the plots deal with bloody violence or murder. In fact, as Pratt (1955) has observed, in fully one-quarter of the stories no legal crime takes place at all. The essentially mundane character of most of the plots clearly demonstrates the observation that the "cycle may be said to be an epic of everyday events" (Nordon 1967, p. 247). It is this everyday setting of the applications of Holmes's "science" and rationality that so astounds and gratifies the reader. And it is not so much the superior ability of Holmes to obtain remarkable insights and inferences from simple observations which so impresses the reader; it is the seeming reasonableness and obviousness of his "method" once it has been explained to the reader.

There are many people who believe

~~One truly believes~~ (at least while under the spell of the narrative) that Holmes's new applied science is ~~possible~~ *also* possible for ~~the diligent~~ *They use* student of his "methods." As has been noted: *by diligent students.*

> The fictitious world to which Sherlock Holmes belonged, expected of him what the real world of the day expected of its scientists: more light and more justice. As a creation of a doctor who had been soaked in the rationalist thought of the period, the Holmesian cycle offers us for the first time the spectacle of a hero triumphing again and again by means of logic and scientific method. (Nordon 1967, p. 247)

This fascination with the possibility of the mundane application of scientific methods to the interpersonal world has captured not only the imagination of the lay readers of the Holmes saga. It has *also* had an appreciable effect upon criminologists and those concerned with the real life problems that parallel those fictionally encountered by Sherlock Holmes. Thus, a representative from the Marseilles Scientific Police Laboratories pointed out that "many of the methods invented by Conan Doyle are to-day in use in scientific laboratories" (Aston-Wolfe 1932, p. 328); the Director of the Scientific Detective Laboratories and President of the Institute of Scientific Criminology has stated that "the writings of Conan Doyle have done more than any other one thing to stimulate active interest in the scientific and analytical investigation of crime" (May 1936, p. x); and, most recently, an expert on firearms has argued that Holmes should be called "Father of Scientific Crime Detection" (Berg 1970). Many famous criminologists, including Alphonse Bertillon and Edmond Locard, have credited Holmes as a teacher and source of ideas, and Holmes's techniques of observation and inference are still presented as a useful model for the criminal investigator (Hogan and Schwartz 1964).[9]

In addition to the very practical consequences of Sherlock Holmes's influence upon modern criminology, the reality of his "method" is even better shown through an understanding of his origins. In his autobiography, *Memories and Adventures* (1924), Doyle clearly states that the character of Holmes was patterned after his memories of his professor of surgery when Doyle was in medical school, Joseph Bell, M.D., F.R.C.S., Edinburgh, whom Doyle recalled as capable of the kind of observation and inference so characteristic of Holmes. Bell's remarkable ability is well exemplified by the following anecdote related by Doyle:

> In one of his best cases he said to a civilian patient: "Well, my man, you've served in the army." "Aye, Sir." "Not long discharged?" "No, Sir." "A Highland regiment?" "Aye, Sir." "A non-com officer?" "Aye, Sir." "Sta-

tioned at Barbados?" "Aye, Sir." "You see, gentlemen," he would explain, "the man was a respectful man but did not remove his hat. They do not in the army, but he would have learned civilian ways had he been long discharged. He has an air of authority and he is obviously Scottish. As to Barbados, his complaint is Elephantiasis, which is West Indian, and not British." To his audience of Watsons, it all seemed very miraculous until it was explained, and then it became simple enough. (Doyle 1930, p. 23)

It is likely, however, that Holmes was only partly patterned after Dr. Bell and is actually a composite of several persons.[10] Ultimately, though, "there is no doubt that the real Holmes was Conan Doyle himself" (Starrett 1960, p. 102). As Michael and Mollie Hardwick have shown in their remarkable study *The Man Who Was Sherlock Holmes* (1964), the parallels in Doyle's life, including the successful solution of several real-life mysteries and Doyle's championing of justice (best seen in his obtaining the ultimate release and clearing of two men falsely convicted of murder, the celebrated cases of George Edalji and Oscar Slater),[11] clearly demonstrate the roots of Holmes's essential character and methods within his creator. Dr. Edmond Locard, Chief of the Surete Police Laboratories at Lyon, stated that "Conan Doyle was an absolutely astonishing scientific investigator," and the criminologist Albert Ullman took the position that "Conan Doyle was a greater criminologist than his creation Sherlock Holmes" (quoted in Anonymous 1959, p. 69).

The important point being made here is that the successes of Dr. Bell and Sir Arthur Conan Doyle demonstrate the fact that the methods of scientific analysis exemplified and dramatized by Sherlock Holmes in his adventures have had their counterparts in the real world. As the well known American detective William Burns put it:

I often have been asked if the principles outlined by Conan Doyle, in the Sherlock Holmes stories could be applied in real detective work, and my reply to this question is decidedly "yes." (Quoted in Anonymous 1959, p. 68)

What, then exactly, is the "method" of Sherlock Holmes, and what are its limitations and implications for a modern applied social psychology? We turn now to an examination of Holmes's views of science, and of man and society, and to his prescriptions for the applications of the former to the latter as these are outlined in the canon.

THE METHOD OF SHERLOCK HOLMES

It is unfortunate that although Holmes's method is central to his character and universal attractiveness, there is no systematic statement of it to be found in the canon. It is also surprising to find that relatively little consideration has been given to his techniques of "deduction" in the massive bibliography of Sherlockiana. Most Sherlockians have been more concerned with their own application of Holmes's techniques to the clues available in the canon than upon an examination of the methods themselves. Therefore, we must turn to a search for the many but scattered statements about his method uttered by Holmes throughout his adventures.

Holmes's "Science of Deduction and Analysis"

It has often been stated that science is but refined common sense. With this Holmes would probably agree for he states that his own approach is a "simple art, which is but systematized common sense."[12] But his view is not a simple or mechanical view of the process, for at another point he notes that a "mixture of imagination and reality . . . is the basis of my art."[13] Though Holmes stresses raw empiricism to a degree reminiscent of the archinductionist Francis Bacon, he does not neglect the importance of creative imagination. "It is, I admit, mere imagination," Holmes states, "but how often is imagination the mother of truth?"[14] "One's ideas must be as broad as nature if they are to interpret nature,"[15] he notes, and

breadth of view . . . is one of the essentials of our profession. The interplay of ideas and the oblique uses of knowledge are often of extraordinary interest.[16]

Although Sir Arthur Conan Doyle was to become a major promoter of spiritualism, Holmes, in a true Comtean manner of positivism and scientific skepticism refuses to seriously entertain hypotheses of supernatural causation. Recognizing that "the devil's agents may be of flesh and blood,"[17] before considering the possibility that "we are dealing with forces outside the ordinary laws of Nature," he argues that "we are bound to exhaust all other hypotheses before falling back on this one."[18] Holmes states of himself that

this Agency stands flatfooted upon the ground, and there it must remain. The world is big enough for us. No ghosts need apply.[19]

Holmes's general philosophical assumptions about the universe are somewhat unclear. Although he apparently believed in a purposeful universe,[20] and hoped for the goodness of Providence,[21] he also expressed a more cynical view when he asked Watson:

But is not all life pathetic and futile? . . . we reach. We grasp. And what is left in our hands at the end? A shadow. Or worse than a shadow—misery.[22]

This view of all knowledge as "shadows," aside from its depressive context here, is very much in keeping with the modern scientific and essentially pragmatic view of man as a creator of "cognitive maps" and theoretical "realities" or "conjectures" rather than as discoverer of objective truths and laws.

Holmes also epitomizes the basically deterministic orientation of most modern social science. As he remarked:

The ideal reasoner . . . would, when he had once been shown a single fact in all its bearings, deduce from it not only all the chain of events which led up to it but also all the results which would follow from it. As Cuvier could correctly describe a whole animal by the contemplation of a single bone, so the observer who has thoroughly understood one link in a series of incidents should be able to accurately state all the other ones, both before and after.[23]

Or as Holmes put it in his seminal article "The Book of Life" (in a magazine Dr. Watson unfortunately neglected to name):

From a drop of water . . . a logician could infer the possibility of an Atlantic or a Niagra without having seen or heard of one or the other. So all life is a great chain, the nature of which is known whenever we are shown a single link of it. Like all other arts, the Science of Deduction and Analysis is one which can only be acquired by long and patient study, nor is life long enough to allow any mortal to attain the highest possible perfection in it.[24]

This determinism was seen as present at all levels of life, but Holmes clearly sides with sociology against many psychologists when he states that

while the individual man is an insoluble puzzle, in the aggregate he becomes a mathematical certainty. You can, for example, never foretell what any one man will do, but you can say with precision what an average member will be up to. Individuals vary, but percentages remain constant.[25]

As with all nomothetic sciences, emphasis is placed upon the search for laws and recurrent events. Holmes is greatly impressed by regularities and repetitions in history, and in speaking of a crime to his friend Inspector Gregson, Holmes echoes Ecclesiastes when he says: "There is nothing new under the sun. It has all been done before."[26] And on another occasion he says of his arch-enemy: "Everything comes in circles, even Professor Moriarty."[27] Holmes seeks out generalizations and will ultimately settle only for universal propositions. As he put it: "I never make exceptions. An exception disproves the rule."[28]

Central to Holmes's basic approach, however, is his concern with the empirical verification of his conjectures. His emphasis on induction — an emphasis more present in his words than in his actual practice, as we shall see — is based on a great fear of conceptual detachment from the "real" world of observable phenomena. "The temptation to form premature theories upon insufficient data is the bane of our profession," he tells Inspector MacDonald.[29] For as Holmes says again and again:

It is a capital mistake to theorize before one has data. Insensibly one begins to twist facts to suit theories, instead of theories to suit facts.[30]
It is a capital mistake to theorize in advance of the facts.[31]
It is a capital mistake to theorize before you have all the evidence.[32]
. . . it is an error to argue in front of your data. You find yourself insensibly twisting them round to fit your theories.[33]

And

how dangerous it always is to reason from insufficient data.[34]

Holmes insists upon the absolute necessity of observable facts.

"Data! data! data!" he cried impatiently. "I can't make bricks without clay."[35]

But he claims even more than this, for his posture is attemptedly a-theoretical in an inductive manner remarkably reminiscent of the sort of posture taken today by some behavioristic followers of B.F. Skinner. But like the Skinnerians, Holmes is forced to assert at least provisional hypotheses or "hunches" about the world. Holmes may cry out "No, no: I never guess. It is a shocking habit — destructive to the logical faculty,"[36] but he is forced to acknowledge that

one forms provisional theories and waits for time and fuller knowledge to explode them. A bad habit . . . ; but human nature is weak.[37]

At base, Holmes puts his trust in the empirical world which he sees as the firm and ultimate arbiter. "I can discover facts, Watson, but I cannot change them."[38] And these facts must always be questioned for "it is as well to test everything."[39]

Holmes's Method

Holmes clearly subscribed to the general rule of the modern scientific community that since scientific knowledge is of its definition *public* knowledge (in so far as it must be inter-subjectively communicable), it should ideally be open to public scrutiny. Holmes generally makes no secret of his methods.

It has always been my habit to hide none of my methods either from my friend Watson or from anyone who might take an intelligent interest in them.[40]

Holmes does occasionally fail to inform his astounded clients of his methods, especially in the early stages of his cases, for, as he put it: "I have found it wise to impress clients with a sense of power."[41] Yet, he usually lets us in on his reasonings and points out that the method is basically quite unmysterious.

It is not really difficult to construct a series of inferences, each dependent upon its predecessor and each simple in itself. If, after doing so, one simply knocks out all the central inferences and presents one's audience with the starting-point and the conclusion, one may produce a startling, though possibly a meretricious, effect.[42]

Holmes was very concerned with the clear presentation of his methods, so much so, in fact, that he complained of Watson's romanticizing his adventures:

Your fatal habit of looking at everything from the point of view of a story instead of as a scientific exercise has ruined what might have been an instructive and even classical series of demonstrations.[43]

He even spoke of his plans to do the job properly himself:

I propose to devote my declining years to the composition of a textbook which shall focus the whole art of detection into one volume.[44]

In speaking of the "qualities necessary for the ideal detective," Holmes noted that they were: (1) knowledge, (2) the power of observation, and (3) the power of deduction.[45] We turn now to an examination of each of these.

The Detective's Need for Knowledge. As we have seen, Holmes stressed the interconnectedness of all elements of the universe in his deterministic view. He also recognized the complexities and sometimes surprising connections that might be found, for he noted that

for strange effects and extraordinary combinations we must go to life itself, which is always far more daring than any effort of the imagination.[46]

Thus, the effective detective must be well informed about a vast spectrum of potentially relevant bits of information. Holmes's own storehouse of information was astounding. As we noted earlier, he placed a great emphasis on breadth of knowledge.[47] Watson indicates that Holmes's mastery of the topics relevant to his profession (including chemistry, British law, anatomy, botany, geology, and especially the sensational literature) was remarkable.[48] Yet, Watson also notes that Holmes's "ignorance was as remarkable as his knowledge,"[49] for Holmes apparently knew practically nothing of literature, philosophy, astronomy, or politics.[50] Holmes explained his lack of concern with these areas as follows:

You see . . . I consider that a man's brain originally is like a little empty attic, and you have to stock it with such furniture as you choose. A fool takes in all the lumber of every sort that he comes across, so that the knowledge which might be useful to him gets crowded out, or at best is jumbled up with a lot of other things, so that he has a difficulty in laying his hands upon it. Now the skillful workman is very careful indeed as to what he takes into his brain-attic. He will have nothing but the tools which may help him in doing his work, but of these he has a large assortment, and all in the most perfect order. It is a mistake to think that that little room has elastic walls and can distend to any extent. Depend upon it there comes a time when for every addition of knowledge you forget something that you knew before. It is of the highest importance, therefore, not to have useless facts elbowing out the useful ones.[51]

Despite this avoidance of the irrelevant (based upon a view of memory with which most contemporary experts on cognitive processes would certainly disagree), Holmes still stocked a vast quantity of information in his memory that was not immediately useful; for as he stated on another occasion:

My mind is like a crowded box-room with packets of all sorts stowed away therein — so many that I may well have but a vague perception of what was there.[52]

What Holmes basically argued for was the need for specialization in the quest for knowledge so that one might gain the maximum in resources relevant to one's analytic needs. The argument is not primarily one for avoiding some areas of knowledge so much as it is for a commitment of one's limited resources to the most efficient ends. As Holmes stated in a somewhat different context:

Some facts should be suppressed, or at least a just sense of proportion should be observed in treating them.[53]

Thus, not all knowledge is equally useful, a viewpoint certainly the dominant motif in education (not only in the study of social psychology but in most areas) today.

The Detective's Need for Observation. Holmes emphasized the need for keen observation, for in detective work "genius is an infinite capacity for taking pains."[54] Openness and receptivity to data is essential.

I make a point of never having any prejudices and of following docilely wherever fact may lead me.[55]

Holmes was much aware of the need to control for subjective distortions even in relation to his clients.

It is of the first importance . . . not to allow your judgement to be biased by personal qualities. A client is to me a mere unit, a factor in a problem. The emotional qualities are antagonistic to clear reasoning.[56]

His greatest emphasis, however, was upon "observing" what others merely "see." Thus, though both Dr. Watson and Holmes had walked the steps leading up from the hall to their room hundreds of times, Holmes had "observed" that there were seventeen steps while Watson had merely "seen" them.[57] As Holmes put it:

The world is full of obvious things which nobody by any chance ever observes.[58]

There is nothing more deceptive than an obvious fact.[59]

I have trained myself to notice what I see.[60]

Holmes's observation extended not only to observed facts and events but also to their absence. Negative evidence is frequently regarded as highly significant. Thus, when Inspector MacDonald asks Holmes if he found anything compromising following Holmes's search through Professor Moriarty's papers, Holmes replied, "Absolutely nothing. That was what amazed me."[61] Or, speaking of the absence of international activity following the theft of an important government document, Holmes noted: "Only one important thing has happened in three days, and that is that nothing has happened."[62] But the classic example is the often-quoted instance during Holmes's search for a missing race-horse wherein Inspector Gregory asks Holmes:

"Is there any other point to which you would wish to draw my attention?"
"To the curious incident of the dog in the night-time."

"The dog did nothing in the night-time."
"That was the curious incident," remarked Sherlock Holmes.[63]

Throughout the canon, Holmes emphasizes the importance of what to the less trained might appear to be trifles. But for Holmes, "there is nothing so important as trifles,"[64] and "to a great mind . . . nothing is little."[65]

It has long been an axiom of mine that the little things are infinitely the most important.[66]

You know my method. It is founded upon the observance of trifles.[67]

Never trust to general impressions . . . but concentrate upon the details.[68]

Attention to minutiae is essential, for

as long as the criminal remains upon two legs, so long must there be some identification, some abrasion, some trifling displacement which can be detected by the scientific searcher.[69]

The Detective's Need for Deduction. Holmes has almost unlimited faith in the power of scientific analysis to obtain a reconstruction of human events, for, as he put it: "What one man can invent, another can discover."[70] For Holmes, "the grand thing is to be able to reason backwards."[71] Reasoning from a set of events to their consequences Holmes calls "synthetic" reasoning, whereas reasoning "backwards" from the results to their causes he calls "analytic" reasoning.

There are fifty who can reason synthetically for one who can reason analytically . . . . There are few people . . . . , if you told them the result, would be able to evolve from their own inner consciousness what the steps were which led up to that result.[72]

The first step Holmes suggests is basic examination and sifting out from the existing information the definite from the less definite data.

The difficulty is to detach the framework of fact—of absolute, undeniable fact—from the embellishments of theorists and reporters. Then, having established ourselves upon this sound basis, it is our duty to see what inferences may be drawn, and which are the special points upon which the whole mystery turns.[73]

It is of the highest importance in the art of detection to be able to recognize out of a number of facts which are incidental and which vital.[74]

Following a sorting of the facts for their reliability, Holmes recommends special inspection of the unique and unusual details present in the situation.

The more *outré* and grotesque an incident is, the more carefully it deserves to be examined, and the very point which appears to complicate a case is, when duly considered and scientifically handled, the one which is most likely to elucidate it.[75]

Singularity is almost invariably a clue. The more featureless and commonplace a crime is, the more difficult is it to bring home.[76]

What is out of the common is usually a guide rather than a hindrance.[77]

It is only the colourless, uneventful case which is hopeless.[78]

Yet, Holmes notes that extreme uneventfulness may itself be a singular event which gives a clue to the mystery:

Depend upon it there is nothing so unnatural as the commonplace.[79]

Holmes is careful in his evaluation of circumstantial evidence. It is not to be ignored for "circumstantial evidence is occasionally very convincing, as when you find a trout in the milk."[80] But the investigator must be very cautious, since

circumstantial evidence is a very tricky thing . . . ; it may point very straight to one thing, but if you shift your own point of view a little, you may find it pointing in an equally uncompromising manner to something entirely different.[81]

Although Holmes's greatest emphasis is upon the objective gathering of facts, he fully recognizes the heuristic value of imaginative reconstruction through role playing by the investigator.

You'll get results . . . by always putting yourself in the other fellow's place, and thinking what you would do yourself. It takes some imagination but it pays.[82]

You know my methods in such cases . . . : I put myself in the man's place, and having first gauged his intelligence, I try to imagine how I should myself have proceeded under the same circumstances.[83]

Holmes emphasizes the need for pursuing several possible lines of explanation any one of which takes account of the facts. Other hypotheses must always be entertained, and when considering an explanation, "you should never lose sight of the alternative."[84]

One should always look for a possible alternative and provide against it. It is the first rule of criminal investigation.[85]

For

when you follow two separate chains of thought . . . you will find some point of intersection which should approximate the truth.[86]

From this reconstruction of alternative explanations which fit the facts, one must move next into what might superficially appear to be guessing but is actually

the region where we balance probabilities and choose the most likely. It is the scientific use of the imagination, but we have always some material basis on which to start our speculations.[87]

Holmes sees arrival at the truth in terms of setting hypotheses into competition with one another. But the weighing of the alternatives includes not only a comparison of them in terms of *probability*. Explanations must always be considered in terms of their *possibility*. The *possible*, however, is determined not only by the feasibility of the suggested events. It is also the remaining result of elimination of those alternative hypotheses perceived to be impossible. Holmes often repeats "the old axiom that when all other contingencies fail, whatever remains, however improbable, must be the truth."[88]

Though the analytic process described above is primarily an exercise in logic without direct recourse to the empirical world, Holmes next demanded the empirical validation of the resulting hypotheses in terms which closely approximate what is today called the *hypothetico-deductive* method.[89]

I will give my process of thought . . . That process . . . starts upon the supposition that when you have eliminated all which is impossible, that whatever remains, however improbable, must be the truth. It may well be that several explanations remain, in which case one tries test after test until one or other of them has a convincing amount of support.[90]

For

when the original intellectual deduction is confirmed point by point by quite a number of independent accidents, then the subjective becomes objective and we can say confidently that we have reached our goal.[91]

Throughout Holmes's approach, logical (mostly deductive) and empirical (mostly inductive) considerations are in constant interrelation. The empirical restricts the theoretical, as in the case where Holmes states that

It *is* impossible as I state it, and therefore I must in some respect have stated it wrong.[92]

But empirical events must be interpreted in terms of established theoretical considerations. Thus,

when a fact appears to be opposed to a long train of deductions, it invariably proves to be capable of having some other interpretation.[93]

In a very real and practical sense, Holmes's method anticipated the contemporary emphasis in sociology upon the intertwining relationships between theory and research (cf., Merton 1957, pp. 85-117).

The Application of Holmes's Method

Thus far, we have outlined Holmes's general approach to the problematic in social life. We turn now to a consideration of the limitations of that approach, especially as exemplified in Holmes's own applications of his method.

Holmes's Uses of Observation. Throughout the adventures, Holmes insists upon intensive familiarization of the investigator with his problem, for familiarity will bring clarification. He notes that "it is a mistake to confound strangeness with mystery." Familiarity is seen as generally reducing the problematic elements in an event. He even states that

as a rule . . . the more bizarre a thing is the less mysterious it proves to be.[95]

Familiarization can also remove fear, for the unfamiliar leaves us room for imagination, and "where there is no imagination, there is no horror."[96]

Holmes attempted to familiarize himself with all possible observable details of life which might have a bearing upon his criminal cases. This familiarization was not just the result of passive observation but includes the active search for new details of meaning which might prove useful in the future. Thus, for example, Holmes was described as having at one time beaten a corpse to discern how bruises might be produced after death.[97]

Holmes argued, as we have noted, that all human actions leave some traces from which the discerning investigator can deduce information. This emphasis on obtaining indirect data from sources through observation of physical traces constitutes an early recognition of the potential uses of what recently have been termed *unobtrusive measures*. (Webb, *et al.,* 1966, p. 35). Again and again, Holmes concerns himself with the small details about those involved in his inquiries.

I can never bring you to realize the importance of sleeves, the suggestiveness of thumbnails, or the great issues that may hang from a boot lace.

Always look at the hands first, . . . then cuffs, trouser-knees and boots.[99]

[T]here is no part of the body which varies so much as the human ear. Each ear is as a rule quite distinctive, and different from all other ones.[100]

It would be difficult to name any articles which afford a finer field for inference than a pair of glasses.[101]

Pipes are occasionally of extraordinary interest . . . . Nothing has more individuality save, perhaps, watches and bootlaces.[102]

Nor does Holmes restrict his observations to things seen or heard. The investigator should develop his sense of smell, too, for

there are seventy-five perfumes, which it is very necessary that a criminal expert should be able to distinguish from each other, and cases have more than once within my own experience depended upon their prompt recognition.[103]

Possibly the most important and frequent among the traces carefully examined by Holmes is the footprint. Of it he says:

There is no branch of detective science which is so important and so much neglected as the art of tracing footprints.[104]

Even the traces of bicycle tires are not left unconsidered by Holmes, who claims at one point that he can differentiate some forty-two different "tyre impressions."[105]

Though Holmes's uses of the observable differences which he notes and conveys to the reader are often fantastic and hardly practicable in the "real world" outside the pages of the canon, the basic approach represented by these fictional narratives has startling parallels in the actual world of criminalistics and forensic medicine (e.g., cf. Stewart-Gordon 1961) where true cases of detection through subtle observation and inference are often far more startling than anything ever suggested by Sir Arthur Conan Doyle.

The Character of Holmes's Inferences. Although examples of Holmes's remarkable uses of inference abound in the Sherlockian literature, as with his basic method, little attention has been given to an examination of the logic of his applications (minor, largely non-critical and merely admiring studies would include those of Hart 1948, Schenck 1953, Mackenzie 1956, Ball 1958, and, especially, Hitchings 1946).

Careful examination of the sixty narratives that comprise the canon reveals at least 217 clearly described and discernible cases of inference (unobtrusive measurement) made by Holmes. Many of these are strung together in logical chains with Holmes gathering a great deal of information from a single object or event.[106] Thus, numerous instances appear in one story (at least thirty in "A Study in Scarlet") with few or none (as in "The Adventure of the Dying Detective") in others.

Although Holmes often speaks of his *deductions*, these are actually quite rarely displayed in the canon. Nor are Holmes's most common inferences technically *inductions*. More exactly, Holmes consistently displays what C.S. Peirce has called *abductions*.[107] Following Peirce's distinctions, the differences between deduction, induction, and abduction can be seen as follows:

DEDUCTION

Case	All serious knife wounds result in bleeding.
Result	This was a serious knife wound.
∴ *Rule*	There was bleeding.

INDUCTION

Case	This was a serious knife wound.
Result	There was bleeding.
∴ *Rule*	All serious knife wounds result in bleeding.

ABDUCTION

Rule	All serious knife wounds result in bleeding.
Result	There was bleeding.
∴ *Case*	This was a serious knife wound.

Abductions, like inductions, are not logically self-contained, as is the deduction, and they need to be externally validated. Peirce sometimes called abductions *hypotheses* (he also called them *presumptive inferences* at times), and in the modern sense, that is what the conclusion in the abduction represents: a conjecture about reality which needs to be validated through testing.

The great weakness in Holmes's applications of inference—at least as Watson related them to us—was Holmes's failure to test the hypotheses which he obtained through abduction. In most instances, Holmes simply treated the abducted inference as though it were logically valid. (Most of the parodies on Holmes are built upon this weakness in the narratives.) The simple fact is that the vast majority of Holmes's inferences just do not stand up to logical examination. He concludes correctly simply because the author of the stories allows it so.[108] Upon occasion, the abductive inferences are strung together in a long narrative series which the startled client (or Watson) confirms at each step. In a sense, this constitutes a degree of external corroboration of the hypotheses (especially where they are made about things correctly known to the listener, which is often the case). Nonetheless, in the vast majority of instances, the basic reasoning process described by Watson whereby Holmes astounds his listeners must, in the final analysis, be judged logically inadequate if not invalid.

Despite the logical inadequacies of Holmes's abductions, it must be noted that Holmes does actually hypothesis test (i.e., seek external validation) in at least twenty-eight instances (though not even all of these occasions are directly related to the minimum of 217 abductions found in the canon). Several of the stories include more than one case of hypothesis testing ("Silver Blaze" and "A Study in Scarlet" both evidence three such tests), but most of the narratives show no such attempts at external confirmation by Holmes. The best example of such testing by Holmes occurs in the story of Holmes's search for the missing race horse Silver Blaze. Postulating that the horse's leg was to be operated upon by an amateur to damage it, Holmes reasoned that the culprit would probably practice the operation beforehand to gain skill and assure success. Since sheep were nearby, Holmes further conjectured that the culprit might have practiced upon them. Inquiring about the sheep, Holmes learned that several of them had recently and inexplicably gone lame. The sheep's predicted lameness thus acted as a confirmation of Holmes's conjectures.[109]

The reconstruction of Holmes's methods and the extraction of the fundamental ideas in his thought is necessarily incomplete. Holmes relates only bits and pieces to us through the narratives of Dr. Watson, and even these items are stated sparingly. Watson noted of Holmes that "he pushed to an extreme the axiom that the only safe plotter was he who plotted alone."[110] And as Holmes put it:

I do not waste words or disclose my thoughts while a case is actually under consideration.[111]

I claim the right to work in my own way and give my results at my own time—complete, rather than in stages.[112]

Despite these obstacles, we have seen that a general reconstruction is possible, and it reveals a systematic and consistent orientation.

HOLMES AND SOCIAL PSYCHOLOGY

Just as with his basic method, examination of the canon reveals a large number of statements and insights, many stated in near-propositional and testable form about many aspects of social and psychological reality. We turn now to a look at some of the observations.

Holmes on Character and Personality

Holmes brings the same skepticism which served him as a detective of crimes into his general orientation towards the social world. As is the case with most social psychologists who term themselves symbolic interactionists (cf. Stone and Farberman 1970), Holmes was much aware that people's definitions of their situations, their phenomenological perception of their worlds, rather than physical realities, may be the important factors which determine their actions.

What you do in this world is a matter of no consequence . . . . The question is what can you make people believe you have done.[113]

Holmes's skepticism of appearances bordered upon the paranoic when it came to women. Holmes was especially cautious in his relations with women and found it nearly impossible to correctly assess their motives.

Women are never to be entirely trusted—not the best of them.[114]

[T]he motives of women are so inscrutable . . . Their most trivial action may mean volumes, or their most extraordinary conduct may depend upon a hairpin or a curling-tongs.[115]

He showed special concern about the socially isolated female.

One of the most dangerous classes in the world . . . is the drifting and friendless woman. She is the most harmless, and often the most useful of mortals, but she is the inevitable inciter of crime in others. She is helpless. She is migratory. She has sufficient means to take her from country to country and from hotel to hotel. She is lost, as often as not, in a maze of obscure *pensions* and boarding houses. She is a stray chicken in a world of foxes. When she is gobbled up she is hardly missed.[116]

Yet, Holmes was no misogynist (as is well seen in his admiration for Irene Adler who bested him in "A Scandal in Bohemia"), and he placed great value on female intuition.

I have seen too much not to know that the impression of a woman may be more valuable than the conclusion of an analytic reasoner.[117]

Holmes mentions several generalizations about women which proved valuable to him in successfully analyzing his cases, but these were highly specific to their situations and probably would not stand up under rigorous investigation in other contexts.[118]

In attempting to read a subject's character and motives, Holmes used a variety of subtle indicators. The movement of the subject's eyes and body were carefully noted (such study of "body language" is today called *kinesics*):

I can read in a man's eye when it is his own skin that he is frightened for.[119]

And, seeing a young lady client's motions on the street as she approached his apartment, he noted:

Oscillation upon the pavement always means an *affaire du coeur*.[120]

Extensive examination was always given not only to the subject under investigation but also to those with whom he associated, including children and animals.

I have frequently gained my first real insight into the character of parents by studying their children.[121]

And

I have serious thoughts of writing a small monograph upon the uses of dogs in the work of the detective . . . . A dog reflects the family life. Whoever saw a frisky dog in a gloomy family, or a sad dog in a happy one? Snarling people have snarling dogs, dangerous people have dangerous ones. And their passing moods may reflect the passing moods of others.[122]

Holmes suggested a number of interesting ideas about personality. Thus, he endorsed the idea of complementarity in mate selection:

You may have noticed how extremes call to each other, the spiritual to the animal, the cave-man to the angel.[123]

He argued that excellence at chess was "one mark of a scheming mind."[124] He claimed that all the misers were jealous men,[125] and that "jealousy is a strong transformer of characters."[126] Recognizing the importance of man's inferiorities, Holmes noted that "weakness in one limb is often compensated for by exceptional strength in the others."[127] Regarding the appreciation of subtle variations by those with expertise, he noted that to the man who loves art for its own sake, . . . it is frequently in its least important and lowliest manifestations that the keenest pleasure is to be derived.[128]

And of a man's stubborn psychological inertia, he generalized that

a man always finds it hard to realize that he may have finally lost a woman's love, however badly he may have treated her.[129]

All these generalizations must remain questionable until empirically tested, but these maxims suggest interesting and potentially fruitful directions for future research.

Holmes as Criminologist

Thus far, we have been primarily concerned with Holmes's general orientation to the investigation and perception of the realities of social life. As a consulting detective, however, his primary concern was with legal and moral crimes. We turn now to examine his insights and observations into this more specialized domain.

Holmes on Justice and Deception. Holmes felt that his personal hardships were "trifling details" that "must never interfere with the investigation of a case."[130] But he was far from the usual stereotype most people have of the daring hero. Though a brave man, Holmes did not ignore adversity, for he thought that "it is stupidity rather than courage to refuse to recognize danger when it is close upon you."[131] Far more contrary to the pure heroic image, however, was the fact that Holmes's activities sometimes ran counter to the law. As an unofficial investigator, he was not bound to the conventions of the police. He had little respect for the abilities of Scotland Yard's men and thought them generally "a bad lot" (though he did display respect for the abilities of the Yard's Inspector Tobias Gregson). He went even further in his disdain for other police, as when he noted that "local aid is always either worthless or biased."[132] Holmes was well aware of the inadequacies of law inforcement and commented that "many men have been wrongfully hanged."[133]

Holmes did apparently have a degree of faith in the ultimate victory of justice, as indicated in his statement that

violence does, in truth, recoil upon the violent, and the schemer falls into the pit which he digs for another.[134]

But Holmes sometimes finds it necessary to go outside the law to assure justice. Thus, he occasionally commits trespass, burglary, and unlawful detention. Of the most serious of these, burglary, he argues that it

is morally justifiable so long as our object is to take no articles save those which are used for an illegal purpose.[135]

He adopted this basically vigilante role because, as he put it:

I think that there are certain crimes which the law cannot touch, and which therefore, to some extent, justify private revenge.[136]

Holmes also recognized that prison was not always an appropriate punishment for a crime, and that it might actually deter the process of reform. Thus, on at least fourteen occasions, Holmes actually allowed known felons to go free (Leavitt 1940, p. 27), for as he said of one such man he released: "Send him to gaol now, and you make him a gaolbird for life."[137]

Holmes was also not beyond deception if he felt it might suit the ends of justice. This went to rather extreme lengths when he attempted to trap "the worst man in London" by disguising himself as a plumber and becoming engaged to the villain's maid to obtain information.[138] Holmes was aware of the need to obtain the full confidence of his informants, and this he sometimes did by passing himself off as one of them. Thus, on one occasion when he needed certain information, he disguised himself as a groom, explaining to Watson that

there is a wonderful sympathy and freemasonry among horsey men. Be one of them, and you will know all that there is to know.[139]

On other occasions, Holmes faked illnesses, accidents, information, and even his own death. He often used the newspapers in a manipulative manner[140] and noted that "the press . . . . is a most valuable institution, if you only know how to use it."[141]

Holmes on Crime. Sherlock Holmes was well aware of the fact that crime rates normally show only *reported* instances of law violation. Thus, in looking at the pleasant countryside through which he and Dr. Watson were moving by train, Holmes remarked to Watson:

You look at these scattered houses, and you are impressed by their beauty. I look at them, and the only thought which comes to me is a feeling of their isolation, and of the impunity with which crime may be committed there ... They always fill me with a certain horror. It is my belief . . . founded upon my experience, that the lowest and vilest alleys in London do not present a more dreadful record of sin than does the smiling and beautiful country-side . . . .

[And] the reason is very obvious. The pressure of public opinion can do in the town what the law cannot accomplish. There is no lane so vile that the scream of a tortured child, or the thud of a drunkard's blow, does not beget sympathy and indignation among the neighbours, that a word of complaint can set it going, and there is but a step between the crime and the dock. But look at these lonely houses, each in its own fields, filled for the most part with poor ignorant folk who know little of the law. Think of the deeds of hellish cruelty, the hidden wickedness which may go on year in, year out, in such places, and none the wise.[142]

As with his views on personality, Holmes offers us numerous maxims about crime and criminal investigation which the contemporary criminologist might well consider. Thus, Holmes claimed that there was a potential relationship between the unusual and the criminal, as when he pointed out that "there is but one step from the grotesque to the horrible"[143] and "often the grotesque has deepened into the criminal."[144] Yet, he also warned us that we should not assume such a relationship to be automatic for

the strangest and most unique things are very often connected not with the larger but with the smaller crimes, and occasionally, indeed, where there is room for doubt whether any positive crime has been committed.[145]

Holmes found two types of crime especially difficult to unravel. He found the "senseless" or motiveless crime the greatest challenge for the criminal investigator.

The most difficult crime to track is the one which is purposeless.[146]

But where a discernible motive is involved, the planned crime presents great difficulties for a detective also, for

where a crime is coolly premeditated, then the means of covering it are coolly premeditated also.[147]

This realization of the hidden complexities potential within a planned crime led Holmes to be most suspicious in such cases, especially of suspects with semingly solid alibis, for, he noted, "only a man with a criminal enterprise desires to establish an alibi."[148] Finally, it might be noted that in addition to seeing these two types of crime as formidable, Holmes also recognized special difficulty with cases where the criminal was an M.D.

When a doctor does go wrong he is the first of criminals. He has nerve and he has knowledge.[149]

Canonical Errors and Anticipations. As might be expected, the adventures sometimes show Holmes stating scientifically erroneous ideas. These largely reflect the popular notions of his time. Thus, Holmes placed far too great an emphasis on heredity as a causative factor in the creation of criminals. He referred to an hereditary criminal strain in the blood of the arch-villain Professor Moriarty[150] and strongly stated his views when he said:

There are some trees . . . which grow to a certain height and then suddenly develop some unsightly eccentricity. You will see it often in humans. I have a theory that the individual represents in his development the whole procession of his ancestors, and that such a sudden turn to good or evil stands for some strange influence which came into the life of his pedigree. The person becomes, as it were, the epitome of the history of his own family.[151]

Holmes also seems to share some of the stereotypes and prejudices of his Victorian world as regarded some minority groups. Thus, he displayed mild prejudice towards Negroes and Jews.[152]

He also had some unusual and false ideas about thought processes. We have already mentioned his view of memory as similar to an attic which can become over-crowded.[153] He also showed a degree of misunderstanding of cognitive processes in the following statements:

To let the brain work without sufficient material is like racing an engine. It racks itself to pieces.[154]

[T]he faculties become refined when you starve them.[155]

And

Intense mental concentration has a curious way of blotting out what has passed.[156]

Despite such occasional lapses into the misinformation common to his historical period, Holmes managed to pioneer in the anticipation of several innovations in scientific crime detection. Since the science of ballistics was unknown to police prior to 1909 (cf. Baring-Gould 1967, II, p. 349, note 51), Holmes's statement about a villain in a story first published in 1903 that "the bullets alone are enough to put his head in a noose"[157] seems to show him to be a true pioneer in this field. Holmes was also an early advocate of the importance of both fingerprints,[158] and the Bertillon system of measurement.[159]

Among the most interesting of his anticipations was his realization of the possibility of distinguishing and identifying different types of communications. He was able to spot identifying differences between a wide variety of printing types in newspapers and magazines, and he stated that

the detection of types is one of the most elementary branches of knowledge to the special expert of crime.[160]

And, more important, he early recognized that typewriters could be identified.

It is a curious thing . . . that a typewriter has really quite as much individuality as a man's handwriting. Unless they are quite new, no two of them write exactly alike. Some letters get more worn than others, and some wear only on one side.[161]

But most of all, Holmes strongly believed in the great knowledge which could be gained through the careful examination of handwritings (cf. Christie 1955 and Swanson 1962). Holmes not only pioneered in this study but went considerably beyond what most graphologists would yet claim for their science when he made the statements that

the deduction of a man's age from his writing is one which has been brought to a considerable accuracy by experts.[162]

And that

a family mannerism can be traced in . . . two specimens of writing.[163]

Finally, it should be noted that Holmes may have anticipated some of the devices of later psychoanalysis. Thus, it would appear that he saw the basis for tests of free-association, for in analyzing a coded message which contained seemingly extraneous and meaningless words, he noted of the writer:

He would naturally use the first words which came to his mind, and if there were so many which referred to sport among them, you may be tolerably sure that he is either an ardent shot or interested in breeding.[164]

Holmes also clearly understood the defense mechanism of projection when he stated of a villain:

It may only be his conscience. Knowing himself to be a traitor, he may have read the accusation in the other's eyes.[165]

And at another point, when speaking of the subtle influences of music, he would seem to have closely paralleled the idea of archetypes within the collective unconscious as later developed by Carl G. Jung when he said:

There are vague memories in our souls of the misty centuries when the world was in its childhood.[166]

Holmes, then, shared many of the errors of the men of his time, but, as we hope has been adequately shown in this essay, he also extended our view of man. Given the extraordinary popularity of the tales of his adventures, created for us through the genius of Sir Arthur Conan Doyle, for many criminologists who recognized the merits of the detective's methods, it is doubtful that Sherlock Holmes could have had a greater impact on the sciences of man had he actually lived.

NOTES

1. The fully accepted Holmes legend appears in four full-length novels and fifty-six short stories. Though a great many editions of the works exist, the most recent and authoritative version of the tales is to be found in William S. Baring-Gould's beautifully edited and introduced *The Annotated Sherlock Holmes* in two volumes (1967). *All reference to the Holmes stories throughout this essay refer to this edition and its pagination.*

In addition to the above works (called the "canon" or the "sacred writings" by Sherlockian scholars), Holmes is also believed to figure prominently in two other stories by Arthur Conan Doyle ("The Man With the Watches" and "The Lost Special") available as *The Sherlockian Doyle* (1968). There also was published a posthumously discovered manuscript which was at first thought to have been written by Sir Arthur Conan Doyle as "The Case of the Man Who Was Wanted" (1948). The authenticity of this piece has since been challenged with the result being general agreement that the story was actually written by a Mr. Arthur Whittaker, who had sold the story to Conan Doyle in 1913. For full details on this episode, see Brown (1969).

Within the sixty narratives comprising the canon, mentions are made of at least fifty-five other cases (for a listing, see Starrett 1960, pp. 90-92). A minority of Sherlockians would therefore be inclined to include twelve other stories among the sacred writings which were written by Sir Arthur's son and official biographer, Adrian Conan Doyle and John Dickson Carr (1954).

In addition to the canon and its apocrypha plus some secondary references to Holmes by Doyle (most notably in several of his plays based on the stories), there is a vast literature based directly on the canon including over twenty-one plays, one Broadway musical, hundreds of radio and television productions, and at least 123 motion pictures. This is not to count the hundreds of books and articles dealing with Sherlockiana or the hundreds of pastiches and parodies of the canon, of which many of the best were anthologized by Ellery Queen (1944).

2. According to Sherlockians, of course, Doyle is not the author of the stories but merely an acquaintance of Holmes's associate, Dr. John Watson, who wrote (narrated) fifty-six of the sixty adventures in the canon. "The Adventure of the Blanched Soldier" and "The Adventure of the Lion's Mane" were apparently written by Holmes himself, and "The Adventure of the Mazarin Stone" and "His Last Bow" were written by

person or persons unknown. Sherlockians have speculated about the authorship of these two narratives, suggesting everyone from Mrs. Mary Watson, Inspector Lestrade, a distant relative of Holmes called Dr. Verner, to Dr. Watson himself merely pretending to write in the third person. Even the rather extreme suggestion was made, first by the great Sherlockian scholar, Edgar W. Smith, that these two stories were written by Watson's friend Sir Arthur Conan Doyle. For full details on this controversy, see Baring-Gould (1967, II, pp. 748-50).

For biographical works on Sir Arthur Conan Doyle see: Carr (1949); Nordon (1967); Pearson (1943); Lamond (1931); and M. and M. Hardwick (1964). See also Doyle's autobiography (1924). Re Doyle's writings, see: Locke (1928); Nordon (1967, pp. 347-51); and Carr (1949, pp. 285-95).

3. The adventures themselves have been chronologized differently by numerous Sherlockians, but Baring-Gould (1967) sees them as spanning from 1874 to 1914. Far more controversially, in his biography of Holmes, Baring-Gould (1962) calculated Holmes's birth year as 1854 and placed his death in 1957. For other chronologies, see: Bell (1932); Blackeney (1932); Christ (1947); Brend (1951); Zeisler (1953); Baring-Gould (1955); and Folsom (1964).

4. E.g., Baring-Gould (1967) and Brend (1951). For a biographical study of Dr. John Watson, see Roberts (1931).

5. E.g., Park (1962) and M. and M. Hardwick (1962). Many other reference volumes on the canon exist including: Harrison (1958); Christ (1947); Bigelow (1959); Petersen (1956); Smith (1940); and Wolff (1952 and 1955).

6. Among the many excellent books and collections of Sherlockiana one must include: Bell (1934); Starrett (1934 and 1940); Smith (1944); and Holroyd (1967). A wide variety of such studies appear in the numerous Sherlockian journals. In addition to the best known *The Baker Street Journal*, published in New York, and *The Sherlock Holmes Journal*, published in London, there are many newsletters and other privately printed publications produced by Sherlockian groups around the United States, including: *The Vermissa Herald*, the *Devon County Chronicle, Shades of Sherlock*, and the annual Pontine Dossier. For an extensive critical bibliography, see Baring-Gould (1967, II, pp. 807-24).

7. The most well-known organization in the United States is the Baker Street Irregulars, born in 1933 in the "Bowling Green" column conducted by Christopher Morley in the *Saturday Review of Literature*. For a brief history of the B.S.I., see Starrett (1960, pp. 128-36). The B.S.I. has Scion Societies (chapters) all over the world including the Orient. Re the Sherlockian organizations see: Baring-Gould (1967, I, pp. 37-42); and Starrett (1960, pp. 128-36).

8. Though these movements have failed thus far, numerous other memorials have been erected to Holmes's memory including plaques in Picadilly, at St. Bartholomew's Hospital, at the Rosslei Inn in Meiringen, Switzerland, and even at the Reichenbach Falls. For full information, see Baring-Gould (1967, I, pp. 43-46.).

9. For a somewhat more critical view of Holmes as criminologist, see Anderson (1903).

10. Nordon (1967, p. 214) has argued that Doyle's description of Bell is "too like Holmes to be true," and that the model for Holmes was "invented" by Doyle *a posteriori* to fit the image of a proper man of science. Pearson (1943) suggested that Holmes was largely patterned after one Dr. George Budd, Doyle's eccentric medical partner with whom he briefly practiced at Plymouth. More recently, it has been convincingly argued that Holmes was basically patterned after the private consulting detective Mr. Wendel Shere (Harrison 1971).

11. *The Spectator* said of him: "The fights that he made for victims of perverted justice will stand alongside Voltaire's championship of Jean Calas and Emile Zola's long struggle for Dreyfus" (quoted in Anonymous 1959, p. 67).

12. "The Adventure of the Blanched Soldier," II, p. 720.

13. "The Problem of Thor Bridge," II, p. 605.

14. "The Valley of Fear," I, p. 507.

15. "A Study in Scarlet," I, p. 179.

16. "The Valley of Fear," I, p. 512.
17. "The Hound of the Baskervilles," II, p. 20.
18. *Ibid.*
19. "The Adventure of the Sussex Vampire," II, p. 463.
20. " 'What is the meaning of it, Watson,' said Holmes solemnly as he laid down the paper. 'What object is served by this circle of misery and violence and fear? It must tend to some end or else our universe is ruled by chance, which is unthinkable. But what end? There is the great standing perennial problem to which human reason is as far from an answer as ever.' " "The Cardboard Box," II, p. 208.
21. "Our highest assurance of the goodness of Providence seems to me to rest in the flowers. All other things, our powers, our desires, our food, are really necessary for our existence in this first instance. But this rose is an extra. Its smell and its colour are an embellishment of life, not a condition of it. It is only goodness which gives extras, and so I say again that we have much to hope from the flowers." "The Naval Treaty," II, p. 178.
22. "The Adventure of the Retired Colourman," II, p. 546.
23. "The Five Orange Pips," I, p. 398.
24. "A Study in Scarlet," I, p. 159.
25. "The Sign of the Four," I, p. 666. In this passage, Holmes indicates his agreement with Winwood Reade's *The Martyrdom of Man* which Holmes actually misquotes. Cf., Crocker (1964).
26. "A Study in Scarlet," I, p. 168. Re this statement, see W. J. Bell (1947).
27. "The Valley of Fear," I, p. 479.
28. "The Sign of the Four," I, p. 610.
29. "The Valley of Fear," I, pp. 481-82.
30. "A Scandal in Bohemia," I, pp. 349-50.
31. "The Adventure of the Second Stain," I, p. 311.
32. "A Study in Scarlet," I, p. 166.
33. "The Adventure of Wisteria Lodge," II, p. 246.
34. "The Adventure of the Speckled Band," I, p. 261.
35. "The Adventure of the Copper Beeches," II, p. 120.
36. "The Sign of the Four," I, p. 614.
37. "The Adventure of the Sussex Vampire," II, p. 467-68.
38. "The Problem of Thor Bridge," II, p. 589.
39. "The Reigate Squires," I, p. 335.
40. *Ibid.*, p. 341.
41. "The Adventure of the Blanched Soldier," II, p. 707.
42. "The Adventure of the Dancing Men," II, p. 527. Along similar lines, Holmes also stated that "every problem becomes very childish when once it is explained to you" *Ibid.*, p. 528) and "results without causes are much more impressive" ("The Stockbroker's Clerk," II, p. 154).
43. "The Adventure of the Abbey Grange." II, p. 491. Holmes stated the matter more strongly when he told Watson: "Crime is common. Logic is rare. Therefore it is upon logic rather than upon the crime that you should dwell. You have degraded what should have been a course of lectures into a series of tales." "The Adventure of the Copper Beeches," II, p. 115.
44. *Ibid.*, p. 492.
45. "The Sign of the Four," I, p. 612.
46. "The Red Headed League," I, p. 419.
47. "The Valley of Fear," I, p. 512.
48. "A Study in Scarlet," I, p. 156.
49. *Ibid.*, p. 154.
50. *Ibid.*, p. 156. Holmes's many statements dealing with these very areas in other stories patently contradict Watson's early impressions of Holmes's astounding ignorance in these realms, and Holmes's statement to Watson that he was unaware of the basic Copernican Theory of the solar system is generally taken by most Sherlockians to have been intended as a joke by Holmes which Watson failed to perceive. Cf., Baring-Gould (1967, I, pp. 154-57, notes 30-44).

51. "A Study in Scarlet," I, p. 154.
52. "The Adventure of the Lion's Mane," II, p. 784.
53. "The Sign of the Four," I, p. 611.
54. "A Study in Scarlet," I, p. 171. For an excellent review of Holmes's uses of observations and their implications for modern criminological investigation, see Hogan and Schwartz (1964).
55. "The Reigate Squires," I, p. 341.
56. "The Sign of the Four," I, p. 619.
57. "A Scandal in Bohemia," I, p. 349.
58. "The Hound of the Baskervilles," II, p. 18.
59. "The Boscombe Valley Mystery," II, p. 137.
60. "The Adventure of the Blanched Soldier," II, p. 708.
61. "The Valley of Fear," I, p. 479.
62. "The Adventure of the Second Stain," I, p. 313.
63. "Silver Blaze," II, p. 277.
64. "The Man with the Twisted Lip," I, p. 379.
65. "A Study in Scarlet," I, p. 187.
66. "A Case of Identity," I, p. 409.
67. "The Boscombe Valley Mystery," II, p. 148.
68. "A Case of Identity," I, p. 411.
69. "The Adventure of Black Peter," II, p. 402.
70. "The Adventure of the Dancing Men," II, p. 543.
71. "A Study in Scarlet," I, p. 231.
72. *Ibid.*
73. "Silver Blaze," II, p. 262.
74. "The Reigate Squires," I, p. 34.
75. "The Hound of the Baskervilles," II, p. 109.
76. "The Boscombe Valley Mystery," II, p. 135.
77. "A Study in Scarlet," I, p. 231.
78. "The Adventure of Shoscombe Old Place," II, p. 636.
79. "A Case of Identity," I, p. 404.
80. "The Adventure of the Noble Bachelor," I, p. 291.
81. "The Boscombe Valley Mystery," II, p. 136.
82. "The Adventure of the Retired Colourman," II, p. 556.
83. "The Musgrave Ritual," I, p. 137. Holmes believed that getting into the same environment could facilitate this process for he said: "I shall sit in that room and see its atmosphere brings me inspiration. I'm a believer in the *genius loci*." "The Valley of Fear," I, p. 508.
84. "The Adventure of Black Peter," II, p. 410.
85. *Ibid.*, p. 408.
86. "The Disappearance of Lady Carfax," II, p. 665.
87. "The Hound of the Baskervilles," II, p. 24.
88. "The Adventure of the Bruce-Partington Plans," II, p. 446. Also cf., "The Sign of the Four," I, pp. 613-38; and "The Adventure of the Beryl Coronet," II, p. 299.
89. The hypothetico-deductive method is by no means new, for it can even be seen in the works of the ancient Greek philosopher Parmenides. For an excellent modern statement on this approach to knowledge, see: Popper (1968, pp. 215-50).
90. "The Adventure of the Blanched Soldier," II, p. 720.
91. "The Adventure of the Sussex Vampire," II, p. 472.
92. "The Adventure of the Priory School," II, p. 620.
93. "A Study in Scarlet," I, p. 194.
94. *Ibid.* At another point, Holmes quotes Tacitus's Latin maxim that "everything unknown passes for something splendid." "The Red-Headed League," I, p. 421.
95. "The Red-Headed League," I, p. 428.
96. "A Study in Scarlet," I, p. 179.
97. *Ibid.*, p. 149.
98. "A Case of Identity," I, p. 411.
99. "The Adventure of the Creeping Man," pp. 762-63.

100. "The Cardboard Box," II, p. 202.
101. "The Adventure of the Golden Pince-Nez," II, p. 356.
102. "The Yellow Face," I, p. 576.
103. "The Hound of the Baskervilles," II, p. 110.
104. "A Study in Scarlet," I, p. 232.
105. "The Adventure of the Priory School," II, p. 617.
106. According to Ball (1958), this ability is epitomized by what Ball argues are Holmes's twenty-three deductions from a single scrap of paper in "The Reigate Squires," I, pp. 331-45.
107. For full clarification of Peirce on abduction, the reader is best referred to: Cohen (1949, pp. 131-53); Feibleman (1946, pp. 116-32); Goudge (1950, pp. 195-99); and Buchler (1955, pp. 150-56). For an excellent brief survey of the general problems of induction, see Black 1967.
108. Noting the logical discrepancies in Holmes's reasoning, one Sherlockian has commented that Holmes's successful conclusions might be accounted for by the suggestion that Holmes had psychic powers of extra-sensory perception (Reed 1970). Holmes remarkable abilities actually approximate the reading of Watson's mind in "The Cardboard Box," II, pp. 194-95.
109. "Silver Blaze," II, pp. 277-81.
110. "The Adventure of the Illustrious Client," II, p. 684.
111. "The Adventure of the Blanched Soldier," II, p. 715.
112. "The Valley of Fear," I, p. 491.
113. "A Study in Scarlet," I, p. 231.
114. "The Sign of the Cour," I, p. 656.
115. "The Adventure of the Second Stain," I, p. 311.
116. "The Disappearance of Lady Carfax," II, p. 657.
117. "The Man with the Twisted Lip," I, p. 380.
118. These include: "[T]here are few wives having any regard for their husbands who would let any man's spoken word stand between them and their husband's dead body." "The Valley of Fear," I, p. 506; "No woman would ever send a reply-paid telegram. She would have come." "The Adventure of Wisteria Lodge," II, p. 238; and "When a woman thinks that her house is on fire, her instinct is at once to rush to the thing which she values most . . . . A married woman grabs at her baby — an unmarried one reaches for her jewel box." "A Scandal in Bohemia," I, p. 364.
119. "The Resident Patient," I, p. 275.
120. "A Case of Identity," I, p. 406.
121. "The Adventure of the Copper Beeches," II, p. 129.
122. "The Adventure of the Creeping Man," II, p. 752. Recent years have seen social psychologists interested in a similar approach, e.g., see Levinson (1966).
123. "The Adventure of the Illustrious Client," II, p. 680. For a modern version of this idea, see Winch (1955).
124. "The Adventure of the Retired Colourman," II, p. 554.
125. Ibid.
126. "The Adventure of the Noble Bachelor," I, p. 291.
127. "The Man with the Twisted Lip," I, p. 376.
128. "The Adventure of the Copper Beeches," II, p. 114.
129. "The Musgrave Ritual," I, p. 137.
130. "The Hound of the Baskervilles," II, p. 110.
131. "The Final Problem," II, p. 302.
132. "The Boscombe Valley Mystery," II, p. 134.
133. Ibid., p. 138.
134. "The Adventure of the Speckled Band," I, p. 261.
135. "The Adventure of Charles Augustus Milverton," II, p. 563.
136. Ibid., p. 570.
137. "The Adventure of the Blue Carbuncle," I, p. 467.
138. "The Adventure of Charles Augustus Milverton," II, pp. 562-63. Holmes commonly obtains information from servants, especially the investigated subject's ex-

employees, for Holmes noted that for information "there are no better instruments than discharged servants with a grievance." "The Adventure of Wisteria Lodge," II, p. 253.
139. "A Scandal in Bohemia," I, p. 356.
140. E.g., in "The Adventure of the Bruce-Partington Plans" (II, p. 449), Holmes planted a false notice in the "agony columns" to get the villain to reveal himself.
141. "The Adventure of the Six Napoleons," II, p. 580.
142. "The Adventure of the Copper Beeches," II, pp. 121-22.
143. "The Adventure of Wisteria Lodge," II, p. 259.
144. *Ibid.*, p. 238.
145. "The Red-Headed League," I, p. 419.
146. "The Naval Treaty," II, p. 179.
147. "The Problem of Thor Bridge," II, p. 600.
148. "The Adventure of Wisteria Lodge," II, p. 252.
149. "The Adventure of the Speckled Band," I, p. 257.
150. "The Final Problem," II, p. 303.
151. "The Adventure of the Empty House," II, p. 347.
152. Holmes apparently accepted the common stereotype of Caucasians that black people have extraordinary body odor for on one occasion he tells the black bruiser Steve Dixie, "I don't like the smell of you," and on another he snidely referred to looking for his scent-bottle. "The Adventure of the Three Gables," II, pp. 723 and 728. Holmes also seems to have accepted an anti-Semitic stereotype for he referred to a client in debt by saying that "He is in the hands of the Jews." "The Adventure of Shoscombe Old Place," I, p. 637.
153. "A Study in Scarlet," I, p. 154.
154. "The Adventure of the Devil's Foot," II, p. 514.
155. "The Adventure of the Mazarin Stone," II, p. 737.
156. "The Hound of the Baskervilles," II, p. 106.
157. "The Adventure of the Empty House," II, p. 348.
158. "The Adventure of the Norwood Builder," II, pp. 425-26.
159. "The Naval Treaty," II, p. 183.
160. "The Hound of the Baskervilles," II, p. 22.
161. "A Case of Identity," I, p. 414.
162. "The Reigate Squires," I, p. 342.
163. *Ibid.*, p. 341:
164. "The Gloria Scott," I, p. 115.
165. "The Valley of Fear," I, p. 473.
166. "A Study in Scarlet," I, pp. 178-79.

REFERENCES

Anderson, Sir Robert. "Sherlock Holmes, Detective, as Seen by Scotland Yard." *T.P.'s Weekly* 2 (October 2, 1903): 557-58.

Anonymous. *Sir Arthur Conan Doyle Centenary 1859-1959*. London: John Murray, 1959.

Ashton-Wolfe, H. "The Debt of the Police to Detective Fiction." *The Illustrated London News,* February 27, 1932, pp. 320-28.

Ball, John. "The Twenty-Three Deductions." *The Baker Street Journal* 8, N. S. (October, 1958): 234-37.

Baring-Gould, William S. *The Chronological Holmes*. New York: Privately printed, 1955.

——.*Sherlock Holmes of Baker Street: A Life of the World's First Consulting Detective*. New York: Bramhall House, 1962.

_____.,ed. *The Annotated Sherlock Holmes.* 2 volumes. New York: Clarkson N. Potter, 1967.

Bell, Harold W. *Sherlock Holmes and Dr. Watson: The Chronology of Their Adventures.* London: Constable and Co., 1932.

_____.*Baker Street Studies.* London: Constable and Co., 1934.

Bell, Whitfield J., Jr. "Holmes and History." *The Baker Street Journal* 2, Old Series (October 1947): 447-56.

✓ Berg, Stanton O. "Sherlock Holmes: Father of Scientific Crime Detection." *Journal of Criminal Law, Criminology, and Police Science* 61 (1970): 446-52.

Bigelow, S. Tupper. *An Irregular Anglo-American Glossary of More or Less Familiar Words, Terms and Phrases in the Sherlock Holmes Saga.* Toronto: Castalotte and Zamba, 1959.

Black, Max. "Induction." In Paul Edwards *et al.*, eds. *The Encyclopedia of Philosophy.* New York: Macmillan and Free Press, 1967. 4: 169-81.

Blakeney, T.S. *Sherlock Holmes: Fact or Fiction?* London: John Murray, 1932.

✓ Brend, Gavin. *My Dear Holmes, A Study in Sherlock.* London: George Allen and Unwin, 1951.

Brown, Francis C. "The Case of the Man Who Was Wanted." *The Vermissa Herald: A Journal of Sherlockian Affairs* [published by the Scowrers, San Francisco, California] 3 (April 1969): 12.

Buchler, Justus, ed. *Philosophical Writings of Peirce* [First published in 1940 as: *The Philosophy of Peirce: Selected Writings*]. New York: Dover, 1955 (1940).

Carr, John Dickson. *The Life of Sir Arthur Conan Doyle.* New York: Harper and Bros., 1949.

Christ, Jay Finley. *An Irregular Guide to Sherlock Holmes of Baker Street.* New York: The Pamphlet House and Argus Books, 1947.

_____.*An Irregular Chronology of Sherlock Holmes of Baker Street.* Ann Arbor, Michigan: Fanlight House, 1947.

Christie, Winifred M. "Sherlock Holmes and Graphology." *The Sherlock Holmes Journal* 2 (1955): 28-31.

Cohen, Morris R., ed. *Chance, Love and Logic* [First published in 1923]. No address: Peter Smith, 1949.

Crocker, Stephen F. "Sherlock Holmes Recommends Winwood Reade." *The Baker Street Journal* 14, N. S. (September 1964): 142-44.

Doyle, Adrian M. Conan. *The True Conan Doyle.* London: John Murray, 1945.

Doyle, Adrian M. Conan, and John Dickson Carr. *The Exploits of Sherlock Holmes.* New York: Random House, 1954.

Doyle, Sir Arthur Conan. *Memories and Adventures* [First published in 1924]. New York: Doubleday, Doran and Co., Crowborough edition, 1930.

_____."The Case of the Man Who Was Wanted." *Cosmopolitan* 125 (August 1948): 48-51 and 92-99.

_____.*The Sherlockian Doyle.* Culver City, California: Luther Norris, 1968.

Feibleman, James. *An Introduction to Peirce's Philosophy, Interpreted As a System.* New York: Harper and Bros., 1946.

Folsom, Henry T. *Through the Years at Baker Street: A Chronology of Sherlock Holmes.* Washington, New Jersey: Privately printed, 1964.

Goudge. *The Thought of C. S. Peirce.* Toronto, Ontario: University of Toronto Press, 1950.

Hardwick, Michael, and Mollie Hardwick. *The Sherlock Holmes Companion.* London: John Murray, 1962.

———.*The Man Who Was Sherlock Holmes.* London: John Murray, 1964.

Harrison, Michael. *In the Footsteps of Sherlock Holmes.* London: Cassell and Co., 1958.

———."A Study in Surmise." *Ellery Queen's Mystery Magazine* 57 (February 1971): 60-79.

Hart, Archibald. "The Effects of Trades Upon Hands." *The Baker Street Journal* 3, Old Series (October 1948): 418-20.

Haycraft, Howard. *Murder for Pleasure: The Life and Times of the Detective Story.* New York: D. Appleton-Century, 1941.

Hitchings, J.L. "Sherlock Holmes the Logician." *The Baker Street Journal* 1, Old Series (April 1946): 113-17.

Hogan, John C., and Mortimer D. Schwartz. "The Manly Art of Observation and Deduction." *Journal of Criminal Law, Criminology and Police Science* 55 (1964): 157-64.

Holroyd, James Edward. *Seventeen Steps to 221B.* London: George Allen and Unwin, 1967.

Lamond, John. *Arthur Conan Doyle: A Memoir.* London: John Murray, 1931.

Leavitt, R.K. "Nummi in Arca or The Fiscal Holmes." In Vincent Starrett, ed. *221B: Studies in Sherlock Holmes.* New York: Macmillan, 1940, pp. 16-36.

Levinson, Boris M. "Some Observations on the Use of Pets in Psychodiagnosis." *Pediatrics Digest* 8 (1966): 81-85.

Locke, Harold. *A Bibliographical Catalogue of the Writings of Sir Arthur Conan Doyle, M.D., LL.D., 1879-1928.* Tunbridge Wells: D. Webster, 1928.

Mackenzie, J.B. "Sherlock Holmes' Plots and Strategies." *Baker Street Journal Christmas Annual,* 1956, pp. 56-61.

May, Luke S. *Crime's Nemesis.* New York: Macmillan, 1935.

Merton, Robert K. *Social Theory and Social Structure* [First published in 1949]. Glencoe, Illinois: Free Press, 1957.

Murch, Alma Elizabeth. *The Development of the Detective Novel.* London: Peter Owen, 1958.

Nordon, Pierre. *Conan Doyle: A Biography.* Translated by Frances Partridge. New York: Holt, Rinehart and Winston, 1967.

Park, Orlando. *Sherlock Holmes, Esq., and John H. Watson, M.D.: An Encyclopedia of Their Affairs.* Evanston, Illinois: Northwestern University Press, 1962.

Pearson, Hesketh. *Conan Doyle, His Life and Art.* London: Methuen, 1943.

Petersen, Svend. *A Sherlock Holmes Almanac.* Washington, D. C.: Privately printed, 1956.

Popper, Karl R. *Conjectures and Refutations: The Growth of Scientific Knowledge* [First published in 1962]. New York: Harper and Row, Torchbook edition, 1968.

Pratt, Fletcher. "Very Little Murder." *The Baker Street Journal* 2, N.S. (April 1955): 69-76.

Queen, Ellery, ed. *Misadventures of Sherlock Holmes.* Boston: Little, Brown and Co., 1944.

Reed, John Shelton. *The Other Side.* Unpublished manuscript (mimeo), Department of Sociology, University of North Carolina at Chapel Hill, 1970.

Roberts, Sir Sidney C. *Doctor Watson: Prolegomena to the Study of a Biographical Problem.* London: Faber and Faber, 1931.

Schenck, Remsen Ten Eyck. *Occupation Marks.* New York: Grune and Stratton, 1948.

_____."The Effect of Trades Upon the Body." *The Baker Street Journal* 3, N.S. (January 1953): 31-36.

Smith, Edgar W. *Baker Street and Beyond: A Sherlockian Gazetteer,* with Five Detailed and Illustrated Maps by Julian Wolff, M.D. New York: The Pamphlet House, 1940.

_____.*Profile by Gaslight: An Irregular Reader About the Private Life of Sherlock Holmes.* New York: Simon and Schuster, 1944.

Starrett, Vincent. *221B: Studies in Sherlock Holmes.* New York: Macmillan, 1940.

_____.*The Private Life of Sherlock Holmes* [First published in a different edition in 1933]. Chicago: University of Chicago Press, 1960.

Steward-Gordon, James. "Real-Life Sherlock Holmes." *Readers Digest* 79 (November 1961): 281-88.

Stone, Gregory and Harvey A. Farberman, eds. *Social Psychology through Symbolic Interaction.* Waltham, Massachusetts: Ginn-Blaisdell, 1970.

Swanson, Martin J. "Graphologists in the Canon." *The Baker Street Journal* 12, N.S. (June 1962): 73-80.

Webb, Eugene J., *et al. Unobtrusive Measures: Non-Reactive Research in the Social Sciences.* Chicago: Rand McNally, 1966.

Winch, R.F. "The Theory of Complementary Needs in Mate Selection: Final Results on the Test of the General Hypothesis." *American Sociological Review* 20 (1955): 552-55.

Wolff, Julian. *The Sherlockian Atlas.* New York: Privately printed, 1952.

_____.*Practical Handbook of Sherlockian Heraldry.* New York: Privately printed, 1955.

Zeisler, Ernest B. *Baker Street Chronology: Commentaries on the Sacred Writings of Dr. John H. Watson.* Chicago: Alexander J. Isaacs, 1953.

MILTON M. GORDON

8

Kitty Foyle and
the Concept of Class as Culture

Christopher Darlington Morley (1890-1957) was a
contributor to many different literary genres, for he wrote
poetry, plays, essays, and novels. He was possibly best
known to many as a contributing editor and columnist for
The Saturday Review of Literature from 1924 to 1941. His
best known novels included *Parnassus on Wheels* (1917)
and its sequel *The Haunted Bookshop* (1919), *Where the
Blue Begins* (1922), and *Kitty Foyle* (1939).

Although Morley considered himself primarily a poet, he
is best known for his novels and, especially, for his many
essays. He authored some fifty books running a very wide
range of topics. He was especially pleased with his play *The
Trojan Horse* (1937) which foreshadowed the events of
World War II.

Because of Morley's association with many whimsical
activities — he was the founder of the Baker Street
Irregulars, the major Sherlock Holmes society in the United
States, and belonged to a small but well-publicized group of
food enthusiasts known as the Three Hours for Lunch Club,
among his many activities — his more serious work was

never properly greeted. But even in the following excerpt from his "Obituary (premature, I hope)" which he wrote for the 1955 edition of *Twentieth Century Authors* in which he complains of this, his comic gifts crept in.

> What interested Christopher Morley most about his own work (in which he was intensely interested) was that his early writing, which was (though not intentionally) imitative and immature, was received with absurd over-praise, whereas his later work, wherever it showed symptoms of originality and power and an attempt to cut below epithelial tissue, was often received with anger or dismay.

In the following essay on social stratification as seen through Morley's heroine Kitty Foyle, Milton Gordon takes a serious look at Morley's work that would probably have delighted the author.

KITTY FOYLE AND THE CONCEPT OF CLASS AS CULTURE*

The traditional approaches to the concept of social class[1] can, on the whole, be placed under one of two categories: (1) economic analysis of income stratification, or the relation of groups to the means of production and (2) class consciousness—that is, concern with the presence or lack of a feeling of class identification. Each has its shortcomings.

Discussion of social class in terms of economic factors alone begs the peculiar function of the social scientist, who should be able to include economic factors in his analysis but not be circumscribed by them, whereas the question of the existence of class consciousness is also a component part of the problem but not an inclusive frame of reference. As Simpson has pointed out:

Class consciousness is a highly important element in class analysis, but it enters as an objective factor to be studied only after we are aware as to what we

---

*Reprinted from *The American Journal of Sociology*, (1947): 210-217, by permission of The University of Chicago Press. Copyright 1947 by the University of Chicago. Quotations from the book *Kitty Foyle* by Christopher Morley. Copyright 1939 by Christopher Morley. Renewal © 1967 by Christopher Morley, Jr., Helen Morley Woodruff, Blythe Morley Brennan and Louise Cochrane. Reprinted by permission of the publishers, J. B. Lippincott Co.

mean by class. The presence of classes in a society could not possibly be dependent upon class consciousness, because the degrees of consciousness of individuals vary even among those of identical relative modes of life and we would be forced to accept what men *think* they are as final indication of what they are. Propaganda concerning the equality of all individuals might lead individuals to accept themselves as equal to each other . . . . whereas their material equality is nowhere evident.[2]

The concept of social class can, however, be best approached through the anthropological concept of "culture." In other words, whatever the means by which they have evolved and whatever the degree of psychological awareness of the process on the part of those concerned, social classes in America constitute somewhat separate subgroups in American society, each with its own cultural attributes of behavior, ideas, and life-situations. From the point of view of "class as culture," then, analysis may subsequently be made of the status differentials involved, the historical reasons for the development of classes, the differential rewards obtained from society by the various classes, the avenues and methods of social mobility, and similar problems.

The cultural approach to class is based on two assumptions: (1) that classes are "little worlds" within which a particular individual carries on most of his important social relationships (the point must be made, of course, that there are innumerable spatially separated units of the same class) and (2) that the experience of growing up in a particular class is reflected in one layer, so to speak, of the individual's personality structure. Warner and Lunt have called this aspect of personality structure directly traceable to group experience the "social personality."[3] A review of the research literature on social class published since 1941 reveals that, although never explicitly stated, the concept of class as culture is implicit in the recent important group of studies carried out by Warner, Lunt, Srole, Davis, and the Gardners.[4] It is interesting to note, too, that the director and initiator of these studies, W. Lloyd Warner, was trained in the discipline of cultural anthropology.

The writer is at present making a study of the concept of social class as it has been handled in the American novel of the period between two World Wars, in which the hypothesis that the cultural implications of social class have been perceptively realized and presented by leading American novelists is being investigated. As an example, the novel *Kitty Foyle*,[5] by Christopher Morley, is analyzed from the point of view of its contribution to the "class-as-culture" concept. *Kitty Foyle* is especially interesting to the sociologist of class because it deals largely with the upper class in American life, a group which, for a number of reasons, has not often been the object of sociological investigation.

The locale of *Kitty Foyle* is Philadelphia; the author himself comes from the upper-class Philadelphia background of which he writes. The plot revolves around the love affair of Kitty, the daughter of a lower-class family of Irish descent living in an industrial section of the city, and Wynnewood Strafford, who lives with his family in Philadelphia's fashionable residential section, the "Main Line." The story takes place during the early 1930's and is told in the first person by Kitty, in retrospect. In a sense, Kitty, in her observations of the mores and behavior patterns of the upper class acts as the anthropological alter ego of Morley, viewing the upper class from the outside. How did Kitty and Wynnewood Strafford meet? As a result of the fact that Kitty's father, now a night watchman, had once been associated in a semiservant capacity with an upper-class institution. He had been groundkeeper at one of the suburban cricket clubs and coach at a private school:

I suppose Philly is the last place in America where it still matters to be a gentleman. Of course, the old man wasn't, but he was on intimate terms with gentlemen on account of cricket. At the clubs, and at the big private school where he was coach, he knew all the Rittenhouse Square crowd when they were just boys. He was invited to cricket club dinners and used to sing Irish songs for them. There's nobody so snobby about keeping up social hedges as somebody who isn't himself quite the real McCoy. For Pop, men who didn't know about cricket hardly existed. . . . .

It was on account of cricket that Wyn first came to the house; he was getting some old scorebooks for that Hundred Years of Philadelphia Cricket they printed . . . . (pp. 14-15)

The association of class position and geographical locale—in other words, some primary group community interaction—is vital to the validity of the class-as-culture concept. This association is repeatedly made in *Kitty Foyle*. The term "Main Line," which refers to the suburban communities strung out along the main westerly tracks of the Pennsylvania Railroad, is used synonomously with "upper class." As a matter of fact, a subtle grading of the class position of various suburbs, including an internal grading of the Main Line itself, is indicated in one passage. Ruminates Kitty:

People who wouldn't live on the Main Line for fear of being high-hatted go out to Oak Lane and Elkins Park. You wouldn't believe how complicated social life can be till you know about the Philadelphia suburbs. It's a riot.

Wyn had a theory about how certain kind of people wouldn't dare live further out the Main Line than Merion. (p. 131)

Wyn's family is pictured as living far enough out on the Main Line— at St. David's—and as having a town house on Rittenhouse Square, in central Philadelphia, the earlier residential locale of the Philadelphia upper class. Kitty's home, on the other hand, is in a distinctly unfashionable industrial section,

just around the corner from Orthodox Street. That's in Frankford, and a long way from the Main Line, if you know what that means in Philly. It's freight trains and coal yards and factories and the smell of the tanneries down by Frankford Creek . . . . (p. 6)

Kitty's mother had come from a section of Philadelphia of higher social standing than her father: "Mother came from Germantown, which is pretty much top shelf compared to Frankford" (p. 2). But perhaps not from the most fashionable part of Germantown:

And the old faded photograph of Mother when she was still a young lady in Germantown before she married into Frankford. That's quite a gulf, if you don't know it; though Pop when he got peeved, would say when you get that far down Wissahickon Avenue it's not Germantown but Tioga. Mother said Nonsense, we even had a station in Germantown named for us, Upsal. Who ever heard of a station called Foyle? Then Pop would call her his little chicken from Wissahickon which always tickled her . . . . (pp. 60-61)

Another geographical identification, the association of shopping areas and downtown streets with class, is interestingly made:

Of course it's no use to think you won't meet people in Philly. All the shopping that amounts to anything socially is along those few blocks on Chestnut and Walnut, and sure enough one day when I went out for lunch I ran into Wyn. There had to be comedy about it, he was standing by the curb scraping one of those beautiful brown shoes on the edge. He said, "Kitty, this is very embarrassing, I walked on some chewing gum, I can't imagine where."

"What were you doing on Market Street?"[6] I asked, and he said, "Kitty, you're adorable." (pp. 215-16)

And in another passage, Kitty, by this time living in New York, discusses class and geography in that city:

Then I walked up Fifth Avenue all the way to the Plaza and back again, looking in windows and trying to figure out whether women looked different from Philly. I was kind of disappointed. Of course I didn't know then what I do now, you don't see the really smart women on Fifth; they're mostly on Madison and Park Avenue. As a matter of fact Fifth Avenue isn't as smart as the right blocks on Chestnut St. [in Philadelphia]. There's too much of it, and a Public Library and Woolworth's, and clearances of Philippine lingerie certainly drag it down . . . .(p. 162)

If our hypothesis of "class as culture" is valid, class patterns of dress should be discernible. Kitty shows an acute awareness of upper-class patterns of attire: informality and simplicity, expensive material, and, among males, an emphasis on casual tweeds and flannels. In her first meeting with Wyn, when he drops in to talk with her father about cricket, she recalls that he was wearing "old gray pants and the soft shirt, and the cricket club blazer." At first, Kitty's reaction to this deviation from her lower-class stereotype of upper-class clothes was not favorable:

I only thought "My God, does he work at a bank in that outfit?" . . . . Darby Mill, Old St. David's meant nothing to me. How could I guess how much swank there is in that intentional shabbiness. (p. 107)

On another occasion she recalls Wyn's first formal call at the house: "All I can see is an attractive tweed suit in a kind of tobacco brown, and the loveliest deep maroon woolen socks" (p. 19).

As it becomes increasingly clear to her that her affair with Wyn is complicated by the separation of their two worlds, she makes an effort to escape by going to Chicago. Wyn follows her and turns up at her room: "Wyn, west of Paoli! Just the few days I'd been away I'd got used to the way men dress in Chicago,[7] pressed very sharp and neat, and provincial snap-brim hats, and Wyn looked almost foreign" (p. 145).

To celebrate the fact that Wyn came to Chicago to be with Kitty, at the cost of missing the Philadelphia Assembly, the annual upper-class ball, they decide to go dining and dancing in evening clothes:

When I was all equipped he sent me back to Molly's in a taxi and got himself a readymade evening suit. I bet it was the only time Wyn Strafford wore ready mades, and he looked almost too Ritzy. He said he did a few somersaults over the bed to take the shine off. (p. 149)

In discussing her Uncle Elmer who lived in the mid-West, Kitty says: "He had genius for choosing the wrong kind of clothes, tweeds that were the color of straw and would have given Wyn apoplexy" (p. 55).

Later in the course of Kitty's life, while she is attempting to break off the affair with Wyn, she goes to New York, and there eventually meets a Jewish doctor named Mark Eisen. Lonely and impressed with Mark's professional competence and intelligence, she begins to go out with him. But the cultural aspects of Jewish middle-class life to which she is introduced bother her. In a paragraph of reminiscing about Wyn, one evening she mentions clothes:

There's a roof of some hotel I can see right from my office desk. The women come out on the terrace and I can see them pause just an instant in the doorway to feel beautiful and sure and to know the dress will float just right as they step off the sill. Their escorts, just like it might be you behind me, following politely right after. You wouldn't be wearing a dentistry coat and a cummerbund, though, and looking like something in café society. Did you make a snob out of me, big boy! I could wring Mark Eisen's neck when I see his clothes, poor sweetheart; and how hard he tries. Always too nifty, always too shiny like cellophane, that's them. (pp. 126-27)

Appraising Mark's appearance at a summer gathering, she writes:

Of course Wyn got me so conditioned about men's clothes that I hate to see them overdressed. Mark's striped pants, creased like a knife-edge, would blackball him at any cricket club, and those black and white yachting shoes with perforated breathing holes were definitely Hollywood. What put Big Casino on the outfit was a polo shirt wide open to the fur and a blue tweed coat with a handkerchief made of the same stuff as the shirt. That's pretty terrible, because a man ought to look like he's put together by accident, not added up on purpose. Poor old Mark, you could just see he'd been spending his Saturday afternoons figuring out this cruising kit. (pp. 232-33)

He's got the same kind of sureness professionally that the Main Line has socially. He's got respect for intelligence like the Main Line has for flannel pants without any crease in them. (pp. 203-4)

About class patterns of women's clothes, Kitty has less to say. On one occasion, however, while demonstrating perfume in a Philadelphia department store, she meets the woman Wyn has eventually married and commenting on her possibilities of attractiveness, says:

She might get that wholesome tweed-skirt, Wayne-Devon and Paoli[8] look . . .
. . Her manners were so pleasant it would be hard to know was she really dumb or not; of course all those vintage Main Liners pride themselves to be just lovely with the lower classes as long as they don't go beyond their proper station, which would probably be Overbrook. (p. 214)

One of the characteristics of Wyn's class (in Warner's terms, it would be the upper-upper class of Philadelphia) is its careful lack of ostentation. Wyn's station wagon (in itself traditionally connected with upper-class status), as he calls at the Foyle house, is described as follows:

I looked out the window and saw a weatherstained old station wagon, and painted on the side of it in small green letters DARBY MILL, OLD ST. DAVID'S.

In line with her early lower-class stereotypes, Kitty evaluates this shabbiness in an amusing mistake:

In the car were some big piles of shingles baled up with wire. Pop had been saying for I don't know how long that we must get new shingles for the backhouse roof, it leaked on him when he was sitting in there. I supposed he ordered some without telling me, and ran downstairs just to see that he wasn't getting cheated.
"Is that the man for the backhouse?" I said as I went into the room. Pop cackled with laughter and the visitor rose politely. I could feel my pure and eloquent blood doing its stuff. It was Wyn. (p. 106)

Years later, when Kitty has begun to see the status implications of a shabby station wagon, she writes as follows of an unexpected encounter with Wyn's wife:

I get off at 30th Street Station and walk out for a cab, and Jesusgod comes a station wagon pulling up under those pillars marked DARBY MILL. Not a nice old tumble-down station wagon neither but bran shiny new. I bet Ronnie wouldn't understand how much smarter the old one was. (p. 208)

And in the scene describing Wyn's call at the Foyle home, when he leaves, Kitty apologizes to her father:

"I thought Mr. Strafford must be in the lumber business," I said.
"Jesusgod," exclaimed the old man. "Don't you ever read your *Ledger?* Strafford, Wynnewood and Company, the oldest private bank in Philly. Darby Mill, that's the name of their country place; there's an old sawmill on the crick out there, where they cut up the logs for Washington at Valley Forge. Honey, those folks are so pedigree they'd be ashamed to press their pants. They hire someone to drive the Rolls for a year before they use it, so it won't look too fresh."
"I think that's just as silly as the opposite." [Kitty notes that she replied.] I think so still. (pp. 107-8)

This drive for unostentation goes as far as using circumlocutions to avoid public identification with names connoting prestige:

Wyn said he was getting a lot of work done because he'd taken leave of absence from the bank and his family were all away at their summer cottage in Rhode Island. He had a funny phobia about saying "Newport." I soon got to spot that habit of the Main Line crowd, kind of ashamed to let on how swell they are. Jesusgod they don't even brood on it in secret, they just know. (p. 110)

An interesting sidelight on the use of the term "Esquire" among the upper classes is thrown in one paragraph; Wyn for a time engages in an eventually abortive attempt to produce a magazine in Philadelphia patterned after the *New Yorker,* and Kitty becomes his secretary:

I learned a lot about letters in the office of *Philly* because when I addressed one to Parry I remembered Pop's talk about the high-toned Esq and I wrote it Mr. Parrish Berwyn Esq which Wyn said was wrong. If you're Esq you can't be Mr. at the same time. I think I was rather cute, I said suppose I'd ever write you a letter would it be Wynnewood Strafford Esq VI or Wynnewood Strafford VI Esq? He said at Old St. David's or even at Rittenhouse Square it was his father was really the Esq and he himself was only Wynnewood Strafford VI, but if writing to an office it was better to put Mr. because there you were just the honest tradesman. It seems a man can't properly be Esq away from his inherited private property. To put Esq on a business letter is New York phony or the Nouveau Long Island touch, he said. (pp. 138-39)

The reason for *Philly's* failure comes from the mouth of Molly, Kitty's shrewd midwestern friend:

It sounds like fun . . . . But if I get the town from what you've told me I don't think it'll work. The *New Yorker's* grand because it's edited by a lot of boys who are both smart and ambitious. You haven't got 'em like that here. If they're really peppy they clear out. And the *New Yorker's* got a readymade public of all kinds of people who have an awful yen to be In the Know. It's a kind of inferiority. But I don't believe Philadelphia gives a damn about being In the Know. It prefers not to be or it thinks it's there already. The people on top are so damn sure they know it all they don't want to learn anything new; and the people underneath know they haven't got a Chinaman's chance. I think it's rather swell to have one town that simply doesn't give a damn except be comfortable. Why does your friend want to give it the needle? If I were you I'd let Philly be like old Pattyshells. Leave it wag its tail on the porch. (pp. 117-18)

Class differences reveal themselves in speech. Morley uses the device of having his lower-class heroine tell the story in racy, slangy prose; but pronunciation and inflection are obviously difficult to present on a printed page without the use of phonetics, and he makes no attempt at it. In one place, however, he has Kitty comment on the speech of Rosey Rittenhouse, one of Wyn's upper-class friends:

I think of Rosey's voice sometimes, that easy well-bred Philadelphia accent that seems to fit them like a suit of good tweeds. The kind of voice people only get when they've had good meals and good sleep for several generations and horses in the stable. (p. 159)

Religious affiliation and class are not dealt with extensively in *Kitty Foyle,* but the close historical association of Quakerism with the upper class in Philadelphia is indicated by the fact that several of Wyn's friends, including Rosey, are specifically mentioned as being members of this sect. A theological discussion is reported:

We sat by a big fireplace and talked . . . . about religion. Wyn said what he liked about Quakerism was the idea of salvation piped direct to the individual, what they called the Inner Light, everybody has it for himself. A kind of neon tubing I guess. Rosey said he wasn't so sure there wasn't something to be said for Indirect Lighting too, like the Catholics. "But don't quote me, I'll be thrown out of Swarthmore Meeting." (p. 159)

What happens when second-generation lower-class Irish tangles with the Main Line? It is to Morley's credit that when Wyn indicates a serious interest in Kitty Foyle to his family,[9] there are no "Go, and never darken my door again," or "You must choose between us" scenes. As a matter of fact, the Straffords' first response to the situation is to invite Kitty to a house party at their country home. Kitty goes reluctantly. As all concerned, with the possible exception of Wyn, had envisaged, Kitty's formal introduction to the Main Line is not a success:

It was a mistake. Of course Wyn had done what any man would, told everybody to be lovely to me and they were so god damn lovely I could have torn their eyes out. I was the only one that wasn't in the union. That crowd, if they stopped to think about it, would reckon that Ben Franklin was still a boy from the wrong side of the tracks, so what could they think about me. Somebody wanted to know if I was one of the Iglehart Foyles from Baltimore or the Saltonstall Foyles from Pride's Crossing. I said no pride ever crossed our family except when the old man carried his bat against Merion C.C. That was Wyn's fault, he tried to ease the situation by making everybody drink too many old fashioneds. But it helped because good old Rosey Rittenhouse turned the talk on cricket and said he wished he could get more girls to show some intelligence about it . . . . I knew either I or the rest of them didn't belong, and the embarrassment went around the dinner table all wrapped up in a napkin like that wine bottle the butlers carried.

Even in a Thanksgiving rainstorm, what a lovely lovely place. When I saw Wyn's old faded station wagon out in a hitching shed I asked him to drive me home. Of course he wouldn't and he couldn't. I was supposed to stay the night and I had to go through with it. "I hope you'll rest well," Mrs. Strafford said, "will you want the maid to undress you?" Jesusgod, I blushed like one of those Cornell chrysanthemums. I wanted to say there's only one person here who's good enough to undress me. Wyn saw me turn red, he kept his eyes on me all evening bless him and came across the room to see what was going wrong.

"You mustn't try to get up in the morning, we'll all sleep late." Mrs. Strafford said.

"I've got to get to the office," I said. "We're closing up and I want to leave everything clean."

"Oh, I'm so glad Wyn is giving up that dreadful magazine," she said. "I don't think Philadelphia enjoys that sort of persiflage."

Either she or I must have been pronouncing that word wrong up to then.

"We know damn well they don't," was what I had a yen to say, but by God K.F. had herself under control.

"I don't know what I would do without Kitty," said Wyn, trying to help. "In fact I *won't* do without her. Maybe she'll come and help me at the bank." (pp. 134-35)

It is then that Kitty decides to leave Philadelphia:

"I'm going to Chicago," I said, unexpectedly. I didn't know myself I was going to say it. I'd had a letter from Molly a day or two before. All of a sudden I saw what came next. Wyn was terribly startled, and what a flash of, well, thankfulness, I saw in Mrs. Strafford's eyes. Poor lady, she was only playing on the signals they'd taught her. I could see that down under she had a respect for me, she'd like to have me around if it could have been allowed.

"Really, that's very interesting," she said. "Do you know people in Chicago? We have some very pleasant acquaintances in Lake Forest."

"My best friend has a job at Palmer's, she's in the furnishing department."

"The modern girls are so courageous, I think it's wonderful how enterprising they are."

I looked around at the enterprising modern girls. They were showing a good deal of knee sprawled on the sofas with brandy and sodas and members of the Racquet Club, or they were screeching at ping pong in the game room, or playing some baby chess they called b'gammon. I felt homesick for a good filing case somewhere. (pp. 135-36)

Kitty expresses her understanding of the endogamous nature of the Main Line:

The Main Line girls Bill and Parry were accustomed to have to spend so much time on clothes and stuff they don't have a chance to figure out a good line of hidden-ball formations. The Assembly gazelles know they're practically doomed to the clutches of someone in their own set, why waste good energy in broken field running? (p. 133)

The reaction of Wyn's family is obviously not personal hostility toward Kitty. It seems simply to represent a realistic understanding of the separate and distinct nature of the different social worlds from which their son and Kitty come and a feeling of the hopelessness of bringing them together. In a later passage Kitty hints that Wyn's family "were working on him" to discourage the match, and she even indicates her belief that for a time when Wyn's visits are infrequent, he has resolved to "shake" her "out of his system" (p. 151). But this effort fails. Kitty is described as being a most attractive young lady, and their relationship has already reached the stage of sleeping together.

Kitty feels increasingly that the situation cannot be resolved in marriage and makes up her mind to accept an offer of a job in New York. The denouement, however, comes when Wyn's family, believing that Wyn is determined to marry Kitty, take the advice of Mr. Kennet, described as a Quaker banker, and an old friend of the family, and, in despair, propose a cultural renovation for Kitty:

"Well then I've got to tell you," Wyn said. "Uncle Kennet has a big idea, he wanted to explain it to you himself. He says you're just exactly the girl for me, Kitty, and the girl the family needs, and he wants to send you . . . . to college for a year and then maybe go abroad a year and meanwhile I'll try to get some education myself[10] and be ready for you."

Oh Jesusgod I don't know exactly how you said it, Wyn. It was something like that. My poor baby, how could you know what that would do to me the way I was just then. Maybe that nice old man with his *thee* talk could have sold it to me; I don't know. I had a kind of picture of some damned family conference and the Straffords and their advisers trying to figure out how the curse was going to be taken off Kitty Foyle. So that was it, they were going to buy the girl with an education, and polish off her rough Frankford edges, were they, and make her good enough to live with stuffed animals' heads and get advertised in the *Ledger*. I can still see your face, my poor baby, when I turned on you. I felt hot inside my throat and on the rims of my ears.

"You can tell Uncle Ken he's a white slaver. Listen, Wyn Strafford, I'll be your girl whenever I feel like it because I love you from hell to breakfast. But I wouldn't join the little tin family if every old Quaker with an adding machine begged me to. No, not if they all went back to college and got themselves an education. So they tried to sell you the idea they'd trim up Kitty so she could go to the Assembly and make Old Philadelphia Family out of her, hey? Cut her out of a copy of *Vogue* and give her a charge account and make a Main Line doll out of her. They can't do that to Kitty Foyle. Jesusgod, that's what they are themselves, a bunch of paper dolls."

Remember, you stopped the Buick just before we cut down a tree with it. Better maybe if we had. You just looked at me, and tried to light a cigarette and your hand shook pushing in the dashboard lighter. You were so rattled you threw the lighter away, you thought it was a match. I loved you specially because you hadn't shaved. I thought how the old man would rise green from his grave if he heard a proposition like that. I felt tears coming like those waves you swam through and I had to hurry to say it: —

"By God, I'll improve *you* all I want but you can't improve me." (pp.174-75)

And so Kitty leaves Philadelphia and becomes a "white collar" girl in New York. Although the affair continues on occasional week ends, both Kitty and Wyn are resigned to the hopelessness of bringing their worlds together. The meetings become less frequent, and one day Kitty reads in the society columns of a New York newspaper of Wyn's engagement to "Miss Veronica Gladwyn of 'Welshwood' near King of Prussia." The tenuous threads of individual attraction that had connected the two cultural worlds have at last broken, and Kitty and Wyn proceed along their separate ways, nursing their wounds but gradually being reabsorbed into their respective social spheres. In a striking introspective dialogue with herself, sometime later, Kitty reflects on the affair and shows an amazingly keen and poignant understanding of the social issues:

Q. Did you make Wyn happy?
A. I think so. Yes, I know so.
Q. Then why did you leave him?
A. If I had done what he wanted, other people would have made him unhappier than I could have made him happy.
Q. What do you mean?
A. He was the product of a system. He was at the mercy of that system.
Q. Is it not your conviction that there are now no systems? That the whole of society is in flux?
A. Not in — I mean, not where Wyn lives.
Q. Was not the way you left him rather cruel?
A. Damn you, I was afraid you'd ask that. Yes, it was. But I *had* to be tough with him, otherwise he'd always have felt he had been unfair to *me,* and it would have made him wretched.
Q. You think, then, he is not unhappy now?
A. Yes. No. Ask that again, please.
Q. You think Wyn is happy now?

A. I think his life is full of delightful routine. He has what the government calls Social Security. Oh, and how. Read the *Public Ledger* on Sundays, or whatever papers they have now.

Q. You think you could have made something more important of him?

A. I could have taught him to do the Wrong Thing sometimes.

Q. What, in Philadelphia?

A. We could have lived somewhere else.

Q. Are you quite fair to Philadelphia?

A. I am thinking of it only as a symbol. Actually I love it dearly.

Q. But are they not the most charming people in the world?

A. Of course. But the enemies of the Future are always the very nicest people.

Q. You think the Future should be encouraged?

A. That's a goofy question, my darling; it's on our necks already. And oh, God, Wyn was so much interested in it when he had a chance. What a man he might have been if everything hadn't been laid in his lap.

Q. Is your mind going to go round and round like this indefinitely?

A. How's about going to bed and try for some sleep. (pp. 28-29)

Kitty Foyle, by means of her literary creator, has played the role of the sociologist of the culture of classes.

NOTES

1. See, e.g., Page's summary of the work of the "Fathers" of American sociology in social class, Charles H. Page, *Class and American Sociology* (New York: Dial Press, 1940).

2. George Simpson, "Class Analysis: What Class Is Not," *American Sociological Review*, IV, No. 6 (1939), 829.

3. W. Lloyd Warner and Paul S. Lunt, *The Social Life of a Modern Community* ("Yankee City Series," Vol. I [New Haven: Yale University Press, 1941]), pp. 26-27.

4. *Ibid.;* Warner and Lunt, *The Status System of a Modern Community* ("Yankee City Series," Vol. II [New Haven: Yale University Press, 1943]); W. Lloyd Warner and Leo Srole, *The Social Systems of American Ethnic Groups* ("Yankee City Series," Vol. III [New Haven: Yale University Press, 1945]); Allison Davis, Burleigh B. Gardner, and Mary R. Gardner, *Deep South* (Chicago: University of Chicago Press, 1941); see also W. Lloyd Warner, Robert J. Havighurst, and Martin B. Loeb, *Who Shall Be Educated* (New York and London: Harper & Bros., 1944), which contains an analysis of "Yankee City" materials not previously published.

5. Christopher Morley, *Kitty Foyle* (Philadelphia: J. B. Lippincott Co., 1939); reprinted in an edition by "Penguin Books" (New York, 1944); all page numbers subsequently referred to are from the "Penguin Books" edition.

6. Market Street in Philadelphia corresponds roughly to Forty-second Street in New York City: shooting galleries, hamburger stands, cheap movie houses, and inexpensive stores.

7. In contrast to Wyn, "men in Chicago" obviously means "middle-class men."

8. Stops on the Main Line.

9. Kitty's own mother and father are dead before the affair reaches its climax.

10. Just what Wyn means by this remark is not quite clear. He is already described as being a graduate of Princeton.

DONALD W. BALL

9

Pottermanship:
The Psychological Sociology of
S. Potter (and the Yeovil School)

Stephen Potter (1900-1969), the great British humorist, began writing in a far more serious vein. A lecturer in English literature at London College and later a book and drama critic for the British Broadcasting Company, he first wrote a novel, *The Young Man* (1929) and a series of literary studies including *D.H. Lawrence: A First Study* (1930), *Cooleridge and S.T.C.* (1935). Referring to this early work, Potter said: "Fifteen years of lecturing and scholarship left me with a kind of repugnance that could account in part for my desire to abandon the field and have a little fun out of it as well." This emotional reaction plus economic necessity (he found himself suddenly unemployed in 1947, due largely to a fuel shortage in England) made Potter embark upon his now well-known ventures into academic parody.

His first volume, *The Theory and Practice of Gamesmanship* (1948), was highly successful, and was soon followed by *Some Notes on Lifemanship* (1951), *One-Upmanship* (1952), *Potter on America* (1957), *Supermanship* (1959), *Anti-Woo* (1965), and *Golfmanship* (1968).

POTTERMANSHIP: THE PSYCHOLOGICAL SOCIOLOGY OF S. POTTER*

This essay is an effort to take the supposedly unserious seriously, the ostensibly satirical systematically, the purportedly fictional functionally. More importantly, it is an attempt, through examination of the well-known occasional papers of the late Stephen Potter — on *gamesmanship, one-upmanship, gambits* and *ploys, inter alia,* to demonstrate their psycho-sociological relevance for the study of social encounters, and thus extend the scope of interaction analysis. Primarily, such a consideration will involve the substantive and conceptual content of Potter's writings on the inter-personal strategies of being "one-up" and/or "one-down," and only secondly some of their social implications as applied to contemporary society. In other words, rather than viewing his works as basically humorous albeit truthful, we would urge the reverse strategy, that they be viewed as basically truthful albeit humorous.[1]

We shall, then, consider these manuals of conduct by S. Potter, as he referred to himself, as *folk psychological sociology:* we view him as a polemical social theorist working in a style or tradition which might be called naive *symbolic interactionism* and even, on another level, *ethnomethodology.* However, his was no "ivory-tower" theorizing, devoid of contact with the empirical realities of everyday life. As Potter himself put it:

As a naturalist I like to think of myself as a field-worker in your domain; and I try to keep my observations as truthful as I can. (personal communication, 1968)

A year after he wrote this Potter was dead and although he had commented on an earlier version of this material, unfortunately, his death occurred (December 2, 1969) before he could see this chapter. That he was favorably disposed toward the earlier draft is, of course,

*This article was especially prepared for this volume.

I am indebted, for both critical comments and encouragement to pursue this analysis, to the late Stephen Potter, Stanford Lyman, and anonymous readers in both the United States and Canada. A working paper embodying many of the ideas presented here was presented to the West Coast Conference for Small Group Research, Long Beach, California, April 1966. While I have been a faculty member of the Department of Anthropology and Sociology of the University of Victoria, British Columbia, financial support for some of this material has been provided by the Canada Council, the University's Faculty Research Grant Programme, and its Social Science Research Centre.

no warranty that he would feel so inclined vis-à-vis this one, for which I alone take full responsibility. Ordinarily sociologists write obituaries rather than appreciations; although strictly neither, the following falls closer to the latter than the former. If this is a less scientific tack, it seems to me a more humane one – and at least as close in terms of conforming to scholarly ideals. In a book of this kind, especially, scientific application should be no more nor less than equal to unsentimental appreciation (Matza 1969, pp. 15-40; Becker 1964, pp.1-6).

It is then, perhaps, an exercise in "taking the fun out" of Potter. This principle, *taking the fun out* appears central to the maintenance of scholarly standards – and even the creation of academic disciplines. That is, the legitimization of the pursuit of knowledge requires that it be taken seriously; and this, by definition, means taking-the-fun-out. Thus, people quit reading novels for pleasure and begin doing criticism or close analysis; such is how an academic discipline and its scholars are born. Similarly a de Tocqueville could look for delights in his travels; the modern social scientist retracing his route would search not for delights, but data.[2]

I

In Potter's case, labelling his writings as interactionist theory is simply to root their perspective in a fundamental emphasis on symbolic communication as the warp and woof of social process. Though basically a *litterateur*, his understanding of face-to-face social conduct is essentially the same conceptualization as that which is manifested in the works of Cooley (1902), of Mead (1934),[3] and their intellectual heirs of the "Chicago School" (Faris 1967; Rose 1962; Manis and Meltzer 1967; Blumer 1969).

We choose to call Potter's work psychological sociology rather than social psychology after Schnore (1961, pp. 132-36), who distinguishes between approaches which (1) view social relationships as emergent functions of the internal (psychological) states of the participants, and (2) see the reverse, e.g., external (social) relationships as determinants of member's internal states. The first he designates as psychological sociology, the latter as social psychology.[4] It is this first which seems closest to much of "Chicago School" symbolic interaction.

That his writings have affinity for the symbolic interactionist school is particularly clear in two of the central conceptualizations of this tradition; each central to the writings of both: role taking (Turner 1956, 1962) along with the related notion of self and identity (Stone

1962). *Role taking* refers to the imaginative anticipation of the lines of action, orientations, attitudes, and definitions of the situation of others, i.e. empathetically putting ourselves in their (psychological) place. *Self* speaks to the experience, knowledge, and feelings we have of ourselves, as selves, socially implicated with others. These others are open to our communications about ourselves, and their responses to us are, at least in part, to the self they perceive us to have—the *identity* they assign us, which may or may not more or less coincide with the self we present (Goffman 1956a). Thus, role taking is based upon our *identification* of the other. And since his self will always involve private, hidden, or otherwise unknown aspects, role taking based upon identity will always be imperfect. The question concerning role taking is never accurate or inaccurate, but how accurate or inaccurate; the answer is not drawn for a dichotomy but a continuum.

It is a characteristic of Potter's advocates that their role-taking ability is high; further that their machinations are centrally concerned with the interdependencies of their own selves and the identities of their others—and thus the selves of their others and their own identities. And much of the materials available for construction, maintenance, or alteration of self come from the identifications of us by our others.

In a word, *we owe ourselves to our others.* Our selves are not something we carry around with us, but somethings (plural) which emerge in situated interactions with our others.[5]

Perhaps the greatest area of divergence between the interactionist school and Potter's own work is in his explicit recognition of inequalitarian relationships and the pervasive nature of the power dimension in interpersonal situations; a matter upon which symbolic interactionists, with some notable exceptions, e.g., Goffman and Blau (1960, 1964) have ordinarily been silent. It is only intellectual arrogance, however, that would suggest that sociologists alone have the procedural and methodological equipage necessary to contribute to the analysis of social conduct; similarly, it would be fatuous to argue that only sociological theory, by certified sociologists, is capable of providing all of the conceptualization useful in such analysis (see Turner 1957).

In treating of the interpersonal, Potter's special concern is in the utilization of strategic communication for the manipulation of definitions of self and identifications of others in social situations; i.e., casting of self and other through tactical vocabularies, one to be "one-up," the alter to be "one-down." His writing shows an explicit awareness that the symbolic nature of social interaction is not only verbal/linguistic and gestural, but also includes such other parataxic elements as the spacing, setting, and the props of the physical environment, e.g., its microecological character (Goffman 1956a, pp. 13-19; Birdwhistell 1952; Hall 1959, 1966; Sommers 1969; Ball 1973). Though originally produced for a British readership, a discussion of what may be called *Pottermanship* seems generally relevant to the North American arena, where its descriptions have been widely disseminated as an element of the popular culture. We can only assert this, but the publication of over a half-dozen books, their going through several printings, and Potter's frequent magazine articles and appearances on television shows originating on this continent seem highly supportive of this inference.

The original, written book versions are of a dual nature: Potter is at one and the same time both a cataloguer and an advocate of the uses of communication *qua* strategy in the mundane encounters of everyday life; albeit in his own case, a classbound, upper-middle milieu—the aspirants to which far exceed the actual membership. Thus, in his work Potter is both descriptive theorist, deductively seeking out centralities, especially of asymmetric, i.e., power-discrepant interaction, and polemicist, urging the application of his findings to conduct in natural settings. This advocacy forms, of course, the satirical core of his writings. By espousing the use of symbolic strategies derived from the conventional normative order of the upper-middle class world of gentlemen sportsmen, Potter is deftly poking fun at this social world. That is one of the more obvious, intended functions of his work; but what is also of some concern herein is a more latent aspect: the view of interaction which Potter presents and espouses as well as some possible consequences of such a view in a society where these interpretations have been subject to mass exposure and consumption.

In the ostensible form of conduct manuals, Potter presents a series of fictional, imaginary cases illuminating particular situational strategies; each example showing the means by which the Potterman controls communication in such a way so as to also control the other(s). Actors in these scenes include ideal-typifications of particular styles of control appropriate for various occasions. Parenthetically, it may be noted that in the course of his presentations, Potter also provides a deft parody of modern scholarship copiously using footnotes, both bibliographic and substantive, as an indicator of the seriousness and import of his work. Justification for his voice of authority is provided by his association with Yeovil University and its world-wide correspondence college (Potter 1952, pp. 3-9). We may speak, then, of Potter and the Yeovil School interchangably in this context.

The question might be raised (and it has been by readers of an earlier draft) whether the ascription to Potter of advocacy is not to be taking his satire so seriously as to miss its basically humorous point. The only answer to this can be Potter's own. Although he denied that his original intent was to propound a "philosophy," he also admitted that reader-reaction was so strong and overwhelming that it had led him to adopt his own writings as a sort of "code of conduct" (television interview, 1968). Put another way, by his own account, his reader's identification shaped his presented self. We can do no more than take him at his own word.

II

If Potter is to be treated in a social scientific context, a word about method is in order. That utilized in this study is what might be called *literal formalism*, i.e., an assiduously exact reading of the satirical so as to emphasize, after Simmel, its sociological *content* rather than its literary *form* (1950, pp. 21-23, 40-43); a sort of fundamentalistic exegesis of secular scripture. This procedure is somewhat analogous to the use of written transcriptions of verbal behavior in order to minimize the effects of other factors which may be deemed extraneous, e.g., intonation, cadence, etc. In other words not only can Potter be read for fun (hardly avoidable), but also for profit; and it is to the latter that this work is directed.

When Potter himself is viewed as a naive sociologist, expectedly, his methods are unorthodox. Drawing admittedly loose parallels with more traditional methodology, his work eclectically combines elements of participant observation, the case study, the manipulation of variables in "naturalistic settings" *via* Weber's imaginary experiment, and the use of ideal-types for heruistic purposes.[6] Essentially, it might be viewed as a creative ethnography of manipulative encounters.[7]

Only a few direct examples of Potter's writings will be used in the following for two reasons: (1) brevity, and (2) so as to avoid the tendency toward discursiveness and anecdotal recitation *which is built into the subject* under consideration, as previous Potter readers will well be aware. Those interested are encouraged to open at random any of the works under discussion for a sampling of Potter's work. Thus the material to follow will be most deficient where the originals are richest: in the description of specific Pottermanic devices. There is, after all, no substitute for primary sources and the work herein proceeds on the assumption of the audience's at least surface familiarity with the style and substance of Potter's writings.

III

The level of analysis Potter stresses is that of the *phenomenal experience* of self and other in the context of intimately situated communication.[8] His concern is with the direct impact associated with a message, especially its reception, and the consequences following this receipt for the receiver's self; specifically as this may affect his identity, the other's self, and the overall tone of the interactive relationship. Focus is upon symbolic process and meaning, particularly as they function to imply selves and identities for the actors involved; these implications having social, i.e., *relational* consequences of their own. In this respect Potter's work is in the tradition of Simmel (1924, 1950), Goffman (especially 1956a, 1956b, 1961, and 1963), Garfinkel (1964), and Schutz (1962, 1964), to link him with only a few.

RHETORIC

A primary linkage between interactionist approaches and Potter's assorted ". . . manships" is constituted by a sociological formalization of the concept of rhetoric, a connection which is admittedly externally imposed, and only implicit in the original.

From a sociological standpoint, *a rhetoric may be defined as a specialized vocabulary of limited purpose or function: it is a set of symbols, verbal and otherwise, which operates to communicate a desired set of meanings organized around a particular image or impression.* Through the employment of such rhetorics, actors, and institutions as well, seek to foster or maintain certain appearances so as to structure and elicit desired responses from audiences of relevant others (Ball 1965, 1967, p. 296).

It seems, incidentally, that it is a tenable postulate for the analysis of social life, that role players, and establishments as well, are under some normative constraint to strive for a situationally determined, maximal presentation of image. Put another way, it is suggested that the homily "put your best foot forward" is institutionalized as a moral imperative in everyday life (Ball 1970). Variations in such rhetorical displays, for whatever reason—skill, access to symbolic resources, perception of the relevant audience(s), etc.—would help to explain differentials in social conduct otherwise not accounted for by a strict demands-and-expectations, reflexive model of role-determined interaction.

Given this normative stress upon strategic presentation, it should be apparent that these purposive vocabularies or *rhetorics always function within a moral context* (over and above their possible universality as postulated above): attempting to highlight the valuable and hide the valueless; emphasizing, or at least paying overt deference (Goffman 1956b) to the demands and expectations considered relevant to the situation, the audience, e.g., through role taking, and the desired outcomes of the exhibition. It follows, then, that rhetorics are an important, indeed the central, constituent of the process sometimes called *altercasting*: the activities involved in attempting to impose a role-determined identity upon the interacting other in the situation in order to maximize one's own lines of action and social self—and the concomitant rewards and perquisites thereof (Weinstein and Deutschberger 1964).

It is a characteristic of rhetorics, as viewed sociologically, that they serve to provide both identities and identifiers, and thus, *presented selves and labels of recognition for both the rhetorician and his audience.* To present a rhetoric is to present a self; to view such a presentation is to be able to evaluate it, and thus to relate to it in such a way as to derivatively define one's own self in terms of this relationship and the identity of the other implied.

With this theoretical excursus as prolegomenon, it is now possible to return specifically to Potter as interactionist.

IV

POTTERMANSHIP

Essentially, the various versions of Potter's interpersonal strategies reduce to a central, primary operation: the subtle employment of an appropriate rhetoric so as to put the relevant other(s) in a state of social discomfiture, thus making the actor *qua* rhetorician "one-up" on this audience of other(s), who are therefore, "one-down." It is the communication of a situationally determined, limited vocabulary for the purpose of placing other interactants in a subordinate, less desirable position vis-à-vis the employer of this rhetoric; always within the episode's context of valued norms and conventions—extreme versions of the everyday process of altercasting, that is, maximizing one's gains in the interpersonal situation through control of others' roles and identities.

It may be noted that in employing the *vertical imagery* of "one-up" and "one-down," the Yeovil School is capturing what appears to be a universal metaphor (Ball 1969; Brown 1965, pp. 78-79). This is the equation of height, elevation, rising and the like with the good, desirable, strong and powerful. "The higher the better," and by implication, "the lower the worse."

In the survival of the fittest Potterman, the race goes to those best able to role take, and thus best equipped to covertly manipulate communication and social convention in such a way as to discredit other interactants, and thereby increase their own social stature. The oblique nature of Pottermanship comes from its dissembling presentation, its "as if" character. While typically served up as only incidental, the rhetorical tactic is actually the primary, intended meaning of the Potterman's message. Implication rather than openness is used to convey the really essential content; a content of managed impression and image likely to be questioned, rejected, or disbelieved if presented in a more direct manner. By taking the role of the other and implying rather than announcing, the rhetorician significantly reduces the possibility of direct confrontation with others as regards his claims and their implicative consequences for the identities situated in the episode or encounter.

Abstractly, the Potterman's strategic utilization of rhetoric involves one of two substantive techniques: (1) a telling, but deliberately discrete and opaque debasement of the other(s), along with a resultant elevation of the rhetorician's own social self, or (2) a similarly subtle gambit communicating an upgrading of the Potterman's self thus comparatively downgrading that of the other(s). This distinction is only analytic, however, and may be impossible to make at the empirical level where the two may intermesh. This blending together of the two tactics is neatly illustrated in Potter's description of "Basic Club Play":

It is essential to belong to two clubs if you belong to one club. It doesn't matter if your second club is a 5/-a year sub. affair on Greek Street; the double membership allows you when at your main or proper club to speak often in terms of regretful discrimination about the advantages of your Other One. (1952, p. 141)

In either the empirical or the analytic case, though, the result is the same: a net gain for Potterman and a loss for other(s): the Yeovil way to social rewards is through the generation of discomfiture in others. The several books on the various themes and settings as regards the use of such techniques are all enlargements by Potter on this central motif.

A caveat is in order at this point. Although the discussion herein is one-sided, it should be remembered that in the mundane world interpersonal episodes are more akin to rhetorical contests or duels than the unilateral description embodied in this paper would suggest. In Yeovil terminology, rhetorical "gambits" may be countered by similarly rhetorical "ploys." The interpersonal is a process involving at least two lines of mutually oriented conduct operating simultaneously and interdependently in a complex and tightly interwoven web; Pottermen are not necessarily rationed one to an encounter, but may vie with one another for control of the contest, the content of identities, the rewards (or costs) of self.

A fundamental to the rhetorician's production of discomfort in relevant others is anxiety; it is the primary mechanism through which the desired discomfiture is induced. As implied above, this is essentially done in one of two ways: by using a rhetoric to imply that others' selves are not what they think they are, i.e., by directly provoking in them a questioning of their phenomenally experienced, but socially bestowed identity; or else by leading them to question the social identity or the rhetorician, and thus only less directly their own self as it is defined in the relationship between themselves and the now questionable, ambiguated user of the rhetorical strategy. In either case the effect is to introduce a redefinition of the situation as regards its participants which promotes precariousness and uncertainty on the part of the target-other, thereby engendering anxiety in this object.

Thus, in the "Counter-Drink Play," Potter's suggested tactical procedure is to

take a young opponent . . . . He must be pleasant, shy and genuinely sporting . . . . Then (1) place him by the bar and stand him a drink. (2) When he suggests "The Other Half," refuse him in some such words as these, which should be *preceded* by a genuinely kindly laugh: "Another one? No thanks, old laddy . . . *No,* I certainly won't let you buy me one." Then (3) a minute or two later, when his attention is distracted, buy him and yourself, the second drink. The boy will feel bound to accept it, yet this enforced acceptance should cause him some confusion, and growing thought, if the gambit has been properly managed and the after-play judicious, that he has been fractionally put in his place and decimally treated as if he was [*sic*] a juvenile, and more than partially forced into the position of being the object of generosity. (1948, pp. 52-53)

Ultimately, the function of such tactics is to hamper the potential lines of action of others to the extent that these are linked to conceptions of own self and others' identity. As existing definitions are called into question, self-anchored action patterns are blurred as their appropriateness becomes uncertain. As ambiguity is experienced, the possibilities of a different, less valuable self are suggested; and by implication, a more valuable one for the rhetoric-manipulating Potterman.

In a large proportion of situations, roughly proportionate to the degree of structuring, behavioral lines are a direct consequence of such self-experienced identities, e.g., "I am a certain (kind of) person, therefore, I should do . . . . " It is the tactic of the Potterman to use rhetoric to discredit these definitions through the provocation of anxiety, and thereby alter or eliminate potential courses of action open to another.

Specialized applications of such strategies explicated by Potter range far and wide, and speak to several areas of conventional sociological investigation. Among them: the practitioner-patient dyad, stratification, industry and management, the family and neighboring, leisure and recreation, and recently, an essay on the termination of love affairs, Anti-Woo, which is strikingly congruent with Goffman's paper on "Cooling the Mark Out" (1952).

ETHNOMETHODOLOGY

Earlier we referred to Potter's work not only as psychological sociology, but also as ethnomethodology. Although there is a good deal of controversy among sociologists as to just what ethnomethodology is all about (Hill and Crittenden 1968; Psathas 1967; Denzin 1969), there seems sufficient consensus concerning at least two of its characteristics to warrant their discussion within this context: (1) the search for the unstated rules, the "background expectancies" (Garfinkel 1967) which make social interaction possible; and (2) the technique of disruption (McHugh 1968).

Broadly, background expectancies refer to those rules of conduct which are typically *assumed* to hold true in social episodes, rather than those explicitly applied to them as situationally appropriate. Thus, they refer to norms which "everyone knows" about social activity in general. An example is the rule that when persons are engaged in face-to-face conversation their eye-gazes should be directed more or less at another's face—not his navel. An interesting characteristic of such strictures is that they ordinarily become evident, i.e., we become consciously aware of them, *only* when they have been breached. They are the "of course, everyone knows" rules which become knowable only when they are behaviorally transgressed. These are the norms making up an etiquette of everyday interaction.

An elaborate code which is written nowhere, known by none, but understood by all. (Sapir, in Mandlebaum 1949, p. 556)

Such rules are a major source of interactional structure, an important minimizer of ambiguity, irrespective of the particular substantive concerns of the participants. They insure order in potential chaos; i.e., they integrate the activities of actors with varied pluralities of motives, definitions of the situation (Thomas 1927, 1928; McHugh 1968; Ball 1972), and behavioral repertoires—thus providing both materials and contexts for selves and identities.

The technique of disruption is an ethnomethodological procedure (Garfinkel 1967, pp. 76-103; McHugh 1968) for getting at these unstated rules, these background expectancies. Briefly, this strategy involves the manipulation of situations so that *anomie* (Durkheim 1951, esp. pp. 241-75) is introduced into them; that is, for participants, they become meaningless, without order, unintelligible. The question then becomes, how do actors in such a situation rebuild or reinvest meaning? How is nonambiguity, predictability, and thus regularity and *normality* restored? Put another way, disruption seeks to produce disorder so that the procedures of reordering will occur. When this has taken place, an "everyone knows of course," normal, social environment will have been reconstituted and the ordinarily unknown will have receded from consciousness.

Ethnomethodology has sometimes been described as the study of "practical sociology." The study of what "everyman" knows, assumes, expects-to-be-the-case about society, social structure, and social process. If ethnomethodology is practical sociology, then *Pottermanship is practical ethnomethodology.* The Potterman *qua* ethnomethodologist exploits the background expectancies of interpersonal encounters, and his exploitation takes the form of disruption, the creation of anomie—but only for his other. By creating anomie the Potterman removes the structural and situational anchorage of the other's self, and thus his implied identity. "Of course, everyone knows" becomes questionable and subject to scrutiny rather than assumed and taken-for-granted. "*I am* the kind of person who . . ." is converted into "*Am I* the kind of person who . . . ?" Thus, Potter describes an example of *patientmanship* between otherwise one-down patient and ordinarily one-up physician. As the physician employs a typical *M.D. Manship* gambit, suggesting [the patient is] being rather trivial since he is exhausted, having been

up all night transfusing a couple of touch-and-go cases of thrombolytopenic purpura.

But, patient counter-ploys with apologies for troubling the practitioner, going on that his friend

Eddie Webb-Johnson (Lord Webb-Johnson is the most O.K. surgical name in Britain) persuaded me to go to a really competent physician if I could find one. He prodded me to let him know the results of a more careful examination and who was doing it, what were his qualifications, and so on.
By the way—just to stop him bothering—what are your qualifications? (1953, p. 36)

STRUCTURE AND FUNCTION

As suggested by the discussions above, the structure of Potterman-ship, expectedly never specified by Potter himself, abstractly involves actors, their selves and identities, and communication within a norma-tively ordered context.

At the analytic level of actors there are three units involved: (1) a Potterman *qua* rhetorician or communicator, (2) a target to be dis-comfited, and (3) an audience composed of at least these two, if not additional relevant others. At the level of communication within a normatively ordered context: a manipulated rhetoric, employed so as to create anxiety and discomfort by its debasement, through the meaning-structure provided by situationally appropriate conventions and values, of the target-other's social identity and his self; thereby ennobling the perpetrator and his self by ignobling the other.

Briefly to review as regards identity, the Potterman endeavors to evoke anxiety leading to discomfort and a sensed loss of worth, both personally and phenomenally as regards self, and socially as concerns identity; these as perceived to exist in the cognitions and evaluations of both the other and his own relevant others. Such communication seeks to play upon valued aspects of the culture and the situation; role taking allows for the summoning up of definitions involving ele-ments of situationally important dimensions of both social self and received identity; causing deflation and disorganization for the target, and thereby enhancement and elevation for the rhetorician. The rules bounding encounters (Goffman 1961, pp. 7-81) are exploited so as to make social identity strategically problematic, as is, therefore, the socially situated self of persons subject to such strategems.

Typically, this is done in such a way that the target is rendered, through discomfiture, incapable of the optimal performance upon which his usual, situationally based status, and thus self and/or iden-tity is anchored, i.e., the artful is made, via anxiety, to become artless; this to the advantage of the Potterman. In this sense a rhetoric is a device for the acquisition of power; a tool for the maximization of one's advantages so as to be at the same time disadvantageous to one's interaction partners.

More generally, the interactional function of Yeovil strategy is to put the rhetorician *one-up* and the target or victim *one-down*, i.e., to create an advantageous power discrepancy; the intervening variable between rhetoric and power being the social elements of identity and self.

We may return now to our earlier employment of Schnore's distinc-tion between social psychology and psychological sociology and assignment of Potter to the latter category. Actually Pottermanship employs both models, but in sequential order rather than as parallel orientations. He begins with a social psychological conception of the structure of the relationship determining the consciousness of the participants (cf. Marx). In an inequalitarian relationship, and these are presupposed as the usual state of social affairs, these internal states will be, *ipso facto*, more rewarding (less costly) for the higher member, more costly (less rewarding) for the lower. Thus, it is the goal of the Potterman's psycho-sociological strategem to invert this relationship, to restructure the social relationship so as to reverse the direction of the psychic rewards—to move from psychologically down to sociologically, and therefore psychologically, up vis-à-vis his downed other.

V

From a more macrosociological view, an important structural question is: in what areas of society are most likely to be found situations and encounters most likely to generate Pottermanic behavior? Translating what for Potter is advocacy of application into the more neutral phraseology of a proposition, it may be expected that the most frequent occurrence of rhetorical strategy will be in those contexts where one actor initially feels disadvantaged in the distribution of status and power. As Potter himself pointed out (in the television interview cited earlier) the Yeovil School's "gambits" and "ploys" are essentially "tools for persons who don't have much else" in the way of personal or social resources—or at least, who feel that way about their situated station.

In such cases, the disadvantaged is, if he is not to accept the *status quo*, under some compulsion to at least attempt equalization of the situation and the relationship therein. Pottermanship offers an opportunity, perhaps the only feasible one, for at least partially redressing such imbalances; and utilizes resources, i.e., communicative skills, the expenditure of which, ordinarily, would not be costly. This is likely to be particularly true when such a technique is compared with alternative strategies requiring the output of scarce resources difficult to acquire or replace, e.g., the accumulation of additional status and power bestowing elements such as skill through practise, material goods, *et cetera*—as these may be utilized in the production of self, and thus the assignment of identity.

A specific example of the potential of Pottermanic rhetoric in such resource-discrepant relationships is derived from Scheler's (1961) classic social psychological conceptualization of *ressentiment* (Ball

1964, 1965, p. 196). In such cases, persons who are the lower members of a disadvantageously differentiated relationship, i.e., the less powerful, are hypothesized to experience feelings of hostility which, because of their positional disadvantage, they are unable to openly express. Given this inability, according to Scheler, the hostility will work itself out via strategies of covert verbal aggression; the medium of such aggression being the superior's values, even while, at the same time, these same values are overtly being given ostensible confirmation by the inferior in the relationship.[9] Where such conditions prevail, Pottermanship is an especially suited method of expressing such aggression: attack being made precisely in terms of the target's values. Where power is unequally distributed, and the expression of direct aggression is likely to invite retaliation or reprisal, the character of rhetoric makes it particularly appropriate; its apparent commitment to situationally correct values and the oblique nature of its communication allow it to be strategically disattended or denied; thus, like sarcasm, providing a foxhole strategy which can be ignored by the target or disavowed by the rhetorician. However, it is precisely a capitalization on the values of the target which makes such utilization difficult to disregard, and thus a potent weapon.

Potter reports, in this vein, the discovery of Pottermanship on 8th June, 1931: after going down 40-love in the first game of the first set of a tennis match and envisioning a long afternoon ahead of himself, a rather poor player called out to his expert opponent, just as the latter was about to serve following the former's return of previous shot some ten feet beyond the base-line, "Kindly say, Sir, whether that was in or out." This so rattled the expert, to have his judgment, sportsmanship, and integrity questioned or impugned—even by implication—that he proceeded to become tense and tighten up, ultimately losing the match to the athletically unskilled, but rhetorically proficient nascent Potterman (1948, pp. 16-17). Thus, Potter recalls, were the techniques first discovered, and their utility in imbalanced relationships given early validation.

It should at least briefly be noted that it is not a little ironic that, given contemporary social structure, those with the fewest resources to cope with power discrepancies in conventional ways, i.e., members of disadvantaged classes and categories, are also those least likely to possess the requisite symbolic and staging skills which are ordinarily essential to the presentation of a rhetoric in a profitable manner (Williams 1970); the analytically mixed becomes, empirically, a zero-sum game.

Also our earlier caveat should be remembered: that we are only writing "as if" we were describing a unilateral situation, when in reality it is at least bilateral. Thus, each is only more or less disadvantaged vis-à-vis the other. This discrepancy may actually become quite fluid and shifting, as when Pottermen face one another. Thus, which is initially "up" or "down" may bear no relationship to a particular moment in the encounter; or its outcome. Consideration of such contests is beyond the scope of this discussion, and worthy of separate examination in their own right. Suffice it to say, the less naive the other, the more complex the situation. As McCall and Simmons have noted,

encounters between particularly adept [Pottermen] often become legendary. (1966, p. 141)

Finally, the example of *ressentiment* suggests another aspect of Pottermanship: its connection with more generalized, global hostility and aggression. Its very use implies animosity and alienation. To be a Potterman is to behave aggressively toward the target-other, and also importantly, toward the very social order in which both are positioned. Even if the Potterman's motive is simple, idiosyncratic, personal dislike, attack upon his target is an attack upon a social actor, and thus, upon a part of the system of which he is a constituent member. Persons cannot be completely divorced from their social-positional contexts; neither then, can attacks upon them.

In summary, Pottermanship may be seen as a theory of communicative strategy for the acquisition of power in interpersonal settings; a technique for manipulating rhetorics within the context of a situationally determined normative order; a mechanism for the engendering of social discomfiture and anxiety so as to at least temporarily reconstitute social and personal identities in deliberate ways; a kind of theory of self-aware symbolic interaction, to be aggressively employed in the social contests and games of mundane, everyday life.

VI

IMPLICATIONS

The following section attempts to spell out some of the implications of Pottermanship in contemporary Anglo-American society; a cultural complex wherein both the original works, and secondary discussions in such widely read periodicals as *Time, Esquire, Holiday,* and *The Saturday Review* have had wide circulation. Additionally, Pottermanship has been exploited via the film "School for Scoundrels," perhaps the ultimate mass cultural tribute.[10]

Basically, Pottermanship is an interactional device for subverting the hierarchical differentiation of social organization; a tool at the disposal of the disadvantaged in their efforts to cope with the powerful. At least this is the message embodied in the polemic of Potter's writings. The typical Potterman is one who uses rhetoric precisely because he has no other weapons at hand; he is, in Potter's portraits, an underdog; he lacks status and power because he lacks traits deemed worthwhile in the social situation. The Potterman is unskilled, disadvantaged; he has less of valued things, and thus, in using a rhetoric, is living by his wits in his efforts to gain power and rewards.

It should also be obvious, however, that rhetoric is also available to the already powerful as well as the powerless. As such, it is a potential social control mechanism; as useful in maintaining the status quo as it may be for eroding the structure of power and privilege.

Of more than a little interest is the image of man which is presupposed in Potter's works. Just as do the theoretical writings of Thomas Hobbes, John Locke—not to mention Freud and Talcott Parsons—so too does Pottermanship imply an assumed character of motivation, personality, etc., i.e., a presumed model of the style of social man as actor in the dramas of the everyday world.[11]

As regards the Potterman, this model or image is of man as covertly hostile, as constantly striving to be one-up in a world where there are no equals. In this sense, the view of the social world is that of the "authoritarian"; one in which status and power relationships are paramount, and being down is morally undesirable; a place in which manipulation of interpersonal relations is not only countenanced, but openly encouraged (Adorno, et al. 1950). Proceeding from such a perspective, Potter becomes a modern Machiavelli of mundane interaction.

In a mass society where the character of interpersonal ties is frequently hypothesized to be decaying,[12] where it is argued that the instrumental overwhelms the affective, Potter's works serve as validation for this trend. They are exemplary tales about the exploitation of other actors in the dramas of social life. His writings suggest a new, post-Durkheimian form of social order. The world as presented by Potter is one organized around biotic competition; a society tied together by the manipulative ability and/or utility of its members; a symbiotic integration reminiscent of the grosser elements of the vulgarized ecological view of society allegedly advanced by Park[13] and his colleagues at Chicago.

In effect, Pottermanship becomes a rhetoric in and of itself; an ideological legitimization of interpersonal manipulation and the instrumentalization of social conduct. Potter as polemicist operates to positively sanction the acceptability of extrinsic satisfactions as the *desideratum* of face-to-face interaction.

As Fred Steele has observed,

> The tradition of his general thesis [is] that all life is a competition—that "He who is not one-up is one-down." His humor helps us to see how often we create relational structures day to day which look suspiciously like we agree with this assumption. (1968, p. 523)

Pottermanship acts to provide a grammar and vocabularies for such manipulative behavior. Its explication serves as a folk-sociology of power, a naive social psychology of anxiety production, discomfiture generation, identity transformation (Strauss 1959), stigma imputation (Goffman 1963), and the like. As such, Pottermanship functions as an antithesis to the misnamed, popular version of group dynamics[14] and the human relations school[15] in industry, although paradoxically, both of these share with Pottermanship, a manipulative orientation. The popularity of such phenomena can tell us much about contemporary society, its values, and its norms.

Finally, for the social scientist, Potter's writings provide a handbook of experiments for testing in naturalistic settings; a body of propositions about conduct in the mundane, phenomenally experienced world which await the application of scientific method. In this sense, Potter as sociologist constitutes a source-book of insight and inspiration for the formulation of hypotheses about social interaction in everyday settings and situations.

NOTES

1. His major statements are *Gamesmanship* (1948), *Lifemanship* (1951), and *One-upmanship* (1952); others include *Supermanship* (1959) and *Anti-Woo* (1965).

2. If truly dedicated to his calling, however, they should be one in the same.

3. That Potter's work has social scientific utility is not merely on *a priori* assumption, e.g. the citations in Thibeaut and Kelley's *The Social Psychology of Groups* (1959), Goffman's *Presentation of Self* (1956a), and McCall and Simmons's *Identities and Interactions* (1966), the titles of which speak to their mutual relevance.

4. Actually, the second label has frequently been used as an umbrella for both perspectives.

5. The writer has recently analyzed data suggesting that our situations, particularly the others in them, are more central to definitions of self than our biographies or our attitudes (Ball 1969)—at least at the beginnings and endings of encounters, i.e., at the initiation of interaction, when selves are presented and the termination, when selves (*via* identities) are derived from the episode.

6. Francis Merrill has recently described the sociology of literature as the analysis of social interaction in the imaginary case, literary creation as imaginary experimentation, in "Balzac as Sociologist: A Study in the Sociology of Literature" (1966).

7. However, as an obituary pointed out, many of the personnel populating his treatises were real, with only slight disguises of their names, e.g., A. Boult was Sir Adrian Bolt, conductor of the London Philarmonic (*Newsweek*, December 15, 1969, p. 50).

8. In psychology this perspective is associated with such names as Synng, MacLeod, and Rodgers; in sociology, especially with the late Alfred Schutz.

9. See, for instance, "How to Make People Feel Awkward About Religion" (1951, pp. 10-14).

10. Stanford Lyman has pointed out that the Manchester sub-school of the "Angry Young Men" novelists frequently describes, without acknowledgment, Pottermanic behavior in British settings.

11. See, for instance, Wrong (1961), McDavid and Harari (1968, pp. 26-38).

12. A representative statement is Nisbet (1962).

13. The greater sophistication of Park's own approach is obvious in Park (1952) and Park and Burgess (1925).

14. For the popular view, see Laird (1956), the rigorous and scientific view is exemplified by Cartwright and Zander (1968).

15. See the works of Elton Mayo and compare the critiques by William F. Whyte and especially of Reinhard Bendix and Lloyd Fisher, reprinted in Etzioni (1961, pp. 100-112, 113-26).

REFERENCES

Adorno, Theodore W., et al. The Authoritarian Personality. New York: Harper, 1950.

Ball, Donald W. "Covert Political Rebellion as *Ressentiment*." Social Forces 43 (October 1964): 93-101.

_____."Sarcasm as Sociation: The Rhetoric of Interaction." Canadian Review of Sociology and Anthropology 2 (November 1965): 190-98.

_____."An Abortion Clinic Ethnography." Social Problems 14 (Winter 1967): 293-301.

_____.Attitude, Biography or Situation: Approaches to Standing, Sitting and Definitions of Self. Doctoral Dissertation, Department of Sociology, University of California at Los Angeles, 1969.

_____."The Problematics of Respectability." In Jack D. Douglas, ed. Deviance and Respectability: The Social Construction of Moral Meaning. New York: Basic Books, 1970. Pp. 326-71.

_____."The Definition of the Situation: Some Theoretical and Methodological Consequences of Taking W. I. Thomas Seriously." Journal for the Theory of Social Behaviour 2 (1972): 61-82.

_____.Microecology: Social Situations and Intimate Space. Indianapolis: Bobbs-Merrill, 1973.

Becker, Howard S. The Other Side. New York: Free Press of Glencoe, 1964.

Bennis, Warren G., et al. Interpersonal Dynamics. Rev. edition. Homewood: Dorsey Press, 1968.

Birdwhistell, Ray L. Introduction to Kinesics. Louisville, Kentucky: University of Louisville Press, 1952.

Blau, Peter M. "A Theory of Social Integration." American Journal of Sociology 65 (May 1960): 545-56.

_____.Exchange and Power in Social Life. New York. Wiley, 1964.

Blumer, Herbert. Symbolic Interaction: Perspective and Method. Englewood Cliffs, N.J.: Prentice-Hall, 1969.

Brown, Roger. Social Psychology. New York: Free Press of Glencoe, 1965.

Cartwright, Dorwin, and Alvin Zander, eds. *Group Dynamics*. Third edition. New York: Harper and Row, 1968.

Cooley, Charles Horton. *Human Nature and the Social Order*. New York: Scribner's, 1902.

Denzin, Norman K. "Symbolic Interaction and Ethnomethodology: a Proposed Synthesis." *American Sociological Review* 34 (December 1969): 922-34.

Douglas, Jack D. *Deviance and Respectability: The Social Construction of Moral Meanings*. New York: Basic Books, 1970.

Durkheim, Emile. *Suicide: A Study in Sociology*. Glencoe: Free Press, 1961.

Etzioni, Amatai, ed. *Complex Organizations: A Sociological Reader*. New York: Holt, Rinehart and Winston, 1961.

Faris, Robert E. L. *Chicago Sociology: 1920-1932*. San Francisco: Chandler, 1967.

Garfinkel, Harold. "Studies in the Routine Grounds of Everyday Activities." *Social Problems* 11 (Winter 1954): 225-50. (Reprinted in Garfinkel 1967, pp. 35-75.

_____.*Studies in Ethnomethodology*. Englewood Cliffs: Prentice-Hall, 1967.

Goffman, Erving. "On Cooling the Mark Out: Some Aspects of Adaption to Failure." *Psychiatry* 4 (November 1952): 451-63. (Reprinted in Rose 1962, pp. 482-505).

_____.*Presentation of Self in Everyday Life*. Edinburgh: Social Sciences Research Centre, University of Edinburgh, 1956a.

_____."The Nature of Deference and Demeanor." *American Anthropologist* 58 (June 1956b): 473-502.

_____.*Encounters: Two Studies in the Sociology of Interaction*. Indianapolis: Bobbs-Merrill, 1961.

_____.*Stigma: Notes on the Management of Spoiled Identities*. Englewood Cliffs: Prentice-Hall, 1963.

Hall, Edward T. *The Silent Language*. Garden City, N.Y.: Doubleday, 1959.

_____.*The Hidden Dimension*. Garden City, N.Y.: Doubleday, 1966.

Hill, Richard J., and Kathleen Stones Crittenden, eds. *Proceedings of the Purdue Symposium on Ethnomethodology*. Lafayette, Indiana: Purdue Research Foundation (Institute for the Study of Social Change, Department of Sociology, Purdue University; Institute Monograph Series, Number 1), 1968.

Janowitz, Morris, ed. *W. I. Thomas on Social Organization and Social Personality*. Chicago: University of Chicago Press, 1966.

Laird, Donald, and Eleanor Laird. *The New Psychology for Leadership*. New York: McGraw-Hill, 1956.

McCall, George J., and J. L. Simmons. *Identities and Interactions*. New York: Free Press, 1966.

McDavid, John W., and Herbert Harari. *Social Psychology: Individuals, Groups, Societies*. New York: Harper and Row, 1968.

McHugh, Peter. *Defining the Situation: The Organization of Meaning in Social Interaction*. Indianapolis: Bobbs-Merrill, 1968.

Mandlebaum, David G., ed. *Selected Writings of Edward Sapir.* Berkeley and Los Angeles: University of California Press, 1949.

Manis, Jerome G., and Bernard N. Meltzer, eds. *Symbolic Interaction.* Boston: Allyn and Bacon, 1967.

Matza, David. *Becoming Deviant.* Englewood Cliffs: Prentice-Hall, 1969.

Mead, George Herbert. *Mind, Self, and Society.* Chicago: University of Chicago Press, 1934.

Merrill, Francis E. "Balzac as Sociologist: a Study in the Sociology of Literature." *Sociology and Social Research* 50 (January 1966): 148-59.

Nisbet, Robert. *Community and Power* (formerly *The Quest for Community*). New York: Oxford University Press, 1962.

Park, Robert E. *Human Communities: The Collected Papers of Robert Ezra Park.* Volume II. Glencoe, Ill.: Free Press, 1952.

Park, Robert E., and Ernest W. Burgess. *Introduction to the Science of Sociology.* 2d edition. Chicago: University of Chicago Press, 1924.

Potter, Stephen. *Gamesmanship.* New York: Holt, 1948.

_____.*Lifemanship.* New York: Holt, Rinehart and Winston, 1951.

_____.*One-Upmanship.* New York: Holt, Rinehart and Winston, 1952.

_____.*Supermanship.* New York: Random House, 1959.

_____.*Anti-Woo.* New York: McGraw-Hill, 1965.

Psathas, George. "Ethonomethods and Phenomenology." Paper presented to the American Sociological Association, San Francisco (mimeoed), 1967. Also appearing in *Social Research* (1968).

Rose, Arnold M., ed. *Human Behavior and Social Processes.* Boston: Houghton Mifflin, 1962.

Scheler, Max. *Ressentiment.* New York: Free Press of Glencoe, 1961.

Schnore, Leo F. "The Myth of Human Ecology." *Sociological Inquiry* 31 (No. 2, 1961): 128-39.

Schutz, Alfred. *Collected Papers, I: The Problem of Social Reality.* The Hague: Martinus Nijhoff, 1962.

_____.*Collected Papers, II: Studies in Social Theory.* The Hague: Martinus Nijhoff, 1964.

Simmel, Georg. "Sociology of the Senses: Visual Interaction." In Park and Burgess, *op. cit.,* pp. 356-61.

_____.*The Sociology of Georg Simmel.* K. Wolff, editor. Glencoe: Free Press, 1950.

Sommer, Robert. *Personal Space: The Behavioral Basis of Design.* Englewood Cliffs: Prentice-Hall, 1969.

Steele, Fred I. "The Instrumental Relationship." In Bennis, *et al., op. cit.,* pp. 505-23.

Stone, Gregory. "Appearance and the Self." In Rose, *op. cit.,* pp. 86-118.

Strauss, Anselm. *Mirrors and Masks: The Search for Identity.* Glencoe: Free Press, 1959.

Thibaut, John W., and Harold H. Kelley. *The Social Psychology of Groups.* New York: Wiley, 1959.

Thomas, William I. "Situational Analysis: The Behavior Pattern and the Situation." Reprinted in Janowitz, *op. cit.,* pp. 154-67.

_____.*The Child in America.* New York: Knopf, 1928.

Turner, Ralph H. "Role-Taking, Role Standpoint, and Reference-Group Behavior." *American Journal of Sociology* 61 (January 1956): 316-28.

_____."The Normative Coherence of Folk Concepts." *Research Studies of the State College of Washington* 25 (June 1957): 127-36.

_____."Role-Taking: Process versus Conformity," in Rose, *op. cit.*, pp. 20-40.

Weinstein, Eugene A., and Paul Deutschberger. "Tasks, Bargains, and Identities in Social Interaction." *Social Forces* 42 (May 1964): 451-56.

Williams, Frederick. *Language and Poverty: Perspectives on a Theme.* Chicago: Markham: 1970.

Wrong, Dennis H. "The Oversocialized Conception of Man in Modern Sociology." *American Sociological Review* (April 1961): 183-93.

BEAU FLY JONES

10

James Baldwin:
The Struggle for Identity

James Arthur Baldwin (1924-   ) is among the most
articulate spokesmen of the Black Revolution. From the
beginning, Baldwin has argued that the civil rights issue is
not a Negro problem but the illness of the white man.[1]
Arguing that the myth of white supremacy prevents white
people from facing their own weaknesses, Baldwin sees
them—along with injured black people—as the victims of
segregation. This theme that what happens to the Negro
happens to everyone in our society runs through all of
Baldwin's novels, essays, and plays. Though born in Harlem
and starting his career as a writer in Greenwich Village, he
spent much of his writing apprenticeship in France with
sojourns in other parts of Europe. He has been active in civil
rights work (especially with CORE) and has visited Africa
several times in conjunction with his work for improved
race relations. He is also active on behalf of the National
Committee for a Sane Nuclear Policy.

NOTE

1. Works by Baldwin other than those cited in the article by Jones include: *Tell Me How Long the Train's Been Gone* (1968) and the essay "Negroes Are Anti-Semitic Because They're Anti-White" which first appeared in *The New York Times Magazine* in 1967 and is reprinted in Nat Hentoff, et al., *Black Anti-Semitism and Jewish Racism* (New York: Schocken Books, 1969), pp. 3-12. Re Baldwin's works, see: Donald B. Gibson, ed., *Five Black Writers: Essays on Wright, Ellison, Baldwin, Hughes, & Leroi Jones* (New York: New York University Press, 1969). For Baldwin's more recent statement, see: Margaret Mead and James Baldwin, *A Rap on Race* (New York: J. B. Lippincott, 1971).

JAMES BALDWIN: THE STRUGGLE FOR IDENTITY*

Who is James Baldwin? That is the question embraced by Baldwin throughout his writings. He seeks desperately to define his identity as an American Negro writer[1] and as a spokesman for his people. In order to know who he is, Baldwin must examine his cultural heritage for "the past is all that makes the present coherent."[2] And we must understand the present before we can look forward to the future. It is this goal that has both guided and driven Baldwin as a Negro and as an American.

Despite his distinct antipathy for sociology, Baldwin's writings are highly relevant to that discipline—perhaps even more than many works by professional sociologists. Though obviously prejudiced on the subject of Negro-white relations, Baldwin's personal experience and literary freedom yield an insight and comprehensiveness that social scientists lack. His definition of the problem and its causes, for example, provides a viewpoint that white writers and academics are simply not in a position to contribute. Equally useful is his knowledge of Negro people and their society. Perceptive and broad in scope, Baldwin's combined writings imply a new system for classifying Negro responses to discrimination. They also furnish a fruitful picture of the Negro social structure. But Baldwin's comments on each subject are scattered, frequently tangential, and sometimes contradictory. It is the purpose of this article to abstract and synthesize his views and, wherever possible, to extrapolate their relevance to sociology.

THE PROBLEM

The alleged "Negro problem" in America as Baldwin sees it is not in fact a Negro problem but a white one. Not only have whites created the conditions which make being a Negro problematic but also a

---

*Reprinted from *The British Journal of Sociology* 17 (1966): 107-21, by permission of Routledge & Kegan Paul, Ltd. and the London School of Economics.

complex syndrome of deprivation, exploitation, fear and guilt has made the prejudiced white a problem to himself and to society. In fact, far from desiring to take white society as a model, the terrible irony is that blacks must learn to *accept* whites for what they are, without trying to change them or copy them—including all the white liberals who are still blind to the fact that when talking to a Negro, one is talking simply to another man.[3]

The great white crime, Baldwin argues,[4] is the white man's innocence of his own brutality. Whites are "innocent" in the Freudian sense that they know not what they do because they have subconsciously blinded themselves to the horrible deprivation they have caused the Negro. This "innocence" gives special meaning to the prejudiced white's definition of the situation when he confronts a Negro. What occurs may be called the "tension syndrome."[5] Every time a white encounters a Negro, tension and confusion are created. Deep down inside that "other country" of their being, where truth is too painful to emerge,[6] whites know that they have acted like savages but cannot admit it to themselves at a conscious level. Strong guilt feelings arise for the actual exploitation as well as for the repression. Those possessing such feelings are bound to be insecure, uncertain of themselves, and oversensitive. In effect, they will be most receptive to misunderstanding and ready to express their tension through aggression.

The error is doubly compounded when the tension is actually released through aggression against the object about which they already feel so guilty. And often, because he is powerless to retaliate, the Negro becomes the scapegoat for other anxieties. Thus, not only does the aggressor further exploit and deprive his helpless victims but he also adds to his own guilt for having done so. This tragically perpetuates in vicious-circle fashion the problem whose resolution is so vital to the white American's own well-being.

What causes this syndrome? Baldwin answers this question in several ways, differentiating between origin and persistence. Economic gain was, of course, the original basis of the need to deprive Negroes of all power so that their vital cheap labour could be exploited. In order to rationalize this exploitation, whites created the myth that Negroes were subhuman. And if this were true, then Negroes could justifiably be exploited in other ways, too. At this point sexual gain became a key causal factor.

Baldwin seems quite preoccupied with this issue (especially in his fiction) and indicates that sexual gain is still a crucial source of tension for many people. In *Blues for Mister Charlie* and elsewhere, Baldwin suggests that white men find Negro women more attractive and satisfying sexually than white women. This is mainly caused by the appeal of the forbidden. And men who do participate in such illicit activities find great pleasure in the power that they can wield over Negro women. Under such conditions white men can engage in forms of sexual behaviour that they would not dare even discuss with their wives. One can imagine the feelings of guilt and fear arising from this kind of situation.

But if white men found Negro women so satisfying, would not white women feel the same way about Negro men? Thus began the myth of the male Negro's sexuality and the great fear of it. And thus began the vicious circle—white people seeing what they feared was there. This, of course, so often provides the necessary challenge to Negroes to live up to the myth: in short what Robert Merton would describe as a self-fulfilling prophecy in which "confident error generates its own spurious confirmation."[7]

One reason why exploitation and deprivation have persisted so long is status-insecurity. Americans are so status-conscious and ambitious that they live in fear of losing that status. "The Negro tells us where the bottom is: because he is there, . . . we know . . . how far we must not fall."[8] And there are other fears—that the individual Negro will challenge the power and masculinity of the white, or that the Negro group will rise in concert to take what they have been denied for such a long time. But perhaps the greatest fear of all is that, somehow, the Negro will force the white to look at himself and admit the ugly realities of his being in this relationship.

Baldwin's definition of the "white problem" and his ideas about its causes, breathe life into what Gordon Allport calls the phenomenological aspects of the situation.[9] Through Baldwin's vivid picture it is possible to see more clearly the relationship between physical tension, guilt, fear and aggression: precisely how guilt and fear generate tension which can explode into aggression and how such aggressive release of tension affects guilt and fear. It is also possible to see how intensely intimate is the chance encounter of the prejudiced white and the Negro: how the white applies abstract generalizations about the other group to his personal situation; how insecurities regarding the white man's own sex and potency make him vulnerable to this stranger who happens to be black; how the white may even invent personal threats from an impersonal situation. Under these circumstances it is not surprising that the white man suppresses the truth about himself. Baldwin, as a Negro, is in a unique vantage point to consider such circumstances.

The brutality of this so-called innocence is not, in Baldwin's opinion, the degradation suffered by the individual Negro. Rather it is the white man's control over his life chances. In a letter to his nephew, Baldwin writes:

This innocent country set you down in a ghetto in which in fact, it intended that you should perish . . . because you were black and *for no other reason*. The limits of your ambition were, thus, expected to be set forever.[10]

For Baldwin this is the root of his dispute with America: that the Negro has so little freedom and power to direct his own affairs simply and solely because of his skin colour. Control over the Negro's life covers several related areas: his education, employment, and income — thus his place in the social structure; his self-image; and his relations with white people.

Furthermore Baldwin is keenly aware that these limitations form what Genevieve Knupfer defines as a double handicap.[11] Not only does the person of lower status lack opportunities to the achievement of his life-goals but this closure tends to stifle the original ambition itself. Baldwin notes how many areas of employment are denied to the Negro due to his lack of education and describes the effects of this on his motivation. More important, each career actually opened to Negroes makes those who choose it vulnerable to special forms of role-conflict so that even the successful are handicapped because of their colour.

NEGRO OPPORTUNITY-STRUCTURES

Education is the key determinant of a person's life-chances. And, according to Baldwin, the education available today for the Negro child is meaningless. In the first place, the standards of learning are so low that it would be impossible to equip Negro children for competition in a white world.[12] More tragically school becomes a farce. "Boys, it was clear, would rise no higher than their fathers. School began to reveal itself, therefore, as a child's game that one could not win (so) boys dropped out and went to work."[13] Without education it is almost impossible to be legitimately employed as anything but a manual worker.[14] Unlike whites in a similar position, Baldwin notes that this makes Negroes more vulnerable "to the incessant and gratuitous humiliation and danger one encounter(s)" if one works every day all day long.[15]

For the ambitious there are only a handful of acceptable avenues to success available to the Negro, whose colour makes his career-choice in this area a unique one. On the one hand, he can compete with whites in sport, entertainment, art or literature. But such competition requires unusual talent for the Negro to be successful. Moreover, it exposes him to professional and social contact with whites that might prove awkward or even dangerous. And although Baldwin suggests a number of reasons why these occupations are possibly the most successfully integrated, his fiction is full of characters who are somehow defeated by that contact.

On the other hand, the ambitious Negro can reject this kind of exposure, in favour of an occupation which will serve only the Negro community—namely business and the service professions. Again, those who manage to acquire the education and training to succeed are in a anomalous position. The black bourgeoisie is in a very precarious position. They are automatically cut off from the white world by colour and the Negro world by class.[16] And although they provide vital services for uplifting the Negro community, if that community became fully integrated it would no longer need those services.[17]

This is also true for Negro preachers whom Baldwin finds particularly dubious. While he was a junior cleric in his teens, he rejected the God that is defined by the Judeo-Christian tradition because he found that God to be malevolent. Therefore, he concludes, those who carry on this tradition are either hypocrites or worse, they have accepted a white God.[18] This fear is no doubt connected with Baldwin's distrust of middle-class culture. In his fiction coloured religious people are extremely similar to their white counterparts in their social values. There is as much appreciation of cleanliness, "godliness," punctuality, social manners, parental respect, observance of the law, thrift and so on in one group as the other. Since on the whole these Negroes accept the identity and the God given to them by white society, they feel that they must prove themselves to be equal to whites in these respects. And this is, of course, what Baldwin seems to resent so much.

Most Negro leaders are put in the extremely difficult position of trying to appease two totally conflicting goals. Whites say "Wait" while Negroes press for "Hurry." Moreover, few leaders, Martin Luther King outstanding, are willing to be honest to both sides. Whites recognize only leaders who urge Negroes to model themselves after white society and more and more Negroes are being attracted to leaders who despise all whites and hold no criticism for Negroes.[19]

The only other possibility seemed to involve becoming one of those sordid people on the Avenue.[20] With the realization that hard work and thrift would not lead out of the ghetto, much less into a world of social equality "crime became real . . .—for the first time—not as a possibility but *the* possibility."[21] Every Negro boy who wants to live realizes that because of this, he stands in great danger and must find a gimmick to start him on his way. "And it does not matter what the gimmick is"; this is the terrible thing.[22] Fortunately for Baldwin at that stage, he found such a gimmick with a career in the church. However short-lived, it succeeded in giving him the start that he needed.

But most people are not so lucky as to have revelation meet with opportunity. Baldwin gives ample reason why the probability of choosing a life of crime is so great among Negroes. His descriptions of the overcrowded ghettos where most Negroes live provide almost ideal-type, empirical examples of modern sociological explanations of crime.

Outstanding in such areas is what Richard Cloward and Lloyd Ohlin have described as the overwhelming abundance of illegitimate opportunity structures. Racketeering is as common in Baldwin's slums as the sale of stolen goods, narcotics and illegal liquors. The network of mutual obligations that results is exactly what Cloward and Ohlin called a criminal subculture. This type of subculture is quite distinct from what they term a retreatist subculture which emphasizes escape from painful realities through the use of drugs and alcohol. Baldwin refers to this anomic existence more imaginatively as the 'netherworld'. Here prostitutes, pimps and homosexuals take refuge with drug addicts and alcoholics in their need to withdraw from conventional roles, in their flight from themselves. Baldwin also recognizes what Cloward and Ohlin termed conflict-cultures, whose members seek status through the use of force and violence; but Baldwin emphasizes the interracial character of these subcultures.[23]

And like Gresham Sykes and David Matza, Baldwin sees the importance of rationalizations in the commission of crime. Baldwin notes that the Negro is furnished with several ready-made justifications for a life of crime, and they are all the more compelling for the truth they contain. First, white people have created the conditions which cause the Negro crime rate. They have imprisoned Negroes in a filthy, limited ghetto and have defined them as despicable so that they must rebel to come to terms with themselves. Obversely these conditions are invincible proof that white people do not live up to their law any more than their own moral standards.[24] Thus, white people rob the Negro of his liberty, and they profit by that theft every day.[25] In this context, it is a wonder that the Negro crime rate is not higher.

Baldwin can speak with considerable authority about this Negro social structure because, unlike all white and most Negro social scientists, he has seen it all. Indeed, each stratum has become an integral part of Baldwin. He was born among uneducated manual workers; but his intellect and ambition drove him to search for another identity.

His journey took him first through that tiny unit of lower-middle class respectability—an island in a fast river of Bohemian individuality on the one side and criminality on the other. His rejection of religion forced him to navigate on both shores until he fled altogether to another country. His travels introduced him to Negro leaders from many nations and exposed him, too, to that even smaller peak of the black bourgeoisie, American and international. By then his fame had made those worlds a part of him as well. So when Baldwin writes about the handicaps of his colour at different levels of society, it is because he knows them personally.

THE MYTH

These experiences have given Baldwin another kind of understanding. More than most Negroes perhaps, Baldwin's search has exposed him to many forms of prejudice. And according to him, the worst thing a Negro can do is to accept the identity given to him by white society—that of worthlessness and inferiority. The myths of Aunt Jemima and Uncle Tom are dead now. But with the growth of environmental determinism they have been replaced by the "New Negro" perfectly revealed by Richard Wright in his novel, *Native Son*—(the title of which is deeply resented by Baldwin). Since Baldwin's eloquent analysis of Wright's novel is so relevant to the whole question of identity, it is worthwhile to quote it at length. In Baldwin's opinion, it is this image of a monster that now lives in prejudiced minds. The main character Bigger Thomas is a poor, uneducated Negro who is consumed with hatred and brutally murders a white woman. "He is the 'native son': he is the 'nigger'." For that is what such whites *believe* exists.[26]

Bigger Thomas is a monster; but it takes a very prejudiced white to believe that he was subhuman by birth. So he is made to be the product of his social environment which, of course, he is. The error arises because Bigger is allowed to symbolize *all* Negroes when in fact he is only one. A second error emerges with the failure to see the full nature of such an environment and the multiplicity of causes for it. But possibly the greatest error is that

... this American image of the Negro lives also in the Negro's heart; and when he has surrendered to this image, life has no other possible reality. Then he ... has no means save this of asserting his identity. This is why Bigger's murder ... (is) an "act of creation" ... [26a]

This image, or variations of it, is often transferred to the Negro child very early by the parents who fear for the child's life if he does not accept this identity and decides to rebel. In doing this, however, the child cannot develop any respect for his parents as his mother and father or as Negroes. As he comes to realize their shame, fear and humility, he comes to despise those qualities, his parents' submission and himself as well.[27]

The realities of Negro life resulting from this myth and others also affect his self-image. One feature is outstanding: *frustration* — because their lives are so controlled by others, because they live in such abominable conditions, because they have no positive or constructive identity. Also constant and demoralizing is *fear* of rejection and betrayal; fear of brutality; indeed fear of his own life.

TYPES OF RESPONSE

How does the Negro respond to these problems? There are two main responses explicitly offered by Baldwin,[28] but close analysis of Baldwin's combined writings can be made to yield an eight-fold typology of response. The consideration of whether acceptance or rejection of white myths is active or passive provides a four-fold table which can be subdivided again on the basis of whether rejection is criminal or essentially within the law. See Table I.

Legal, passive, acceptance and rejection of the white myth are hardly distinguishable externally because of the passivity and legality. Only the individual knows whether he is slowly dying inside from a sense of his own shame and degradation or whether he is afflicted inwardly with an embittered rage caused by frustration and hatred of whites for their myth. It is probably in these two categories that most Negroes fall and Baldwin implies that the vast majority tragically accept the myth. The others are those individualists described by Baldwin as "partly criminal" in their rejection of the dominant values. These are the Bohemians whose fight against those values is restricted mainly to themselves.

TABLE I. Responses to the myth of Negro inferiority within Negro communities.

Passively Accept		*Actively Accept*	
Legally	Illegally	Legally	Illegally
Vast majority of essentially law-abiding Negroes		Preachers and social service workers	Aggressive criminals
Bohemian individualists	"Netherland" criminals	Non-violent leaders	Black Muslims
Legally	Illegally	Legally	Illegally
Passively Reject		*Actively Reject*	

Similarly there is very little external distinction between passive acceptance or rejection that is illegal. Into this category fall all the pimps and "queers," prostitutes and whores, drug addicts and alcoholics who seek escape from normal relations among their own kind or interaction with the world that causes them so much harm and frustration. Here again only the individual knows whether he is trying to escape from himself (in the image as defined by the white world); or whether he is there because, while rejecting the white myth, he cannot bear the pain of contact or of trying to change a hopeless situation.

Those who are active are more easily discerned. Preachers and social service workers actively perpetuate the white myth by perpetuating the doctrine of the white God. And by their very legal missionary effort, they try to persuade other Negroes to emulate white values and behaviour. Then there are those who actively reject the white myth by trying to lead Negroes to accept their black identity as defined by *Negro* culture, African and American, and by leading them non-violently to demand what is rightfully theirs as human beings as well as citizens of the United States. No doubt Baldwin himself would fit into this group along with Martin Luther King and all the lesser-known individuals who have apparently come to terms with themselves and stand up for their rights within the bounds of what King calls "acceptable law" (law which is just, as opposed to all the unjust segregation laws unsanctioned by the constitution).[29]

Acceptance that has exploded into aggressive illegality is typified by Richard Wright's character, Bigger Thomas, discussed earlier. And rejection of the white myth that supports violent aggression is perfectly typified by the Black Muslims, whose militant and revolutionary demands Baldwin thinks are quite unrealistic. (Baldwin ultimately rejects them for their eagerness to debase white society, for "*whoever debases others* is debasing himself."[30] For him separation of the races is no more valid from Malcolm X than from Senator Byrd.)

Clearly there is some correlation of the Negro social structure as Baldwin sees it, with whether the individual accepts or rejects the myth. Those with the greatest education, the Bohemians and non-violent leaders, are placed very high in the social structure and tend to reject the myth legally. The Black Muslims are not an exception to this because although a number of leaders in the movement are fairly well educated, the great bulk are converted criminals and uneducated workers.[31] The only other correlation worth noting is the obvious fact that virtually all of those whose reaction is not legal are of lower-class background.

The salient feature of the relationship between the social structure and one's attitude toward the myth is that acceptance or rejection of the myth seems to determine one's place in the social structure. That is, those Negroes most highly placed in that social structure generally *acquired* their status through education and achievement. Whether education of these groupings led to non-violent rejection of the myth or whether rejection of the myth led to a desire for education and social advancement is not clear. Nevertheless the important point is that rejection of the myth was functionally important in achieving high social status. Obversely, acceptance of the myth tends to limit one's social status — undoubtedly because acceptance lowers motivation.

Is it not ironic that social position may be more dependent on what one *thinks of oneself* than on ascribed status? It is possible to argue that generally among whites only the lower classes have a double handicap, whereas nearly all Negroes are handicapped in a unique way whatever their class. White people may lack motivation for many reasons. Only the Negro begins life struggling against such a negative and depressing myth. His handicap is not merely a double one but a triple one.

NEGRO-WHITE RELATIONS

Whatever effect the myth has on social position, it is crucial in determining the Negro's relationship with the white. Negroes acquire much aggressive energy from constant frustration, tension and defeat. This energy must be expressed somehow. Those who are not able to express it actively through non-violent leadership or constructive service, burst into violent aggression by individual crime or group movement against white society. Or they can release these energies through passive revenge and hatred.

This means that constructive communication between black and white is limited to two groups of Negroes. Those who accept the white myth and want to use white society as a model, communicate by virtue of their emulation. This kind of communication, of course, is not considered constructive by those who reject white society as a model. But because they reject the myth also, they can see whites as they are and accept them without trying to emulate them. And although these Negroes would hardly rush to marry whites if they had the opportunity, they unquestionably want the right to do so if they should ever desire such a relationship.

Negro-Jewish relations, states Baldwin,[32] are complicated by the existence of many Jewish tradesmen in Harlem. On the one hand, the Negro identifies with the Jew because he too has been discriminated against. On the other, Negroes resent the fact that these Jews operate as other American capitalists—for profit. The edge of the resentment is that much sharper because of the common experience they have shared. They think the Jew should "know better."

Colour barriers are perhaps at their weakest among Bohemians. Baldwin does not state explicitly why relations are possible in this context but one can deduce from his novels several explanations. First and foremost, the Negroes and whites who compose this world are rebels because they do not accept society's values and judgments. This common bond leads to understanding amongst themselves. At the same time, it leads to hostility from those outside this world. This hostility serves to cement in-group ties. Also, inhabitants of this world tend to be highly individualistic, so that their feelings are more typically formed from evaluation of individual characteristics than by accepting traditional group values.

The heavy emphasis on freedom of individual expression apparently holds true for sex relations. Consequently there seems to be much free participation amongst peoples of both colours in heterosexual and homosexual activities. This suggests that a lot of aggressive physical energy is released sexually. Moreover, it means that among heterosexuals at least,[33] everyone is on an equal footing. If anyone does have the advantage, it is the Negro, due to his alleged prowess in this area.

Another equalizer in this world is occupation and material standard of living. Since discrimination from the larger white society is likely to be at a minimum in these occupations, Negroes can compete more equally with their white colleagues. Also, material wealth is more equally distributed between the two groups than in other occupational areas. These factors, in turn, give Negroes more confidence and courage, and ease social relations between themselves and whites.

Some of the problems involved with mixed relations are poignantly portrayed by Baldwin in *Another Country*. Two of the main characters are Negroes: Rufus, a musician, and his sister Ida. Each is fighting in his own way to find his identity. Rufus begins to have an affair with a white divorcée before he realizes fully how such an event would be received in the white world. When he discovers the looks of disgust and distaste, he knows it is because he is black and finds this challenging; he *will* have her not so much despite this reaction but because of it. Then he actually falls in love with her. But because he accepts the pronouncement of the white world of his worthlessness as a human being, he cannot present himself as a self-respecting man to her. He becomes paranoid and begins to abuse her physically and emotionally. Highly unstable to begin with, she has a complete nervous breakdown. Realizing what he has done, he knows that he cannot accept himself and he commits suicide.

Ida was very close to Rufus and decided upon his death that the only thing that would make life worth living, the only way she could survive in such an ugly world of prejudice and discrimination, was to live by revenge. She decided to use the only things she had, her beauty and her sex, to succeed materially in the white world. She did not accept the myth so she could use the whites to profit by their weaknesses but never give of herself. This way she would triumph or so her mind warped by pain told her. But she, too, falls in love with a white, the very man who had been Rufus' best friend, Vivaldo, a writer.

Rufus and Vivaldo, perhaps because their world was formless, were also successfully to cross the colour barrier in genuine friendship—despite the fact that deep down in that other country Vivaldo knows he could not be free enough to marry one, if indeed he ever married. But he is enormously attracted to Ida and falls in love with her even though he lacks the courage to marry her. He knows in any case that she is playing with him, that she refuses to give of herself to him. Finally she realizes the hopelessness and ultimate barrenness of such a narrow, destructive world. At the depth of her despair, she reveals her true self to Vivaldo and finds that in so doing, she had not only rejected the myth but also accepted herself. She could then proceed from there to construct a fruitful relationship with Vivaldo if he could still love her knowing the truth about her—and if he can accept himself. The book concludes with the promise that with time he can do both.

It is only in *Blues for Mister Charlie*[34] that Baldwin defines the prejudiced Negro as irresponsibly and hopelessly provoking white hostility. One of the main reasons this play is so powerful is that Baldwin sees the dangerous frailty in both Richard, the Negro who is murdered, and Lyle, the killer. *Both are compelled* to provoke hostility in each other *for reasons they do not understand*; and they are drawn to each other as magnets. The tragedy in Richard's case (like that of Bigger Thomas) is that although he had rejected the myth, he was so consumed by hatred for whites that he was made incapable of love—even of himself.

Whatever the difficulties of relations with white Americans, Baldwin feels that such relations are much less problematic than those with Negroes from other countries. On his first trip to Paris,

Baldwin felt that he could identify himself simply as a Negro. "There *was* something which all black men held in common . . . – their unutterably painful relation to the white world . . . the necessity to remake the world in their own image."[35] At the same time, however, he discovered that he could not identify with African Negroes. The emergence of Africa meant that all Negroes were related to "kings and princes in an ancestral homeland far away."[36] This raised considerably the status of Negroes everywhere. But African Negroes are a product of African history. American Negroes are not. On the other hand, he found to his surprise that he felt closest not only to American Negroes but American whites; and he realized that if he did not identify with America, he had no identity at all.

> The one thing that all Americans have in common is that they have no other identity apart from the identity which is being achieved on this continent . . . . The necessity of Americans to achieve an identity is a historical and a present personal fact and this is the connection between you and me.[37]

EVALUATION

Baldwin's analysis of "The" problem has several weaknesses. First, he exaggerates the extent and intensity of white prejudice and vilification of the Negro. The Negro has not made satisfactory gains, for nothing is satisfactory short of real integration – i.e., the withdrawal of prejudice. But he has begun substantially the hard road to desegregation on a national scale and is making major breakthroughs everywhere, especially in the south. Baldwin virtually dismisses all this. Conversely he tends to minimize the responsibility of Negroes for their own situation. He seems not to see the need for the Negro to do what he can to reduce the crime rate, which has such a destructive impact not only on the Negro community but also on the whites. The crime rate provides proof to the prejudiced white that the Negro is inferior and dangerous. *Whatever the causes* of the despicable socioeconomic conditions producing sick and unhappy people, it would seem that *whoever* has the opportunity, the facilities and the desire, *therefore has the responsibility* to attempt at least to remedy the situation. White people may have caused the conditions and by all rights they should do everything they can to remove them. But in the meantime, until their efforts become effective, countless Negroes are suffering. This seems a high price to pay for a principle. Furthermore, as Milton Gordon has noted, white people are not always in the best position to know how to handle the problem.[38]

Baldwin's refusal to see this is closely related to his complete rejection of middle-class values, especially traditional religious ones. On the one hand, Baldwin often "attributes the evils (of exploitation and oppression) to Christianity and to whiteness rather than to the condition of fallen individuals"; in this sense he "has turned the white person into an invisible man."[39] On the other hand, Baldwin implies that acceptance of religious and other middle-class values means acceptance of the myth. But this does not have to be so. Many middle-class values are more a function of occupation and material standard of living than of any religious or ideological commitments. Moreover, the expansion of these high standards will ultimately reduce the status insecurity that Baldwin criticizes. The real issue is that people in this class, black and white, can help the race problem on both sides.

Whatever its flaws, Baldwin's work is both relevant and useful to the social sciences. His definition of the problem as *white* throws new light on the physical strain and mental perspective of the prejudiced white when he encounters a Negro. Baldwin's comments on the peculiar vulnerability of the different socioeconomic groupings certainly broaden our understanding of role-conflict as it applies to Negroes and to other unintegrated minorities. Also his explanation of crime rates adds depth and insight to existing sociological theories.

But perhaps the most useful aspect of Baldwin's writing is his understanding of the special problems created for Negroes by whites. He was one of the first writers to define extensively the details of what it is like to be a Negro in a white society. He is one of the only Negro writers to portray such a wide range of Negro characters in his fiction; to discuss with such insight the psychological handicaps that most Negroes must face; and to realize the complexities of Negro-white relations in so many different contexts. White analysts, scientific or literary, lack the experience to achieve this perspective.

Baldwin's most outstanding triumph is, however, a personal one. He has made a great contribution to the identity of his race, his nation and his profession—mainly because what he says rings true. In redefining what has been called the Negro problem as white, he has forced the majority race in America to look at the damage it has done, and its own role in that destruction. At the same time, he has lifted the burden of humiliation from the shoulder of the Negro. This gives the Negro a greater sense of self-respect. It also could free him, or at least the next generation of Negroes, from much of the psychological power wielded by whites. And if this freer atmosphere produces better communication and more integration, then Badwin has served his country well. It is not within the scope of this paper to evaluate Baldwin's literary talent; but if his work achieves the effect of cre-

ating greater racial understanding, then Baldwin will certainly have
succeeded in the prime function of the writer's profession — communication.

NOTES

1. Baldwin's works include three books of essays:
Notes of a Native Son (New York: Dial Press, 1949), *Nobody Knows My Name*
(New York: Dell, 1954), and *The Fire Next Time* (New York: Dial Press, 1963). His
novels are: *Go Tell It on the Mountain* (New York: Dial Press, 1952), *Giovanni's
Room* (New York: Dell, 1956) and *Another Country* (New York: Dial Press, 1962).
He has also written two plays: *The Amen Corner* (New York: unpublished) and *Blues
for Mister Charlie* (New York: Dial Press, 1964). *Going to Meet the Man* (New York:
Dial Press, 1965) is a book of short stories. Important articles which have not been
incorporated into one of his books are: "On Catfish Row: "Porgy and Bess" in the
Movies," *Commentary*, 1959, vol. 28, pp. 246-8; "The Dangerous Road Before Martin
Luther King," *Harpers*, February, 1961, vol. 222, pp. 33-42; "A Talk to Teachers,"
Saturday Review, 21 December 1963; and "Liberalism and the Negro" (Roundtable
Conference), *Commentary*, 1964, vol. 37, pp. 25-42.
2. *Notes of a Native Son*, op. cit., p. 10.
3. Baldwin also criticizes white liberals whose efforts stop short with desegregation
rather than integration — i.e., the removal of prejudice. See the Roundtable Conference,
"Liberalism and the Negro," op. cit., p. 38.
4. *The Fire Next Time*, op. cit.
5. The following analysis is drawn from a number of Baldwin's writings — both from
direct statements and by implication. This "tension theory" was based specifically on
Notes of a Native Son, op. cit., p. 27 especially, and *The Fire Next Time*, "My Dun-
geon Shook," op. cit.
6. That "other country" is a reference to Baldwin's definition of *Another Country*
as the secret place where each man keeps his most important truths about himself. *Another Country*, op. cit.
7. Robert K. Merton, *Social Theory and Social Structure* (Glencoe, Ill.: The Free
Press, 1957), p. 128. See also Chapter XI, "The Self-Fulfilling Prophecy," pp. 421-438.
8. *Nobody Knows My Name*, op. cit., p. 111. See also *Notes of a Native Son*,
"Stranger in the Village," op. cit.
9. The definition that a person gives to the situation *immediately* preceding his
conduct. This definition involves visual as well as mental perception. Gordon Allport,
The Nature of Prejudice (New York: Doubleday Anchor Books, 1958), p. 210.
10. *The Fire Next Time*, op. cit., p. 21.
11. Genevieve Knupfer, "Portrait of an Underdog" in Reinhard Bendix and S. M.
Lipset, eds., *Class, Status and Power* (Glencoe, Ill.: The Free Press, 1953).
12. At least this is the implication in "Letter from the South," in *Nobody Knows My
Name*, op. cit., and "A Talk to Teachers," op. cit.
13. *The Fire Next Time*, op. cit., p. 32.
14. Baldwin's fiction especially implies that these are usually the most unpleasant,
the dirtiest, the hardest, the most exhausting, the least rewarding psychologically. Negroes are the first to be "laid off" as well. This means that family life for the Negro
male can at best be minimal; when he has time for it, he is exhausted physically and
defeated psychologically.
15. *The Fire Next Time*, op. cit., p. 33.
16. Baldwin said this more explicitly in "Liberalism and the Negro," op. cit., p. 34.
17. *Nobody Knows My Name*, op. cit., pp. 112-13.
18. *The Fire Next Time*, op. cit., pp. 44 ff.

19. "The Dangerous Road Before Martin Luther King," *Harpers*, February 1961, vol. 222, pp. 33-42.

20. *The Fire Next Time*, op. cit., p. 38.

21. Ibid., p. 35.

22. Ibid., p. 38.

23. See Richard Cloward and Lloyd Ohlin, *Delinquency and Opportunity* (Glencoe, Ill.: The Free Press, 1960).

24. Sykes and Matza argue that such rationalizations neutralize the effect of moral judgment from the larger society. See "Techniques of Neutralization," *American Sociological Review*, 1954, vol. 22, pp. 664-70.

25. *The Fire Next Time*, op. cit., pp. 36-7 and "A Talk to Teachers," op. cit., p. 43.

26. *Notes of a Native Son*, op. cit., pp. 35 ff.

26a. Ibid.

27. *The Fire Next Time*, op. cit., pp. 40-2.

28. "A Talk to Teachers," op. cit., pp. 43 and 60.See also *Notes of a Native Son*, op. cit., p. 12.

29. Martin Luther King, Jr., "Letter from Birmingham Jail," *American Friends Service Committee*, May 1963.

30. *The Fire Next Time*, op. cit., pp. 97 ff. Baldwin admits that the Black Muslims have made a great contribution to the Negro community. Their form of racism has at least given the Negro some pride in his colour. And their efforts to convert criminals have been extremely successful where others have failed miserably. Moreover, their strong cohesiveness has given the Negro a sense of belonging and their emphasis on morality has redefined the whole family system for Negro members.

31. C. Eric Lincoln, *The Black Muslims in America* (Boston: Beacon Press, 1961).

32. *Notes of a Native Son*, op. cit., pp. 60-62.

33. It is also true of homosexuals if one discounts the differentiation of active and passive roles in this context.

34. Mister Charlie is the generic name given to white men by Negroes. Miss Anne is the female equivalent.

35. *Nobody Knows My Name*, op. cit., pp.28 and 29.

36. Ibid., p. 81.

37. Ibid., p. 137.

38. Milton Gordon, *Assimilation in American Life* (New York: Oxford University Press, 1964), p. 261.

39. James Finn, "James Baldwin's Vision," *Commonweal*, 26 July 1963, vol. 17, pp. 447-9.

CLARICE S. STOLL

11

George Plimpton:
The Journalist as Social Observer

George Ames Plimpton (1927-   ), editor-in-chief of the
Paris Review, is certainly one of the most remarkable
journalists of today. He is probably most widely known for
his highly successful book *Paper Lion* (1966), which
describes his experiences as a rookie on a professional
football team, and his other works dealing with his
experiences in professional sports, especially in *Out of My
League* (1961) with baseball and *The Bogey Man* (1968)
with golf. He has recently carried his participant reportage
to television where he has demonstrated what it is like to
perform in a circus as part of a flying-trapeze act and as a
stand-up comedian in a Las Vegas night club. But such
versatility is hardly new to Plimpton whose remarkable life
has aready included graduate work at Kings College in
Cambridge, England, editing the *Harvard Lampoon*,
teaching at Barnard College, appearing in several motion
pictures, writing for children (*The Rabbit's Umbrella* in
1955), and producing a host of articles for magazines
ranging from *Sports Illustrated* to *Vogue* and *Horizon*.

GEORGE PLIMPTON: THE JOURNALIST AS SOCIAL OBSERVER*

Ethnomethodology is a sociological perspective concerned with the study of man's practical activities, of his common-sense knowledge, of his ordinary affairs. Although the approach is rooted in the work of such phenomenologists as Husserl or Schutz, its flourishing in sociology was during the sixties, as represented by such writers as Harold Garfinkel (1968), Aaron Cicourel (1970), David Sudnow (1968) and many others (see Douglas, forthcoming). In their empirical research these investigators generally eschew quantitative methods and favor instead observational techniques. Their analyses focus upon everyday behavior in its most ordinary forms.

Ethnomethodologists are interested primarily in how society gets put together on the basis of mundane activities. A key concept is the "taken-for-granted," that is those societal arrangements or rules so embedded in people's view of the world that they are not problematic. These form the bedrock of society, the components of "recipes for living."

To understand the existence of these rules, one need only violate them: move gradually closer to a person during a casual conversation and note how both you and the other respond. Very likely at some point you will feel "too close" to the other. And if you continue to move toward him as though nothing unusual were happening, you may incur in him anger, nervousness, or flight.

Seldom in daily life will you stand "too close" to others or think them encroaching upon you. How "too close" comes to be defined is an example of a question an ethnomethodologist might seek to answer. Needless to say, "too close" has many meanings and depends upon one's situation or circumstances; consequently, the question is also a practical concern for all of us in our everyday lives, and is always salient whenever we enter a new situation. Problems in living are multiplied many times over to include, for example, the choice of words we select, whom we can talk to, where to sit, whom to avoid, whom we can look in the eyes, and so forth. Whenever we can say that we "belong" to the new scene, perhaps we are simply indicating that we now understand its taken-for-granted rules.

It follows then that one prodecure for identifying what is taken-for-granted in a setting would be to study how a newcomer enters and perceives it. Hence, in reporting the results of his own participant observation research, the social scientist would detail the ways in which

---

*This article was prepared especially for this volume.

he learned to adapt to the group. In practice this seldom is found in ethnographic reports, which typically omit discussion of how the investigator managed his entry and acceptance as a newcomer. (In fact, many observers would explain that the early weeks are too fraught with potential misunderstandings and errors simply because they are new to the scene—consequently the data is "unreliable.") Unlike sociologists, journalists are not hampered by such methodological dicta and can describe the tenderfoot stage of experiences with all their bunglings and confusions reproduced in full for our enjoyment and enlightenment.

THE WRITINGS OF GEORGE PLIMPTON[1]

George Plimpton is one of a number of journalists and writers who emerged in the sixties and spoke in such a way that those with ethnomethodological concerns listened. There are three characteristics of this group. First, the reporting methods go beyond the standard observation-interview techniques of the older journalist to include participation in the setting under study. Second, the topics of the reports are seldom "newsworthy" in the sense that their purpose is other than to provide additional information on current events. Third, the content of the reports consists of descriptions of the mundane, rather than the unique or sensationally bizarre. The resulting essays, based on personalized accounts of participation, have produced smatterings of ethnography on such diverse topics as arsonists and gangsters (Jimmy Breslin), life in Los Angeles (Tom Wolfe), the Pentagon March (Norman Mailer), and the Detroit Lions (George Plimpton).[2]

Methodical social scientists would likely find Plimpton to appear the most respectable on the basis of general scientific standards for ethnographic reporting. Jimmy Breslin's case studies are too brief, and often form a springboard for personal opinion. Wolfe's reports are detailed yet also are sometimes so stylized as to obscure the clarity of his observations. And most social scientists would charge that Mailer's egocentric commentaries too much embody—as the jargon goes—observer-bias. In contrast, Plimpton's straightforward works provide good examples of ethnography for its own sake: his literary style is to let the case provide its own lesson.

Plimpton has had an unusual background for his role as participant observer. As one reviewer noted,[3] he was

. . . friend of Marianne Moore, friend of the Kennedys, friend of everybody, gifted, personable, energetic, bright, with-it, rich.

Furthermore, his occupation as editor of *Paris Review* allowed him to take on journalistic assignments requiring investments of blocks of time. (He was also unmarried at the time of preparing the works discussed here.)

Three of Plimpton's books describe his experiences as participant in the professional sports world. *Out of My League* (1967a) narrates the events leading up to and including an afternoon when he took the mound at Yankee Stadium to pitch to a full All-Star line-up. Following the success of this piece, he joined the training camp of a professional football team. The result, *Paper Lion* (1967b), was eventually the basis for a popular motion picture. The third volume, *Bogey Man* (1969), recounts his exposure to several professional golf tournaments. What Plimpton provides, then, is the basis for a comparative ethnography of social groupings where display of physical prowess within a game structure is the major problem at hand.

The style and flavor of the works are distinct from one another. *Out of My League* is terse and compelling, as Hemingway's quoted reaction testifies:

Beautifully observed and incredibly conceived, this account of a self-imposed ordeal has the chilling quality of a true nightmare. It is the dark side of the moon of Walter Mitty.

The nightmare motif was struck by other reviewers as well. *Paper Lion* by contrast was repeatedly described as "the best book about football" for such features as its "air of reality" or "warmth, wit, and style." Because Plimpton spent a number of weeks at the Lions camp, he was able to describe the full variety of often-humorous extra-training activities the players indulge in. *Bogey Man* was similarly described as the most "funny" or "entertaining" book about golf ever written. Here the content is often a recounting of anecdotes from the various golf books Plimpton read during the tournament. To summarize, each successive book is increasingly entertaining or diverting, and also more circumscribed by the particular sports context.

These differences in style and context raise two questions. First, why is *Out of My League* the most serious, that is, more about life than about baseball? And for all the diverting qualities of all three volumes, why should the reviewers and myself deign to describe them as having dark, even nightmarish, qualities? After all, Plimpton hardly endangered his life or suffered the profound personal loss we attach to situations of terror. He was simply out to play some games—or so it seems.

There are several quick answers as to why the baseball book might be the most "serious." One is that Plimpton was less certain of his role as a journalist-participant, so that he was not as comfortable about the reactions of the others as he showed himself to be in later books. Also, his actual baseball skills were much less advanced than the other sports, for his actual play experience had ended in childhood. Well-informed of football technique and lore, he also happened to play "touch" regularly as an adult. Golf was a sport he had played since childhood, although he performed erratically, and at his best in the 90s. Thus *Out of My League* falls into the general class of books concerned with One Man's Tragic Struggle Against the World.

Yet at close look these explanations appear glib, for in themselves they incorporate taken-for-granted assumptions. For example, what does "being comfortable" mean? Who were the "others" that Plimpton oriented toward? What does it mean to be forced to perform in public a physical task for which one is essentially unprepared? These are exactly the kinds of inquiries Plimpton himself made as he was moving through each setting. And this is the stuff that ethnomethodologists thrive on.

Being Accepted

The baseball undertaking was freakish by anyone's definition: to pitch to each of the All-Star team members just prior to the actual All-Star game. Plimpton was willing, in the words of his editor, to be a "fool guinea pig" for the story. The football mission was less unusual in that he was to observe and participate as a team member in training camp through to an exhibition game. For the golf story he was to play a fully legitimated role, that of an amateur player in several pro-am competitions.

The baseball volume, then, is essentially a phenomenology of the entry process. Forced to perform a task he was scarcely able to perform adequately, let alone with accomplishment, he strove for impression management. In his own words, his goal was simply to "survive without shame" (1967a, p. 66). If ultimately he was to fail through his performance on the mound, he would try to achieve respectability in all other respects. How did Plimpton handle his self-imposed problem and what does his behavior tell us about the procedural rules of entry? His descriptions lead to the conclusion that a new member's successful acceptance by group members will proceed from two sets of role-related behaviors.

To illustrate the first role, consider the following reviewer's comments, which capture well the self Plimpton portrays through the narratives:

As this book reveals him, he is a man compounded of, among other things, endless curiosity, unshakable enthusiasm and nerve, a deep respect for the world he enters. As a writer he is truthful without betraying anyone, modest but never falsely so.

It could be that this characterization is not a description of Plimpton in general, but rather, fitting of many people who would happen to do what he did—play novice. In other words, there may be a general expectation in our society that a newcomer should behave inquisitively toward the new setting and subordinately toward the others within it. There is good logic behind such a stance, because it permits the participant to be on the periphery of the scene: observing, yet not committing one's self too early in the game to what might later prove to be unacceptable stances.

The second constellation of activities bears upon self-presentation in perhaps a more profound sense. When Plimpton states his goal in *Out of My League* as "to survive without shame," he implies that he wishes to avoid being labeled a fool. How does he manage not to be a fool? What did he worry about in order to avoid a foolish appearance? He seems to have discovered two features of the entry process that gave him a strategy for being accepted unfoolishly in all three settings.

First, early in *Out of My League* he becomes aware that there are elements of his audience for whom acceptance will not be a problem. He soon realizes that he does not have to account for himself in many situations because he displays cues to others that he is in fact a professional sportsman. Thus, when he parks in the players' lot, the youngsters in the area assume that he is a player despite his unfamiliar appearance (1967a, pp. 35-36).

Even in situations where he exhibits counter-evidence that he is not a player, he discovers that the others are quick to find reasons to deny the discrepancies. For example, during warmup at the All-Star game, Plimpton overhears fans' remarks which indicate that they wonder about his identity as a real player. Then, when Toots Shor (a New York celebrity of sorts) calls Plimpton over to the fence for a chat, he hears the fans change their conversation. They decide that Plimpton must be someone after all because, "Toots Shor talking to a bat boy? You nuts?" (1967a, p. 68)

These patterns of normalization would hardly be surprising to a sociologist, but they were surprising to Plimpton. What is important is that having learned of these patterns, he turned them to his advantage. He recognized that there would be many in the audience for whom his presence would not present a problem, and this enabled him to focus upon those situations where appearances would be more problematic.

In fact, Plimpton soon recognized that he would cause problems with the fans if he did *not* try to pass.

Always after practice, the crowds moved across the sidelines and grouped around the players as they started across the wide fields for the gym. Some of them wanted autographs . . . I had refused to sign anything at the beginning, but it was too difficult to explain why my autograph was not one they'd be especially keen to have. So I signed what they offered—their books, scraps of paper, and once the cast on a small girl's arm. The scraps of paper were used for trading. I'd hear someone calling: I'll give you a Morrall for a Terry Barr. Sometimes a familiar hand, overly grubby, with a Band-Aid of the thumb would appear among the books and pencils with a notebook sheet identical to one presented a moment or so before. And then, after I'd sign it, the hand would withdraw and I'd hear just within earshot: "I'll give you two of these . . . for one Morrall.

"Never heard of this guy."

"He's a rookie. That tall guy."

"Listen I can't even *read* this guy's name. What is it?" . . . "Pumpernickel."

I didn't write my name very distinctly.

"He could make it with Detroit," the first youngster said. "He could make it big with them."

"Well, I'll give you one Plum for three of your guy's."

So the same notebook paper would appear, held under a bandaged thumb, and I'd sign it, pretending I hadn't heard anything. (1967b, p. 129)

Plimpton seems to have realized that personal accountability was most salient with regard to the players themselves, for they were the ones who were to provide the most information for the research. After all, failure to be accepted by players could mean that his participation might be cut prematurely. In order to be taken seriously by players, his strategy was to take seriously things of concern to them. This meant being alert to small cues of language, ritual, ecology, and so forth.

I began to envelop myself in the fiction of actually being a ballplayer. I knew that with the first question I asked, I would be marked for what I really was an observer, a writer, an outsider. So I stubbornly refused to betray the image of myself as a ballplayer by asking questions, and I began to strengthen the fiction as the afternoon progressed by adopting a number of curious mannerisms I associated with ballplaying: my voice took on a vague, tough timbre—somewhat Southern in tone . . . I created a strange, sloping, farmer's walk . . . I was sorely tempted to try a stick of gum, despite my dislike of the stuff, in order to get the jaws moving professionally. Sometimes I just moved the jaws anyway, chewing on the corner of the tongue.

The trouble with the role was that my responsibilities as a writer were eclipsed. (1967a, p. 71)

On the other hand, it should be pointed out that taking others' concerns seriously caused Plimpton often to behave in ways that he would generally consider as foolish in his "real" life. This is implicit in the chewing example above. A more involved series of events occurred as a consequence of his hearing that baseball players are superstitious about having their personal equipment touched. He then purchased a glove, which was stolen overnight from his car. Since it was a Sunday morning, he could not buy another; so he called seven of his friends, awakening many, in order to borrow one. He eventually located a glove with a missing thumb, no lacings, and mold growing in its pocket, or looking "like a seal's flipper." Once he reached the locker room he couldn't rid his mind "of the spectacle I'd present on the mound with the black piece of leather draped from my hand." Finally, he located a trainer who borrowed a glove for him from a boy attending the game (1967a, chap. 5).

Thus for the most part Plimpton followed the lead of the sportsmen around him. He followed a general strategy for avoiding foolishness: (1) managing his physical presentation so that he would not look different from other players; (2) controlling his actions so as to avoid any disruptions of usual practices.

It is noteworthy too that Plimpton made no special demands on the basis of his status as a journalist. This accounts partly for the tone of modesty exhibited throughout the volumes. An excellent example is his interview with the golf champion, Arnold Palmer. He says that he approached Palmer at practice tee and asked:

. . . if he had a moment. He looked at me quickly. I explained that I was a writer. (1969, p. 291)

Actually, at the time Plimpton was a representative for a prestigious sports medium, *Sports Illustrated.* Yet nowhere in the books is there an indication that he appealed to this membership as a means for facilitating entry. In not making these special claims he was in fact not asking for anything out of the ordinary, and hence avoiding a potentially disruptive encounter. To understand the importance of modesty, imagine how the books would be had Plimpton retained the force of his real identity, such as requesting a private room or dispensation from team curfew regulations. We would probably have "just another sport book."

The Mind-Body Problem

If Plimpton learned how not to appear a fool before the others, he nevertheless *felt* foolish in certain situations. The common theme across the books is description of the occurrence of his uncomfortable feelings, as well as a theory as to why they arose.

The theme begins when Plimpton describes his behavior on the mound at the All-Star game. He notes how his own voice served to distract him from other sounds and sights in the stadium:

Mostly you hear your own voice — chattering away, keeping you company in the loneliness, cajoling and threatening if things go badly, heavy in praise at times, much of everything being said half aloud, the lips moving, because although you know you're being watched, no one can hear you, and the sound of your voice was truly a steady influence — the one familiar verity in those strange circumstances. I recall the first to be O.K., bo, you're goin' to be O.K. Nothin' at all to worry about, nothin', nothin'." (1967a, p. 89)

The situation soon changed:

It was while Hodges was at the plate that the inner voice, which had become mumbling inaudibly at first, and calmly, began to get out of control . . . . The mind seemed situated in a sort of observation booth high above the physical self. (1967a, p. 113)

And then this curious thing happened. *It turned traitor.* The voice went defeatist on me. It escaped and ran off, washing its hands of the whole miserable business . . . . Much worse, it capered around out there on the periphery — jeering and catcalling. "You fat fool! . . . You can't pitch yo' way out of a paper bag." (1967a, p. 119)

Plimpton wondered why his mind had scorned him in this manner, and presumed at first that it was merely the harmless expression of anguish. Sometime later, thinking back to the event, he realized that more had been involved:

I found out that if your faculties don't stay around to help you, it simply means you're inadequate to the task, running from it shamefully . . . The physical self was left to face the music alone, disembodied and empty of mind. (1967a, p. 121)

In other words, to display physical incompetency at a task where skill is expected can lead the mind to dissociate itself from the offending body. Plimpton's mind continued to rail him during the pitching, with so little connection to his physical state that only when his hand drifted up to touch his brow and found it damp, did he realize that he was on the verge of fainting.

The situation was repeated at the Lions' exhibition game. He walked to the huddle in full confidence with steady nerves, and *"feeling* like a quarterback" (1967b, p. 194). On his first attempt he fumbled the ball, recovered it, and was downed by his own men. Yet,

> my inner voice was assuring me that the fault in the fumble had not been mine. "They let you down," it was saying. "The blocking failed." But the main reason for my confidence was the next play on my list . . . a play I had worked successfully in the practice scrimmages. (1967b, p. 198)

On this play, upon receiving the snap he fell down.

> The schoolmaster's voice flailed at me inside my helmet. "Ox!" it cried. "Clumsy oaf!" (1967b, p. 198)

We may in charity note that the rest of his plays were also failures.

Afterward the voice appeared again:

> "You didn't stick it," it said testily. "You funked it." (1967b, p. 202)

Bogey Man begins with a metaphor that Plimpton's body is

> a *mechanical* entity, built of tubes and conduits, and boiler rooms here and there, with big dials and gauges to check, a Brobdingnagian structure put together by a team of brilliant engineers, but manned entirely by a dispirited, eccentric group of dissolutes, — mean with drinking problems who do not see very well, and who are plagued by liver complaints. (1969, p. 15)

In contrast, his mind or self

> is an unsteady group (as I see them) of Japanese navymen — admirals, most of them . . . . In their hands they hold ancient and useless voice tubes into which they yell the familiar orders: "Eyes on the ball!" "Chin steady!" (1969, pp. 15-16)

The problem is that at the control center, which is to convey messages from self to body, is posted by such men as

> a cantankerous elder perched on a metal stool, half a bottle of rye on the floor beside him, his ear cocked for the orders that he acknowledges with ancient epithets, yelling back up the corridors, "Ah, your father's mustache!" (1969, p. 16)

Plimpton hoped that he could "overhaul" himself through the steady competition of the professional golf tour. Nothing happened, of course; the volume is filled with the familiar miffs, bungles, and embarrassments of his earlier adventures.

Some Lessons for Sociologists

What can this very selective purview of Plimpton's writings teach us as professional social ethnographers? His contributions are both to social theory, or the understanding of social behavior, and to method, our approach to studying behavior. These necessarily interwine, because the devices we use to view the world filter the images we receive.

Perhaps the most unusual feature of his work was the reporting of interior conversations. This is hardly an unusual style for a nonfiction writer, but it is certainly so for the social scientist. The latter deletes virtually all subjective data from his ethnographic reports, believing that to do otherwise would be unscientific or show bias. Social scientists prefer to write as though they had been omniscient observers — overlooking that this style itself diminishes the validity of the work. *We should reconsider again the traditions of writing as though the subjective element were missing, as though its role as a source of error were trivial.* Would it not be more accurate to include our personalities in our accounts, just as they had been during the real observation period?

Not only might reports gain validity, but new theoretical areas could be explored. Plimpton's analysis of his self-body relation is without doubt a breakthrough in the empirical study of the self and social performance. He has demonstrated aptly how interior conversations vary with one's displays of competence. Furthermore, his data show how fully conscious control of performance is never possible, if only for the reason that we are incapable of the performance. In such cases one's conversational self—while imagining the grandeur of accomplishment—can only detach and freak out in response.

This type of phenomenological insight is rare, yet it comes from observation of very ordinary events of the kind all of us experience. Even more, Plimpton has captured the tensions and drama of these simple events with an effectiveness seldom found in sociological writings. In contrast, sociologists have been noted for their ability to make the queer, abnormal, and perverted phenomena of society seem matter-of-fact. Until ethnomethodology came along they generally ignored the normal course of affairs. Yet Plimpton is much more successful at capturing the reality of everyday life than most ethnomethodologists, and for a good reason: he is a skillful writer. No matter how fine-honed an ethnographer might be at dissecting a group's affairs, he is useless unless he can translate his results for others to understand. *The only time ethnography should have a dull and ponderous flavor is when the actual event being reported upon was tedious or plodding in structure.* I realize that I am raising a popular straw-man battered about in any critical discussion of the profession. Good writers like Plimpton only prove that there is reason for it.

A second contribution is Plimpton's detail on the process of entry. Perhaps most striking is that he was willing to feel foolish in order to pass; he did not let his "real self" inhibit his attempts. Thus, he did not bring his considerable social status into the scene. I suspect that social scientists have been less inclined to give up their signs of upper-middle class status when they observe new settings. It is true that there are cases where maintaining our separate identity is important whether for ethical reasons or even for personal safety. Research on deviant groups is relevant here. But how many of us would let down our pretenses in studying middle-class groups? Could we study an *average* political or religious group with the respect Plimpton displayed toward his subjects?

Finally, it is worth noting certain features of Plimpton's reporting methods. To begin, as might be expected of his journalistic training, Plimpton typically describes the settings surrounding his conversations or observations. As a matter of course he recalls details of physical setting, ecology, and his own position in any scene. For example, his narration of his first dinner at the Lions training camp starts by depicting the room, the seating patterns (e.g., that rookies are informally segregated), and his own position (at a table with the equipment manager and other staff) (1967b, pp. 17-24).

Although Plimpton recognized the value of reporting how he fit in each scene, perhaps more cogently he informs us of those experiences he missed. At the Lions camp we know that he did not interact much with rookies informally, nor did he follow coaches beyond the training settings nor did he practice with interior linemen, and so forth. Typically he presents accounts for not participating or observing in the full variety of activities and these accounts are important data in themselves. For example, his infrequent participation with rookies was partly a result of his dorm assignment with veterans. However, it also resulted from his own expressed feelings of distance that rookies display toward one another as a defense for the time when squad cuts occur (1967b, pp. 85-92). Because Plimpton was so much a participant, his shared experience of distance from others introduced a structural obstacle to his obtaining certain kinds of informant information. This situation is all the more evident in *Bogey Man*, in which his concerns about his golfing performance resulted in excessive self-isolation from others. Hence the book fails to document much of the rich social backdrop found in the other two books. (Yet it captures the phenomenology of golf, namely, that the pro golfer is a man who leads a lonely life in competition with himself.)

Perhaps Plimpton's strategies for becoming accepted appear to elaborate the obvious, but that is because they invoke commonsense. *It is probably because field researchers assume that we all know the obvious, i.e., how one manages to obtain entry, that this stage in reports has been ignored.* While Plimpton's cases do elaborate entry and provide new insights into the process, further reports of this type are yet needed. We do not know how much generality can be made, or where generalities can be drawn. Certainly there are many forms of entry and stance to take. Perhaps the various forms of presentation share common procedures, but only further documentation can secure these patterns.

Furthermore, additional documentaries can give us a basis for codifying those slices of social reality that are cut by any particular stance. It has been shown how Plimpton's strategies for entry limited both the type and quality of information he was able to obtain. What is important is that he provided us with sufficient information about his presentation to evaluate its effects upon his data collection. The potential errors of omission are thus more apparent.

But more important than these contributions is Plimpton's attitude: his willingness to display his humanity with all its imperfections. In accepting his own humanity he could not help but grasp that of his subjects. And one senses that his observations are more valid than they would have been had he objectified his approach. Maybe it is through our errors, not in spite of them, that we find the truth.

NOTES

1. I am grateful to Donald Ball for urging me to try taking Plimpton seriously as he had done with the works of Stephen Potter. Colin J. Williams and Paul T. McFarlane both responded to an early draft with helpful suggestions.

2. Rather than refer to exact citations here, let me note that Breslin and Wolfe wrote many excellent articles for the late New York *Herald Tribune*, and continue to write for the offspring of its Sunday magazine, *New York*. Other *New York* contributors can be added to this group, such as Gail Sheehy, or in some of her articles, Gloria Steinem. Some of the regular *Cosmopolitan* writers have also produced unusual observational studies. There is no need to expand about Norman Mailer, whose personal renewal as a writer through the nonfiction format stimulated a renaissance of the form itself.

3. All quotes attributed to reviewers are taken from book jackets and related advertisements for the volumes.

REFERENCES

Cicourel, Aaron V. "Basic and Normative Rules in the Negotiation of Status and Role." In Hans Peter Dreitzel, ed. *Recent Sociology No. 2: Patterns of Communicative Behavior.* New York: Macmillan, 1970, pp. 4-45.

Douglas, Jack D., ed. *Understanding Everyday Life.* Chicago: Aldine, 1970.

Garfinkel, Harold. *Studies in Ethnomethodology.* Englewood Cliffs: Prentice-Hall, 1968.

Plimpton, George. *Out of My League.* New York: Pocket Book, 1967a.

_____.*Paper Lion.* New York: Pocket Book, 1967b.

_____.*Bogey Man.* New York: Avon, 1969.

Sudnow, David. Untitled discussion. In Richard J. Hill and Kethleen Stones Crittenden, eds. *Proceedings of the Purdue Symposium on Ethnomethodology.* Lafayette, Ind.: Institute for the Study of Social Change, Purdue University, 1968, pp. 52-86 passim.

JERRY M. LEWIS

12

McLuhan: A Sociological Interpretation

Herbert Marshall McLuhan (1911-) is certainly one of today's most controversial thinkers. Formally trained in English literature, primarily at Cambridge University, his work leaps across normal disciplinary lines into literature, art, philosophy, education, sociology, and physiology. He characterizes himself as an intellectual *explorer*, one who wishes to examine, unearth, and provoke, not one who claims to explain or prove. In essence, he argues that many of today's radical social changes can be attributed to the effects of electronic communications. Starting with his *The Mechanical Bride: Folklore of Industrial Man* (1951) and *The Gutenberg Galaxy: The Making of Typographic Man* (1962),[1] the impact of his writing captured its widest audience with his *Understanding Media: The Extensions of Man* (1964) wherein he tried to show that the new electric media (radio, TV, telephone, motion pictures, etc.) are restructuring civilization.

Admitting that his works often contain overstatements and obscurities, McLuhan argues that even these "defects" are important in promoting discussion of the issues he raises.

Following an attempted clarification of his ideas in *The Medium is the Massage: An Inventory of Effects* (written with Quentin Fiore in 1967), McLuhan has written and produced a host of other works (including a multi-media "magazine") expounding his ideas, including: *Verbi-Voco-Visual Explorations* (1967); *War and Peace in the Global Village* (with Quentin Fiore in 1968); *Through the Vanishing Point: Space in Poetry and Painting* (with Harley Parker in 1968); and *From Cliche to Archetype* (with Wilfred Watson in 1970).

NOTES

1. One might also include among these early efforts the journal *Explorations* which McLuhan edited with Edmund Carpenter. Some of the most interesting pieces in this periodical were anthologized in *Explorations in Communications* (1960).

McLUHAN: A SOCIOLOGICAL INTERPRETATION*

A book review in the *New York Times* questions, "Are the Days of McLuhancy Numbered?" (*New York Times Book Review*, September 8, 1968, p. 3) The purpose of this chapter is to show that the influence of Marshall McLuhan's thought is neither numbered nor lunatic and further represents a rich source of propositions for sociologists. In the recent years McLuhan has managed to startle, enrage, excite, and mystify a great many people in almost every field from government to academe. Most of the furor over McLuhan came as a result of his book, *Understanding Media: The Extensions of Man* (McLuhan 1965) in which he suggests that the media themselves, independent of the information they carry, shape and change society. Since *Understanding Media*, which *Time* magazine listed as one of the top ten nonfiction books of the sixties, McLuhan has become a product of his own subject matter. McLuhan is a media personality. He has been the subject of a cover story for *Newsweek* and *Saturday Review* as well as an hour-long program on NBC-TV. TV appearances that come to mind have been on the Dick Cavett and David Frost talk shows.[1]

*This article was prepared especially for this volume. I am greatly indebted to the following students and colleagues for their contributions to this effort: Joseph Albini. Joyce Bohlander, Charles Etlinger, James Lawless, Diane Lewis, Peg Ruffner, Sue Schroeder, Morris Sunshine, and Marcello Truzzi.

The interest in "McLuhancy" or the more neutral McLuhanism has been wide ranging from ad-men to students to politicians. To illustrate a most interesting example of McLuhanism, I turn to a recent best seller *The Selling of the President, 1968* (McGinniss 1970). This book is a study of the place of media and advertising in Richard Nixon's campaign. McGinnis (1970, p. 197) suggests that McLuhan's ideas were influential on Nixon's staff. One staffer responded to *Understanding Media* in this manner:

mcluhan etc: (*sic*) so what does all this mean in practical political terms? for one thing, we're talking at the same time to two quite differently conditioned generations: the visual, linear older generation; and the aural, tactile, suffusing younger generation.

McLuhan's influence has been tremendous, yet he has been largely ignored by American social scientists. The works of Kenneth Boulding (Stearn 1967, pp. 56-64) and James W. Carey (Rosenthal 1968, pp. 270-308) discussed below, are notable exceptions to this statement. Sociologists *per se* have generally ignored McLuhan and this essay attempts to remedy this situation.

HERBERT MARSHALL McLUHAN

Marshall McLuhan, a professor of English and Director of the Center for Culture and Technology at the University of Toronto, has co-authored several books on the impact of media on society. While *Understanding Media* has been the most influential, *The Gutenberg Galaxy* (McLuhan 1962), *The Medium Is the Massage* (McLuhan and Fiore 1967), and *War and Peace in the Global Village* (McLuhan and Fiore 1968), also represent sources of insights and propositions for sociologists.

McLuhan was born in Edmonton, Alberta, Canada, on July 21, 1911, but during his boyhood, his family moved to Winnipeg. He entered the University of Manitoba in the early 1930s, with intentions of becoming an engineer, but later became interested in English and received his B.A. (1933) and M.A. (1934) in this field from the University of Manitoba. Shortly after receiving these degrees, McLuhan left for England to study at Trinity Hall in Cambridge University and received his B.A. in 1936. He then left campus, but continued his studies of medieval education and Renaissance literature at Cambridge University and ultimately received his M.A. (1940) and his Ph.D. (1942).

It was in 1936 that McLuhan began his teaching career, at the University of Wisconsin, and it is apparently also at this time that he took his first interest in popular culture. As quoted in *News-*

week (March 6, 1967, p. 54): "I was confronted with young Americans I was incapable of understanding. I felt an urgent need to study the popular culture in order to get through."

Although McLuhan was born of parents of Methodist and Baptist religious faiths, he was, through his childhood, exposed to various denominations. In the late 1930s he converted to Roman Catholicism and has remained a rather devout Catholic since. It is not certain as to what caused this conversion but according to Rosenthal (1968, p. 17), it was said to be largely due to a collection of essays by G. K. Chesterton, *What's Wrong with the World,* and further strengthened by the work of Gerard Manley Hopkins.

Regardless of the causes of his conversion, it is apparent that religion does play an important role in his thought and writings. McLuhan's religious convictions, in fact, are the impetus for his interest in and writings about media. He felt that media affect everyone and bring about total involvement of people in people. The media, in essence, affect human development. As he (Stearn 1967, p. 267) stated:

Here perhaps my own religious faith has some bearing. I think of human charity as a total responsibility of all, for all. Therefore, my energies are directed at far more than mere political or democratic intent. Democracy as a by product of certain technologies, like literacy and mechanical industry, is something that I would take very seriously. But democracy as it belongs very profoundly with Christianity is something I take very seriously indeed.

James Joyce had considerable influence on McLuhan. He credits Joyce, the great Irish novelist who wrote *Ulysses* and *Finnegans Wake,* for showing him the effect of technology on society. In *War and Peace in the Global Village* McLuhan (1968, pp. 4-5) writes:

The frequent marginal quotes from *Finnegans Wake* serve a variety of functions. James Joyce's book is about the electrical retribulation of the West and the West's effect on the East:

The west shall shake the east awake...while ye have the night for morn...

Joyce's title refers directly to the Orientalization of the West by electric technology and to the meeting of East and West. The *Wake* has many meanings, among them the simple fact that in recoursing all of the human pasts our age has the distinction of doing it in increasing wakefulness.

Joyce was probably the only man ever to discover that all social changes are the effect of new technologies (self-amputations of our own being) on the order of our sensory lives. It is the shift in this order, altering the images that we make of ourselves and our world, that guarantees that every major technical innovation will so disturb our inner lives that wars necessarily result as misbegotten efforts to recover the old images.

Finally, in discussing the major influences on McLuhan's thought, the work of Harold Innis should be noted. McLuhan met Innis, a political economist, at the University of Toronto. Innis, like McLuhan, felt that transformation of society, and history of civilization at large, was caused by mass media. In 1951, Innis completed his book, *The Bias of Communication*, in which he elaborated on his theory of the centrality of communication technology. McLuhan has occasionally characterized his own work as an extension of Innis's.[2]

McLUHAN'S IDEAS

In examining McLuhan's ideas one can be criticized for attempting to derive sociological propositions out of a body of thought that is based essentially on literature. Yet, the entire thrust of this volume legitimates this approach since all the works are concerned with the development of propositions from unexpected sources.

It is not my purpose to submit all of McLuhan's ideas to the ordering of propositions, for this would simply not be possible. Further, the charm and insight of some of his (McLuhan 1965, p. 229) aphorisms such as ". . . ads are carefully designed by the Madison Avenue frogmen-of-the-mind . . . " would be lost.

McLuhan writes about all forms of technology. The propositions that follow provide an ordering of his ideas on how the mass media of newspapers, magazines, movies, radio, and television shape society. This search for propositions follows in part that of Kenneth Boulding (Stearn 1967, pp. 56-64) who has written what I consider to be the best secondary treatment of McLuhan available.

The basic idea underlying McLuhan's approach is that media independent of content are the determinants of social systems. He writes in *Understanding Media: The Extensions of Man* (McLuhan 1965, p. 9) that:

it is the medium that shapes and controls the scale and form of human association and action. The content or uses of such media are as diverse as they are ineffectual in shaping the form of human association. Indeed, it is only too typical that the content of any medium blinds us to the character of that medium.

This suggests these propositions about the mass media of any social system.

A. Mass media are extensions of human sense faculties. Man communicates through extensions of himself. For example, the book which is based on print is an attempt to extend the capabilities of the eye. Radio and television, based on electric circuitry, are logical extensions of man's central nervous system.

The logical question here is one of whether the complexity of media varies directly with the complexity of society or vice versa. McLuhan, of course, would say that the complexity of the media determines the nature and potential for complexity in the society.

McLuhan points out that we "march backwards into the future" with our eyes on the past because we don't understand the implications of the effect of electronic media on our way of life. He calls attention to the popularity of the cowboy shows on TV as an example of our general unwillingness to cope with electronic media. It is possible that much of the alienation in society today stems from the fact that man made the technological leap into the electronic age long before he was prepared to deal with its psychological implications. One must have sympathy for the man who considers his home a place where he could leave the world's problems behind him when he closed the door, only to find his TV set bringing the problems of the world right into his living room.

B. Mass media can be classified on a two-dimensional scale from "hot" linear to "cool" mosaic. The classification is based on two criteria. First, the form in which the image comes to the individual and second, his participation with the medium.

McLuhan (1965, p. 22) defines a hot medium as "one that extends one single sense in high definition. High definition is that state of being well filled with data." A cool medium such as television provides the sense faculties with incomplete information and thus requires participation by the user to complete the message.

C. Mass media are determinants of social systems. This is, of course, McLuhan's (1965, p. 22) famous statement: the medium is the message.

This is merely to say that the personal and social consequences of any medium—that is, of any extension of ourselves—result from a new scale that is introduced into our affairs by each extension of ourselves or by any new technology.

Media alter sense-ratios of individuals, and this forces individuals to alter their relationships with others which in turn alter social structures. For example, McLuhan concludes that the auditory sense and the sense of touch have been heightened by television while the visual sense has been depressed by this medium.

D. Linear media, notably print, exploded primitive society, while mosaic media, notably television, are imploding society. Of most interest to students of popular culture today is this imploding effect of electronic media. McLuhan feels that society is no longer one of individuals detached from each other. McLuhan calls this the "electronic global village" which suggests that media are so pervasive that society must be viewed, according to McLuhan, as existing within a total atmosphere of electronic media that surrounds and pervades our whole existence. We are no longer a world of nations.

This analysis should not suggest that McLuhan has written only on mass media for this would be a much too narrow interpretation of his work. For example, his treatment of the lightbulb as "pure information" in *Understanding Media* is most valuable. Generally, however the analysis of media dominates his thought and particularly the argument that the mass media are most influential in shaping social structure.[3]

CRITICISMS OF McLUHAN'S THOUGHT

While it is not likely that sociologists would say: "Who's Marshall McLuhan," his work, in its implications for sociology, has been generally ignored. There are four reasons for this which can be characterized as (1) the problem of style; (2) the problem of scholarship; (3) the problem of content; and (4) the problem of measurement.

Style

McLuhan's nonsociological style of writing leads one to believe that his world-view is based on a table of random numbers and that he learned to write through careful study of the yellow pages. Sociologists disdain his work because they are not accustomed to taking seriously the thought of any scholar who so blithely and admittedly contradicts himself. They tend to regard this as anti-intellectual. In his own defense McLuhan (Stearn 1967, p. viii) has noted about his style:

I am an investigator. I make probes. I have no point of view. I do not stay in one position. Anybody in our culture is regarded as invited as long as he stays in one fixed position. Once he starts moving around the crossing boundaries, he's delinquent, he's fair game. The explorer is totally inconsistent. He never knows at what moment he will make some startling discovery. And consistency is a meaningless term to apply to an explorer. If he wanted to be consistent, he would stay home.

Scholarship

Many writers have attacked McLuhan for his habit of taking quotes out of context and misquoting to support his points. An illustration of this "sloppy" scholarship can be found in Nathan Halper's harsh criticisms of McLuhan's use of Joyce. Halper is quite disturbed by the fact that McLuhan dropped one word out of the passage he quotes from Joyce earlier in this essay. Halper (Rosenthal 1968, p. 79) writes:

Now, in *Finnegans Wake* this is not a couplet. It is set as prose. There are two consecutive sentences and McLuhan has deleted the first word (walk) of the second.

Halper discusses at length what is wrong with this quote pointing out among other things that this quote has nothing to do with electric circuitry. Halper (Rosenthal 1968, pp. 80-81) concludes his critique of McLuhan thus:

As I said in the beginning, I am interested in Joyce. My concern with McLuhan is only with McLuhan as the "man who knows his Joyce" — the man who, potentially, might tell us something about Joyce.
   Alas, he fails to do this. He has read his Joyce. He reads books about him. (*Books of the Wake* is a good one.) He has Joyce on his mind and, certainly, on his tongue. As the word is nowadays used, he may be called an expert. But McLuhan is not a scholar. He is not even a man who, though he is careless, sometimes has a brilliant idea. All he does is dabble. This does not give him authority. A man who is always singing in the shower is not necessarily a tenor at the Met.

While I know of no public response from McLuhan to this particular criticism, his "sloppiness" can be understood in terms of a type of "literary pattern recognition." Since McLuhan is interested in patterns in media, quoting out of context or misquoting would not violate standards based on pattern recognition although it would be a serious violation of more traditional scholarly rules of the road. For example, in *Understanding Media* McLuhan suggests that a complete handbook on studying media extensions of man can be found in the works of Shakespeare. He writes in regard to television and Shakespeare:[4]

Some might quibble about whether or not he was referring to TV in these familiar lines from *Romeo and Juliet*:

'But soft! What light from yonder window breaks?
It speaks, and yet says nothing'.

In the preface to the second edition of *Understanding Media* he (McLuhan 1965, p. xi) defends himself in this way:

there are some lines from Romeo and Juliet whimsically modified to make allusion to TV. Some reviewers have imagined that this was an involuntary misquotation.

Quoting lines that are in fact separate as being together is literary pattern recognition. I think it is safe to say McLuhan would not make the mistake of knowingly misquoting such well known lines, and, consequently, I am willing to settle for his explanation. Whether the modification can be considered whimsical or not is left to the reader. However, students of McLuhan should adopt an attitude of *caveat emptor* particularly in evaluating his examples and his literary pattern recognition techniques.

Content

Most sociologists would be willing to live with his unreadable style, obvious inconsistencies and sloppy scholarship if it weren't for the more serious problem of McLuhan's media deterministic model of social systems. The basis of this model is the idea that media, independent of content, determine social systems.

A sociologist instinctively views this kind of statement with suspicion because he devotes much of his time to extracting information about society from the content of media. Books, films, magazines, and electronic media have always represented important vehicles by which the sociologist learns about society. It is not that McLuhan thinks content is irrelevant. He is simply saying that greater understanding of society can be achieved by analyzing each medium as being unique and having a characteristic impact on society, completely independent of its content. To suggest that the media are more important to the study of society than the information they carry presents sociologists with a serious theoretical challenge. Many writers have looked critically at McLuhan's attempt to eliminate content from his analysis. An illustrative example can be found in the work (Stearn 1967, p. 225) of Ben Lieberman, a New York critic, who writes:

The greatest defect of McLuhan's theory, however, is the complete rejection of any role for the content of communication. One can only assume that the irony that his own work creates "content" exclusively is lost upon McLuhan. At any rate, he ignores the power of ideas, of values, of emotions, of cumulative wisdom—to say nothing of the hard facts of geography, economics, politics, and the human glory and tragedy of life and death. "The medium is the message," and there is no other. Just like that. The truth is overwhelming in its pristine simplicity, as great a stroke of genius as Einstein's $E=mc^2$. And the result, unleashed, is a comparable radioactivity that creates horrible mutations. McLuhan bombs a landscape already in critical condition, and then strews his special seed for the growth of the new truths he sees.

The language is strong, but Lieberman does catch the passion of some about McLuhan's treatment of content. Frankly, it is difficult to determine where McLuhan is on this issue because he continually uses "content" illustrations to support his arguments. Nevertheless, the guts of his argument is that media, independent of content, shape society.

But McLuhan's analysis can be interpreted as asking scholars to be aware of the additive influence of media on content. I doubt if any sociologist would study only the effect of media independent of content. McLuhan tells us to "tease" out the effect of media *qua* media. I think viewing the media as having an additive effect on content is supported by McLuhan (Stearn 1967, p. 268) himself when he notes about his method of analysis that:

I discovered that when you take anything out of daily newspapers and put it on the screen people go into a fit of laughter . . . . People never notice the outrageous humor until something is removed from its form. Because it's environmental and invisible. The moment you translate it into another medium it becomes visible—and hilarious.

Movies on TV are, in a sense, a parody. Just using one over another form creates that comic effect. When movies were new it was suggested that they were a parody of life. The transcript of ordinary visual life into a new medium created hilarious comedy. The word parody means a road that goes alongside another road. A movie is a visual track that goes alongside another visual track creating complete terror.

Measurement

The problem of testing McLuhan's ideas is probably the most relevant to sociologists and at the same time the most difficult to solve. Theodore Roszak, an historian who writes from a sociological perspective (Rosenthal 1968, pp. 261-62) has looked harshly at this difficulty. He writes:

It is perhaps the most remarkable aspect of McLuhan's career that so few of his critics (and of course none of his admirers) have ever asked him for proof of his central thesis. Perhaps because they are so readily intimidated? For to hear McLuhan hold forth, you would assume there is some large body of incontrovertible experimental evidence somewhere to support the assertion — and that everybody who is anybody knows all about it. There isn't. And yet, on the basis of this unexamined thesis, McLuhan is prepared to make extremely ambitious proposals.

To deal with this criticism one must first order McLuhan's thought into propositions that are amenable to testing. This essay reflects a first step in that direction. Second, the sociologist must integrate McLuhan's media deterministic model into the probablistic model that sociologists use. This is quite difficult. However, I shall suggest in the next section how McLuhan's model can be used by the sociologist to study important problems, particularly in areas related to mass communication.

SOCIOLOGICAL PROBLEMS

There are three general areas wherein McLuhan's thought could provide sociologists with an exciting research challenge. They are: (1) comparing McLuhan's ideas with other social theorists; (2) popular culture studies; and (3) McLuhan's influence on mass media professionals.

Comparative Theory

McLuhan's ideas, as I have tried to show in a previous section, can be expressed in the form of nomothetic propositions. When he argues that media are the determinants of all social structures, he is clearly putting forth a proposition at the most general level. Therefore, I think it is useful to compare his thought with the work of such sociological grand theorists as Georg Simmel, Max Weber, Emile Durkheim, Talcott Parsons, and Pitirim Sorokin. They, too, were attempting to develop theory at the general level.

A profitable enterprise would be to explore the methodology of McLuhan in comparison with Weber's ideal-typical model of analysis. The foundation of McLuhan's analysis is clearly the use of the ideal type. However, the most important comparison that one could make with classical sociological theory is between the work of Durkheim and that of McLuhan.[5]

Durkheim was deeply concerned with social integration. Talcott Parsons (1960, p. 118) noted:

It can be said, I think, that it was the problem of the integration of the social system, of what holds societies together, which was the most persistent preoccupation of Durkheim's career.

Durkheim proposed that there are two basically different types of solidarity, varying in degree and state within various societies. One type of solidarity Durkheim depicted is that of "mechanical" solidarity — characterized by likeness. The individual of such a society acquires the habits, attitudes, beliefs, and values which comprise the common or collective consciousness of the group. The second type he describes is that of "organic" solidarity — characterized by specialization and interdependence through the division of labor. Rather than based on sameness, "organic" solidarity is based on complementary differences, and the strength of this solidarity increases with the development of the individual personalities.

McLuhan's theoretical approach cannot be classified as easily or as thoroughly as Durkheim's. McLuhan is not, literally speaking, a sociologist, and would be actively disregarded by many sociologists. One reason for this is that, according to Carey, he emphasizes the individual rather than institutions (Rosenthal 1968, p. 281). However, comparison of McLuhan and Durkheim along three lines is justified.

First, both men are concerned with the disorganization they saw in the world about them. Durkheim's work is greatly influenced by the tragedy and upheaval in French society. McLuhan, likewise, is observing and writing during a period of great and rapid change and influx. They both felt a need for improvement and both, to a degree, pass social comment upon the times in which they write. This suggests that these writers can be studied and compared from a sociology of knowledge perspective.

Second, it is interesting to compare McLuhan and Durkheim on a methodological plane. Both writers operate at the highest levels of abstract theory. Durkheim works at the macro-level of analysis when he shows how the division of labor holds society together. McLuhan operates at the macro-level as well, as can be seen in his treatment of media and its influence on society. McLuhan argues that media are the determinants of the social structure of society. I am suggesting then, that McLuhan and Durkheim are writing at the same conceptual level and can be so compared.

Another parallel aspect of methodology is that of paired concepts, the use of which both McLuhan and Durkheim employ. Paired concepts have been prevalent in social sciences throughout the history of the discipline. As stated by Bendix and Berger (1959, p. 98):

Such paired concepts are attempts to conceptualize what we know about the range of variability of social phenomena so that we are enabled to deal abstractly with their known extremes, regardless of whether we focus on the level of interaction, of institutions, or of societies as wholes.

The use of paired concepts can be considered a valid technique providing they are taken as a total relationship and not viewed merely as designating one extreme or the other. Both McLuhan and Durkheim used their paired concepts in such a total relationship.

Durkheim's paired concept is the familiar "mechanical" and "organic" solidarity. He intended to show a relationship between the two, and maintained that even in the extreme conditions of a complex society, social solidarity would not be exclusively "organic" in nature. There would remain elements of collective consciousness.

McLuhan employed the use of paired concepts to show how the individual deals with media. One of these paired concepts is that of his linear and mosaic forms. In his analysis of the media, the linear form is print, and the mosaic pattern is television. McLuhan does not consider one totally without the other. In fact, according to McLuhan, our present period of history is a combination of the two.

Finally, it would be of value to compare the idea of the collective consciousness to McLuhan's idea of synesthesia. In *The Division of Labor in Society*, Durkheim (1933, p. 79) defines the collective consciousness as "the totality of beliefs and sentiments common to the average citizen of the society." McLuhan defines synesthesia as the condition of a unified sense and imaginative life based primarily on television. A comparative analysis of these two concepts in the respective theories of social integration would be of great value. This analysis should focus on the question of media as an integrative force in society. To what extent is it possible to see media, particularly television, as one of the functional alternatives to the division of labor for integrating society?

There's no question that McLuhan sees television as having a central or core relationship with the rest of mass media. He sees television as evolving from the other media and having much greater impact on social life than the other media—particularly in relation to his concept of synesthesia.

It seems, then, that a comparison of the theories of McLuhan and Durkheim emphasizing the problem of social integration is possible. Such a comparison can be justified along three lines: from the perspective of the sociology of knowledge, in terms of methodology, and in relation to their views of the mechanisms of social integration.

Popular Culture

There have been few objective sociological studies of popular culture because of the value oriented thrust of much of the theory and research. Most of the studies of popular culture have been couched in the framework of the good/bad—optimistic/pessimistic debate about the effects of popular culture on American society. A most influential work in the field, *Mass Culture*, edited by Bernard Rosenberg and David Manning White (1964), begins with two essays stating the issues on whether popular culture is good or bad for American society.[6] In this collection, Bernard Rosenberg's (1964, p. 5) thought represents the bad/pessimistic point-of-view. He sees popular culture, particularly as represented by mass media, as a major threat to man's autonomy. He writes, in evaluating the power of the mass media that

no art form, no body of knowledge, no system of ethics is strong enough to withstand vulgarization. A kind of cultural alchemy transforms them all into the same soft currency. Never before have the sacred and the profane, the genuine and specious, the exalted and the debased, been so thoroughly mixed.

Rosenberg (1964, p. 6) believes that the reduction of popular culture to a common denominator of understandability has serious implications for alienation in American society. He argues that Americans turn to the mass media to be uplifted and come away feeling nothing at all. He bolsters his point with a quote from Flaubert's *Madame Bovary*:

" . . . By moonlight in the garden she recited all the love poetry she knew and sighed and sang of love's sweet melancholy. But afterwards she found herself not a whit more calm, and Charles not a whit more amorous or emotional."

Rosenberg notes (1964, p. 7) that, "nothing goes more directly to the core of mass culture than this. Any indictment of sleazy fiction, trashy films, and bathetic soap operas, in all their maddening forms, must come to rest finally on Flaubert's prescient insight."

A counter-view to Rosenberg's pessimistic position is found in the statements of David Manning White (1964, p. 17). White argues that no society has ever had such opportunities to be culturally uplifted as American society. He writes that the mass media

hold out the greatest promise to the "average" man (in providing) a cultural richness no previous age could give him . . . . If television (or the other media) provided only a diet of the tried and true stereotyped programs, that is, allowed the majority taste to mandate every choice then I would argue with these critics in their fear for the future. But the variety and quality of what is available to national audiences show this is not the case.

White then gives examples appropriate to the time when he wrote the essay in the late fifties. Today he would probably cite the New York Philharmonic Young People's Concerts.

The controversy on the good or bad effects that popular culture has on American mass society interferes with good sociological research on popular culture.[7] The ideas of Marshall McLuhan provide alternative ways to look at popular culture because the continuing battle between the good and bad effects of popular culture has tended to lock theorists into models that have been used to prove positions rather than describe social phenomena.

Media and Popular Culture. McLuhan and the traditional popular culture theorists agree that mass media provide the basic structure of popular culture, but the emphasis on the differential influence of media is not the same. McLuhan clearly feels that television, because of its sense-ratio altering capacities, has the greater effect on our electronic based society than do other media. While traditional theorists note the presence of television, they do not clearly indicate its important influence as does McLuhan.

One of the reasons why a general theory of mass media and popular culture has not been developed is because scholars have attempted to organize their theoretical concerns around the idea that all media are about equal and have similar impact. However, when one develops a model, perhaps an equilibrium model with television as the core medium and the other media in a satellite position, then the theoretical prospectives begin to change. I believe, stemming from McLuhan's thought, that the meaningful development of theory of mass media and popular culture will begin only when we view television as more theoretically important than the other four media (radio, movies, magazines, and newspapers) of mass communication.

There's no question that McLuhan sees television as having a central or core relationship with the rest of mass media. He sees television as evolving from the other media and having much greater impact on social life than the other media. There is some evidence to support this idea. For example, the pervasiveness of television is demonstrated by the fact that 95 percent of all households with electricity in standard metropolitan statistical areas have television sets. Further, recent research on mass media credibility shows television as being rated the most credible medium.

Passive Man and Popular Culture. The passive man model of traditional popular culture theory is seen in the work of both the pessimistic and optimistic theorists. Both argue that people do not get terribly involved in popular culture but rather "sit back and take it." Popular culture seemingly does its thing and the audience are simply receivers. McLuhan's ideas clearly reject this notion. Individuals, particularly through television, get very involved in popular culture. This in turn may have considerable effect on social structure.

Popular culture attracts people to media and this "turns the set on." When this happens then the additive effect of the medium can take place. This raises the possibility that popular culture, in combination with media, may represent an integrative force in electronic society. McLuhan has noted that one of the basic effects of mass media is the movement of electronic society towards synesthesia, which is the condition of a unified sense and imaginative life based primarily on television. McLuhan (1965, p. 315) writes about television in England and America that

the TV image has exerted a unifying synesthetic force on the sense-life of these intensely literate populations, such as they have lacked for centuries.

McLuhan argues that TV man can no longer be seen as passive. He (1965, p. 336) writes:

For people long accustomed to the merely visual experience of the typographic and photographic varieties, it would seem to be the synesthesia, or tactual depth of TV experience, that dislocated them from their usual attitudes of passivity and detachment.

Is it possible to see media, particularly television, as one of the functional alternatives to the division of labor for integrating society? What may hold society together is not the fact that we must depend on each other to carry out tasks that we are unable to do, but rather that we have a common framework of integration based on a unified sense and imaginative life. With the notion of synesthesia McLuhan's ideas suggest that sociologists should look at social basis of perception particularly in terms of the impact of mass media as a medium and not in terms of content. The synesthesia hypothesis provides a new way to look at popular culture. This hypothesis, I believe, is interesting enough to encourage sociologists to do research on television and popular culture that is not so value oriented as previous research efforts. McLuhan (1965, p. 315) clearly supports this position when he writes in regard to synesthesia that

it is wise to withhold all value judgements when studying these media matters, since their effects are not capable of being isolated.

Media Professionals and McLuhan

The third problem area relates to the interest in McLuhan's thought by media personnel. As I noted earlier, his work has received considerable attention in *Newsweek, Saturday Review*, and many major newspapers, as well as all three national television networks. This attention needs to be understood.

One of the major reasons for this is that McLuhan provides a professional legitimation for media personnel. When he states that media are the only determinants of social structure, he provides a powerful value system for media personnel. We have seen throughout occupational structures a widespread development of professional values and attitudes. Media organizations are no exception. In their quest for professional status, media personnel find in McLuhan a system of thought which provides acceptable world-view. This idea could be tested in part through this hypothesis:

The greater the commitment to McLuhan's thought, the greater the commitment of media personnel to the values of professionalism.

Though the gatekeeper function of the mass communicator is widely known, very little is known empirically about the attitudes and feelings of the mass communicator which influence the gatekeeper process. McLuhan's thought validates the mass communicator and gives him a place in the sun. Therefore, it is important to study the dimensions of influence of McLuhan on the communicator.

CONCLUSIONS

This essay has attempted to order the thought of Marshall McLuhan into some workable general propositions. I have argued that it is important for sociologists to consider McLuhan's ideas on what I have called the additive influence of media on the content of messages. While I have been critical of McLuhan's thought in several ways, I feel his ideas are of great value in the sociological study of mass media. In particular, I have suggested lines of inquiry ranging from questions of social integration to matters of popular culture.

William R. Catton (Lange 1969, p. 258) in discussing the effects of mass communication has written that

serious investigation is needed now to determine what long-range unintended consequences will occur from the way we have organized our lives around the mass media and especially around the simulation of primary groups, television.

I think Catton's statement should provide sociologists with a sense of mission vis-à-vis McLuhan's work. It is time to stop arguing the pros and cons of McLuhan and get down to a systematic empirical examination of his thought. I believe the most successful test of McLuhan will come through an examination of his ideas in regard to long-run impacts of mass media, and particularly television, on society.

NOTES

1. The appearances were on ABC-TV during the month of December 1970.

2. For an excellent study of the influence of Innis on McLuhan see James W. Carey, "Harold Adams Innis and Marshall McLuhan," reprinted in Rosenthal (1968, pp. 270-308). While I do not agree with many of Carey's conclusions about McLuhan's thought, his study is a good comparative analysis of McLuhan's work.

3. It should be noted that in *War and Peace in the Global Village* (McLuhan and Fiore 1968, *passim*) McLuhan develops his ideas on the influence of computers, which he sees as an extension of the central nervous system.

4. The lines which are spoken by Romeo when Juliet appears at the garden window are below. The italics are mine.

> *But soft! What light through yonder window breaks?*
> It is the east, and Juliet the sun
> Arise, fair sun, and kill the envious moon,
> Who is already sick and pale with grief,
> That thou her maid art far more fair than she:
> But not her maid, since she is envious;
> Her vestal livery is but sick and green
> And none but fools do wear it; cast it off.
> It is my lady, O, it is my love!
> *She speaks yet says nothing: What of that?*

See *The Complete Works of William Shakespeare*, ed. William George Clark and William Aldis Wright (New York: Cumberland Publishing Company, 1911), p. 892.

5. The idea to compare McLuhan and Durkheim was suggested in a paper, "The Sociological Implications of Thought of Marshall McLuhan" which I gave at the Ohio Valley Sociological Society meetings in 1968. One of my students, Joyce Bohlander, developed the comparison in more detail. This part of the study is based on a paper we jointly wrote entitled, "The Theories of Social Integration of Emile Durkheim and Marshall McLuhan: A Comparative Analysis." Unpublished manuscript, Department of Sociology and Anthropology, Kent State University, Kent, Ohio, 1970.

6. For an updated version of the Rosenberg-White debate see *Mass Culture Revisited* (1971).

7. Gans (1966) attempts to deal with the problem of values in popular culture research with his notions of taste publics and cultures.

REFERENCES

Bendix, Reinhard and Bennett Berger. "Images of Society and Problems of Concept Formation in Sociology." In Llewellyn Gross, ed. *Symposium of Sociological Theory*. Evanston, Illinois: Row, Peterson and Company, 1959, pp. 92-118.

Bohlander, Joyce W. *The Theories of Social Integration of Emile Durkheim and Marshall McLuhan: A Comparative Analysis*. Unpublished Master's Thesis, Kent State University, Kent, Ohio, 1971.

Duffy, Dennis. *Marshall McLuhan*. Toronto/Montreal: McClelland and Stewart Limited, 1969.

Durkheim, Emile. *The Division of Labor in Society*. Glencoe:Free Press, 1933.

Gans, Herbert J. "Popular Culture in America: Social Problem in a Mass Society or Social Asset in a Pluralist Society." In *Social Problems: A Modern Approach*, ed. Howard S. Becker. New York: John Wiley, 1966. Pp. 549-620.

Lange, David L., Robert K. Baker, Sandra J. Ball. *Mass Media and Violence*. Washington, D.C.: Superintendent of Documents, U.S. Government Printing Office, 1969.

McGinniss, Joe. *The Selling of the President 1968:* New York: Pocket Books, 1970.

McLuhan, Marshall. *The Gutenberg Galaxy*. Toronto, Ontario, Canada: University of Toronto Press, 1962.

_____.*Understanding Media: The Extensions of Man*. New York: McGraw-Hill Paperback Edition, 1965.

McLuhan, Marshall and Quentin Fiore. *The Medium Is the Massage*. New York: Bantam Books, 1967.

_____.*War and Peace in the Global Village*. New York: Bantam Books, 1968.

Miller, Jonathan. *Marshall McLuhan*. New York: Viking Press, 1971.

Rosenberg, Bernard and David Manning White, eds. *Mass Culture*. New York: Free Press, 1964.

_____.*Mass Culture Revisited*. New York: Van Nostrand Reinhold, 1971.

Rosenthal, Raymond, ed. *McLuhan: Pro and Con*. Baltimore: Pelican Books, 1968.

Stearn, Gerald Emanuel, ed. *McLuhan: Hot and Cool*. New York: Dial Press, 1967.

Theall, Donald F. *The Medium Is the Rear View Mirror: Understanding McLuhan*. Montreal and London: McGill-Queen's University Press, 1971.

GLENN A. GOODWIN

13

On Transcending the Absurd: An Inquiry in the Sociology of Meaning

Like Marvin Scott in his essay on the Marquis De Sade and the sociology of the absurd,[1] Glenn Goodwin independently developed rather similar ideas through his study of the existentialist writers like Samuel Beckett,[2] Albert Camus, and Jean-Paul Sartre. In this essay, however, Goodwin turns this framework to a consideration of some contemporary changes in American society and towards the development of a radical sociology of human relevance.

NOTES

1. See also: Stanford M. Lyman and Marvin B. Scott, *A Sociology of the Absurd* (New York:Appleton-Century-Crofts, 1970).
2. Re Beckett and sociology, see: Robert N. Wilson, "Samuel Beckett: The Social Psychology of Emptiness," *Journal of Social Issues* 20 (1964): 62-70.

ON TRANSCENDING THE ABSURD: AN INQUIRY IN THE SOCIOLOGY OF MEANING*

The ideas in this paper owe a debt to activist students with whom I have talked over the past two years. Not the least important of these student groups are our own radical and black caucuses which have made their presence known since the American Sociological Association meetings of 1968 in Boston. Convinced that these groups are truly native products, I attempted to "tune in" on why they appeared to be "tuning out" sociology. I was especially curious about the source of their intellectual direction, whom they were reading, from what body of ideas they were drawing their unity. In the course of informal conversations on various university campuses, I discovered their interest in a body of literature generally referred to as "the literature of the absurd." Following their direction I set out to read and re-read this literature, attempting to share their situational definitions. As I reviewed this literature I developed the thesis of this paper which argues that meaning in contemporary American society may be directly related to man's ability to consciously realize dissonance for himself to which he must react.

Drawing upon the general framework of this literature, I will argue for its use in generating new theoretical directions in sociology and present some examples of the "absurd syndrome" as well as sociological insights which may be drawn from it. I will then apply this framework to a critical appraisal of American sociology generally and conclude with some comments in support of an action orientation on the part of American sociologists.

THE LITERATURE OF THE ABSURD

The literature of the absurd, as used in this paper, refers to the body of ideas which concludes that man's existence in society cannot escape being absurd. Man, in this literature, is viewed as attempting to function in an environment continually steeped in contradiction from which there is no possible meaningful resolution. All that remains for

*Reprinted from *The American Journal of Sociology* 76 (1971): 831-46, by permission of the University of Chicago Press. Copyright 1971 by the University of Chicago. A revised version of a paper read at the annual meetings of the American Sociological Association, September 1969, San Francisco, California. A special note of thanks is owed Jim Rinehart and Merl Coon for their stimulating and challenging conversations concerning the thesis of this paper. I also wish to thank Moshe Schwartz for reading the manuscript and offering many helpful comments and suggestions. Of course, the shortcomings of the paper remain entirely my own.

him is the realization, that is, the *conscious ascertainment,* that the final and definitive synthesis—the "good life"—is an impossibility. Choosing to act in the face of this realization, it is argued, becomes the determinant of man's freedom. In other words, man's choosing to act, *with the definite understanding that his action will resolve nothing,* is what determines his freedom.[1] This position may *itself* be a source of meaning in contemporary American society. Predicated on this realization, social man consciously creates dissonance to which he can then react, and thus he achieves a semblance of meaning. The process, it will further be argued, is continuous—it never ceases. Once the dissonance has been reacted to, and perhaps consonance achieved, man soon creates further dissonance, and so on.

Various currents of thought have been concerned with this theme. They have been known historically as the "theater of the absurd,"[2] dialectical thought,[3] and existentialism, to mention only three. Some of their intellectual mentors have been such thinkers as Kierkegaard, Nietzsche, Camus, Sartre, Beckett, and Marcuse. In a general sense, contemporary existential thought can act as an anchor point for discussing the theme of the absurd. At least the term "existentialism" manages to call forth *some kind* of theoretical image when it is presented to social scientists, although the typical reaction is usually one of distaste, especially for American sociologists. Carruth (1964, p. v) sums up well the traditional reaction when the term "existentialism" rears its head:

Existentialism entered the American consciousness like an elephant entering a dark room: there was a good deal of breakage and the people inside naturally mistook the nature of the intrusion. The commonest opinion was that it was an engine of destruction, perhaps a tank that had somehow failed to hear of the end of the war. After a while the lights were turned on and it was seen to be an elephant, whereupon everyone laughed and remarked that a circus must be passing through town. Only later did it become apparent that the elephant was here to stay. Then gradually people recognized that although he was indeed a newcomer and a rather odd-looking addition to the ménage, he was not a stranger: they had known about him all along.

One argument of this paper is that this "theoretical elephant" known as existentialism, and especially its concern with the absurdity of man's being, should finally be recognized by American sociologists and, further, should be put to creative heuristic work in sociology. Hughes (1961) has indicated that "the post-1945 vogue of French existentialism grew directly out of a situation in which a concern with social problems appeared an inescapable necessity" in European social thought. It could be argued, in view of our contemporary concern with social problems in American sociology, that we might also turn to the theoretical and/or heuristic help of existentialism. It is clearly evident to anyone familiar with the literature of the absurd generally, and existentialism in particular, that Carruth (1964, p. xi) is correct when he states that this literature insists that man *confront* the absurd and that this literature, accordingly, is truly a philosophy of our age.

The theoretical framework prescribed by dialectical thought also contributes to the perspective of the absurd. In his now classic work on the social theory of Hegel, Marcuse (1968, p. ix), in discussing dialectical thought, notes that:

Dialectical thought starts with the experience that the world is unfree; . . . man and nature exist in conditions of alienation, exist as "other than they are." Any mode of thought which excludes this contradiction from its logic is a faulty logic. Thought "corresponds" to reality only as it transforms reality comprehending its contradictory structure . . . . Freedom is the innermost dynamic of existence, and the very process of existence in an unfree world is "the continuous negation of that which threatens to deny freedom." Thus freedom is essentially negative: existence is both alienation and the process by which the subject comes to itself in comprehending and mastering alienation.

The perspective of identifying contradictions in one's existence, necessary to the thought of any dialectician,[4] when carried to its logical conclusion, leads to the position of the absurd. What I am referring to here is the view that every thesis contains its own antithesis from which emerges a synthesis. This synthesis, at the moment of its emergence, then becomes a thesis, and the process continues *ad infinitum*. The "absurd position" is the *conscious realization* that there is no final resolution—no final synthesis[5]—but only a kind of social game whose purpose it is to create theses that will eventually destroy themselves. Thus, "absurd theorists" like Sartre (1956) can conclude that man is never *being* but only *becoming*. But, again, it should be emphasized that it is the *realization* that matters. Then and only then, the argument has it, is man truly free. Then and only then can he choose to act or not to act.

It is my suspicion that the reaction of most sociologists to what has been presented hitherto will be extremely negative inasmuch as the argument presented so far reeks heavily of that most horrible of sins in sociology—reductionism. I shall argue, however, that there is a sociology here if we only activate our sociological imaginations. In the interlude it would be helpful to remind ourselves that no matter how we cut the theoretical pie, any discipline concerned with man and society will inevitably be confronted with subject-object relationships. This realization is certainly the legacy, as I see it, of contemporary *social* social psychology.[6] That is, if we are ever to achieve a science of society, it will have to be, simultaneously, a science of man. This is hardly a revolutionary discovery in sociological thought. Simmel (1963, pp. 84-87), writing in 1908, for example, noted:

The individual can never stay within a unit which he does not at the same time stay outside of, that he is not incorporated into any order without also confronting it . . . [thus]: to be one with God is conditioned in its very significance by being other than God . . . . The individual is contained in sociation and, at the same time, finds himself confronted by it . . . he exists both for society and for himself . . . . The "within" and "without" between individual and society are not two unrelated definitions but define together the fully homogeneous position of man as a social animal.

The point I am emphasizing here is that there is an inherent subjective element involved in any analysis of social action and, further, we have, in sociology, tended to ignore this element out of fear of falling into the throes of reductionism.[7] Accordingly, we tend to ignore, *ipso facto*, any body of literature which orients itself to *only* a reductionistic or psychologistic perspective. The literature of the absurd, and especially contemporary existentialism, is in this category. I am suggesting, however, that this type of literature can be extremely functional in forcing us to reexamine our own perspectives concerning man and society. If it does nothing else, this brand of conceptualization at least forces us to remind ourselves that social action requires some attention to a subjective element.[8] The exercise of continuing to examine our basic assumptions concerning man and society, as Madge (1964, pp. 152-53) explicitly suggests, can *only* be valuable for the growth of sociology as a scientific concern. The literature of the absurd, if it does nothing else then, at least forces this reexamination.

The significance of the subjective element in social action and social existence has recently been commented upon by Tiryakian although it still remains relatively untouched as an area of theory *creation* in sociology. Tiryakian (1965, pp. 686-87) has noted:

Not only does sociological knowledge require subjective understanding and objective cognizance of the social situation . . . but it should also be seen as an essentially *radical description* of social reality. Existential phenomenology applied to sociology seeks the *roots* of social existence . . . . Sociological theory can remain true to itself and yet renovate its formulations by focusing on the existential horizon of social life. [Emphasis in the original]

Accordingly, existentialist novelists could be a source of theoretical stimulation (rather than intellectual disdain) for the sociologist. Lee (1966, p. 66), along these lines, has written:

Novelists have done more than social scientists to sensitize readers to the tyranny of social roles over individual behavior, emotion, and thought . . . . The perceptive artistry of the novelist can be very helpful in making us more precisely aware of how we and others cope with the problems of life.

Regardless, then, of its reductionistic undertones (a "dictatorship of the subjective," it might be called), the literature which concerns itself with the absurdity of man's being ought to be searched for its sociological heuristic value. Most of the remainder of this paper takes its direction from the comments of Lionel Rubinoff (1968, p. 11):

Instead of facing up to the absurd, we either counterfeit or ignore it. Many of our current myths and images of man [such as underlie the practice of the social sciences] have been surreptitiously manufactured for the purpose of counterfeiting the experience of the absurd. I propose to confront the absurd directly by imaginatively living through it . . . a mind which has achieved a . . . critical awareness of the absurd . . . may be said, therefore, to have transcended it. [Brackets in the original]

THE SOCIOLOGY OF THE ABSURD: IS THERE ONE?

A major theme of the literature of the absurd is a preoccupation with death. Death is often presented as the only important occurrence in the life of man. Conversely, life is seen as an experience wherein man merely waits for this event. Beckett, in his novel *Malone Dies* (1965a, p. 194), writes: "Coma is for the living. The living. They were always more than I could bear . . . . I stop everything and wait." The novel, in fact, portrays its major character as one who is waiting for the "big event," waiting to die. Death is viewed then, as an event to be celebrated in the life of man as he wades through the absurdity of his existence. Camus (1961, pp. 33-37), in his novel *The Fall*, pursues this same position, as witnessed in the following conversation of Jean-Baptiste Clamence, the judge-penitent:

Do you know why we are always more just and more generous toward the dead? The reason is simple. With them there is no obligation . . . . If they forced us to anything, it would be to remembering, and we have a short memory. No, it is the recently dead we love among our friends, the painful dead, our emotion, ourselves after all . . . . Something must happen — and that explains most human commitments. Something must happen . . . hurray then for funerals!

The message here is that the central concern is death inasmuch as death brings relief from the absurdity of life. Much of the current unrest in American society may be a result of this *realization*, and its accompanying social forms may be attempts at meaning-acquisition so as to avoid the position of Malone and Jean-Baptiste Clamence.

Samuel Beckett, among others, attempts to identify man's existence as one of almost continual suffering, of continual despair. He writes, in his novel *The Unnamable* (1965b, pp. 304-5): "I, of whom I know nothing, I know my eyes are open, because of the tears that pour from them unceasingly . . . . I'll dry these streaming sockets too, bung them up, there, it's done, no more tears, I'm a big talking ball, talking about things that do not exist, or that exist perhaps, impossible to know, besides the point" (*sic*). Beckett's concern with man's existence as suffering and despair[9] is carried to its logical conclusion in Sartre's account of the diary of Antoine Roquentin (1964, pp. 33 ff.) wherein Sartre concludes that nausea *is* existence. Sartre writes:

Nausea . . . spreads at the bottom of the vicious puddle, at the bottom of *our* time. . . . I have known it for twenty years. . . . So this is Nausea: This blinding evidence? I have scratched my head over it! I've written about it. Now I know: I exist—the world exists—and I know that the world exists. . . . The Nausea has not left me and I don't believe it will leave me so soon; but I no longer have to bear it, it is no longer an illness or a passing fit: it is I. [Emphasis in the original]

Again, the *awareness* here is as significant as the perception. Once an awareness is achieved we can at least choose to act. There are any number of avenues of social action which can materialize on the basis of the absurd syndrome recognition. What is crucial, however, is the conscious *recognition* of the absurd in order to then transcend it. One avenue of reaction, predicated on this recognition, may be rebellion. It may be possible, I am suggesting, that rebellion is a quest for meaning, a quest to transcend the absurd.

Camus (1954, pp. 21-23) has argued that rebellion underlies the very conception of the individual and that, further, the rebel, from his very first step (i.e., his first act of rebellion), is fighting for the integrity of his being. Implicit in this statement is the idea that the individual has become aware of what his "being" is—aware, that is, of what it is he must rebel against. Part of this recognition, as suggested earlier, is the position that the absurd is *never* overcome—all that occurs is the creation of new theses which in turn have *their own contradictions*. A *meaningful* existence, then, could become one of continual rebellion, or as Camus (1954, p. 219) has stated: "I rebel, therefore *we* exist" (my sociological emphasis—the word is from

Camus). It is important to note that I am not arguing that nihilism is the source of meaning, nor is that the position of Camus. The argument should *not* be interpreted as "rebellion for rebellion's sake." Rather, rebellion is a meaning-seeking, goal-oriented activity—it is, in essence, a testimony that life has meaning in the continual fight (read "rebellion") for order and unity. As such, it is the very *antithesis* of nihilism. Camus (1954, pp. 72 ff.) sums this position up clearly:

> Human insurrection . . . can only be a prolonged protest against death . . . the protest is always directed at everything in creation which is dissonant, opaque or promises the solution of *continuity*. Essentially, then, we are dealing with a perpetual demand for unity. . . . The rebel does not ask for life, but for reasons for living. . . . To fight against death amounts to claiming that life has a meaning, to fighting for order and for unity. . . . Every rebel, by the movement which sets him in opposition to the oppressor, therefore pleads for life, undertakes to struggle against servitude, falsehood and terror and affirms . . . that . . . [rebellion] is the only value which can save them from nihilism.[10]

Rebellion may be a clue, then, to the source of meaning for contemporary social man. Given the conscious realization of the *inevitability* of contradictions in his life, he can transcend what would, under these conditions, be a meaningless existence by rebelling against those very conditions. There is meaning, here, in the *act* of rebellion—a continuous protest to what Camus calls "servitude, falsehood and terror." The *act* itself also must be continuous. If the object of the rebellion is alleviated, another object will be created so as to maintain the process.

There is a sociology implicit here. The "creation" of dissonance, to then react to, is oftentimes considered a wholly subjective affair and thus dismissed on sociological grounds. What I would argue is that the institutional structure of society can be the "dissonance creator," and this appears to have special significance in contemporary American society (especially among students and black Americans in many of our large cities). Accordingly, any analysis of social institutions has inherent within it a subject-object framework. Consistent with my argument then, contemporary American society may be characterized by *institutional absurdity* (the "object" aspect), and many members of those same institutions have reached a conscious realization of that absurdity (the "subject" aspect), the end result of which may be a rebellious quest for the non-absurd—for meaning. Inherent in this position, however, is an increasing awareness of the "message of dialectic" which states, in effect, that no definitive solution (in the sense of freedom from contradiction) is ever possible. Thus, meaning becomes related to man's ability for perpetual rebellion or, stated differently, the *act* of rebellion becomes a source of meaning within a social structure of institutional absurdity. These ideas are, again, found in Camus's comments (1954, pp. 26 ff.) concerning rebellion. He notes:

The spirit of revolt can only exist in a society where a theoretic equality conceals great factual inequalities. . . . Man's solidarity is founded upon rebellion and rebellion can only be justified by this solidarity . . . the unhappiness experienced by a single man becomes collective unhappiness. . . . Rebellion is the common ground on which every man bases his . . . values. . . . The most elementary rebellion . . . expresses an aspiration to order . . . the generosity of rebellion . . . refuses injustice without a moment's delay. . . . Rebellion proves . . . that it is the very movement of life and that it cannot be denied without renouncing life. Its purest outburst, on each occasion, gives birth to existence.

There would be, I am certain, very little argument among social scientists concerning the fact that American society today is increasingly cognizant of "theoretic equalities" existing next to "great factual inequalities." Summarily, then, what I am arguing is that this reality is becoming increasingly recognized by members of our society, and their response to it is taking the form of rebellion. Further, these same members of our society are realizing increasingly that the "final synthesis"—the good society—is an unattainable goal. The only route to meaning in such a state of mind (and society) is, accordingly, the *act of reacting* to this situation—that is, the *act* of rebellion.

Given the plausibility of my argument so far, then, a theoretical reorientation concerning our traditional conception of man in society as a "consonance seeker" (cf. Sumner 1959, pp. 5-6; Steiner and Fishbein 1965, p. 3) is in order. It is necessary, in fact, to *reverse that very assumption* concerning social man in favor of the assumption that he is, rather, a dissonance seeker.[11] Man has meaning in society, this perspective would state, to the extent that he has dissonance for himself to react to. In propositional form this might be stated in the following manner: the greater the absurdity of the institutional structure (i.e., the more *obvious* the inherent contradictions), the greater the probability of awareness (the "catalytic" factor), and the greater proportionately (relative to other structures) the *acts* of rebellion (in search of meaning) within that structure.

Lionel Rubinoff offers some *theoretical* justification for the position that man, once aware of the absurdity of his existence, seeks and acquires meaning by way of acts of rebellion. In discussing the works of Sartre, Rubinoff (1968, pp. 161-78) notes Sartre's conception of man as one of wanting "to-be-what-he-is-not" and "not-to-be-what-he-is." From this conception of man, Rubinoff goes on:

We are driven to the realization that every human act is fundamentally ambivalent. . . . [But] as Sartre says, man is freedom. Yet he seeks to escape from freedom through deliberate acts of bad faith . . . man is free because he can choose either to accept his fate with resignation or else to revolt against it. This revolt takes the form of . . . an act through which we come to a lucid consciousness of the human condition. . . . This freedom is the real source of anguish. Anguish is *not* so much the *effect* of freedom as the *consciousness* of it . . . far from being an obstacle to action, anguish is its very condition. [Brackets and emphases mine]

The argument presented earlier in this paper logically concludes this position of Sartre's in the following manner: our freedom is defined in our desire to act *insofar* as we are aware that our acting will not *finally* resolve anything. The anguish that Sartre writes of is due to the *conscious realization* of the latter,[12] in essence, to an awareness of the absurd syndrome; this awareness, coupled with the *act* of rebellion, results in the transcending of the absurd.

It was the body of literature which concerned itself with man's existence being one of absurdity—the plays and novels of Samuel Beckett, the novels and short stories of Camus and Sartre, the philosophical insights of Herbert Marcuse, among others—which gave rise to the theoretical position concerning man in society presented above. I should now like to utilize that same body of literature and its insights as a frame of reference for briefly commenting upon American sociology generally, and, on the basis of those comments, to argue for an action orientation on the part of American sociologists.

THE ABSURDITY OF SOCIOLOGY: TOWARD A TRANSCENDENCE[13]

The causes of contemporary unrest among the student population generally, and sociology graduate and undergraduate students specifically, continues to be debated by sociologists as well as other social scientists. Beckett's comments concerning Pupil Mahood, in his novel *The Unnamable*, perhaps should be thought about when we, in fact, bother to think about what we like to call "our students." Beckett (1965*b*, p. 337 ff.) writes:

Orders, prayers, threats, praise, reproach, reasons. Praise, yes, they gave me to understand I was making progress. Well done, sonny, that will be all for today, run along now back to your dark and see you tomorrow. . . . Pupil Mahood, for the twenty-five thousandth time, what is a mammal? And I'll fall down dead, worn out by the rudiments. But I'll have made progress, they told me so. . . . Mahood, repeat after me, Man is a higher mammal. I couldn't. . . . Frankly, between ourselves, what the hell could it matter . . . that man was this rather than that? . . . But this is my punishment, my crime is my punishment, that's what they judge me for, I expiate vilely, like a pig, dumb, uncomprehending, possessed of no utterance but theirs.

What needs to be emphasized here is *not* a debate as to whether or not Pupil Mahood *is* the contemporary student but, rather, we ought to ask to what extent the contemporary student sees *himself* as a Pupil Mahood. The same commentary and question, I would insist, can apply to militant blacks in our society. In the latter instance, the term "they" in the preceding citation would refer to white society. To the extent that students (and blacks) perceive *themselves* in a Pupil Mahood image, then, they will *act* in order to salvage some semblance of meaning. This interpretation, it would appear, applies especially to students of social behavior. What they are saying, in effect, is they are aware that, hitherto, they have been "possessed of no utterance but theirs" and, accordingly, desire to transcend the social and intellectual nausea which such an awareness brings. A *dialogue* must replace the existing monologue for meaningful understanding to occur, and it must replace it *soon*.

What students of social behavior appear to have said in increasing numbers, concerning their disciplines, is found in the words of Jean-Baptiste Clamence (Camus 1961, pp. 86-87) when he states, "I have never been really able to believe that human affairs were serious matters. I had no idea where the serious might lie, except that it was not in all this I saw around me — which seemed to me merely an amusing game, or tiresome." Students (and many younger sociologists) have, in essence, realized human affairs *are* serious matters — too serious to simply leave to "investigation" with no action. They have gone on record as declaring, again with the judge-penitent (Camus 1961, pp. 131-36): "In philosophy as in politics, I am for any theory that refuses to grant man's innocence and for any practice that treats him as guilty. . . . When we are all guilty, that will be democracy." The plea for action on the part of students and many younger sociologists may be a result of the recognition of "guilt" and an attempt to transcend that result. I am suggesting that we listen very closely to that plea. Toward that end, I would suggest that we exert our social consciences and act, in accordance with the younger vanguard, in initiating necessary changes in this society.

The emphasis of this paper has been on *action*, and that emphasis also applies to initiating necessary societal change. Simply *arguing* for social reforms in society is no longer good enough. As Rubinoff (1968, p. 170) has suggested, stressing the importance of social reform can easily become a way of minimizing our own personal involvements in the life of this society: complaining simply becomes a substitute for positive action. Accordingly, "scientism" can lead to the same position—it can be an apology for nonaction in the sphere of social problems. In discussing the neglect of humanism in American sociology Lee has reached a similar conclusion. Lee (1966, p. 352) writes:

Positivism has done much to stimulate the growth of what might be called weeds in sociology . . . positivism became the rationalization for the abdication of the social responsibilities of the sociologist both as scientist and as human being. Sociology thus became choked . . . with uncritical apologies in the trappings of "science" for what exists in society.

Rubinoff has argued, similarly, that the social scientists' concern with a value-free social science has played the role of making these same scientists morally sterile. In discussing the idea of a "value-free" inquiry Rubinoff (1968, pp. 3-21) notes that:

Under the influence of this rapidly spreading "scientism," social scientists often lose their sensitivity to the absurdity of things—especially as they become the more expert at constructing explanations. They know the causes of order and disorder, and it no longer fills them with outrage that disorder continues to prevail. . . . The argument that the social sciences are value-free *because* they are scientific falls to the possibility that they have become scientific *in order to be* value-free. Suspicion mounts that the driving force of scientism is now fed by the unconscious need to escape from the responsibility of taking a moral stand and of evaluating the human condition from a moral point of view. [Emphasis in the original][14]

The same author concludes (Rubinoff 1968, p. 21) that there is nothing more dangerous to the health of society than to be influenced by uncritically accepted values and that is precisely what follows, in his opinion, from the dogma that the social sciences are value free. We must, in the words of Nietzsche (1967, p. 254), shoot at existing morality and values. It is only then that the way can be paved for a new system of values and morality to enter. The sociologist of today would do well to move rapidly toward the conscious realization of the inherent contradictions in his society and, accordingly, to take his direction from those *already at that stage*—many of whom are or, increasingly, *were* his students. In effect, transcending our own absurdity lies in joining the action—not in simply "investigating" it.

A RADICAL EXISTENTIAL TYPOLOGY OF MEANING[15]

A review of meaning acquisition, based upon the thesis of this paper, might reveal four general types:

1. The "dissonance creators." This is the type I would refer to as the "radical existential sociologists." These are the social thinkers (students and too few professors!) who have recognized the absurdity of the social structure and who *continue to act with full awareness* of the absurd. Their action, thus, results in transcending the absurd and functions to supply them with meaning. The "dissonance creators" are the ones on the "front lines," so to speak. They are the individuals who see their *act of rebellion* as the only source of meaning and who, accordingly, refuse to relinquish that source of meaning.

2. The "consonance seekers." Generally the young, concerned, reform-oriented, social science types. Their "reform-orientation" tends to make them minimally pragmatic (vis-à-vis the realization of reform), but they are also characterized by a certain amount of confusion coupled with hopefulness. They are hopeful, that is, of implementing their reforms but confused when "all remains basically the same." Accordingly, their action, without recognition or awareness of the absurdity of social life, characterizes them as "searchers for meaning." As I implied earlier in this paper, this "type," by not transcending the absurd, continuously creates it by attempting to achieve consonance. The participants in "the New Politics" (the McCarthy movement, the followers of the late Robert Kennedy, etc.), the more radical social workers, and the Saul Alinsky organization-type fall for the most part within this group.

3. The "defeatist-oriented." Refers to those who have recognized the absurdity of social life but who have failed to act and, accordingly, have failed to transcend that absurdity. The recognition of the absurd results, rather, in a retreat or, perhaps, an escape from reality. There is little hope, here, for any meaning. Thus, this type is characterized by a continuous struggle to survive in the face of this hopelessness. Subcultures, such as hippies, artists, and drug addicts, as well as the high-risk suicide-prone, are also to be found in this group. It is here that the characters in the novels and short stories of Camus, Sartre, Franz Kafka, and others are found.[16] These are the individuals who, once the recognition and awareness of the absurd is realized, are characterized by apathy and, oftentimes, withdrawal.

4. The "academic-traditional." Here are located the individuals, usually social scientists, who are neither aware of the absurdity of their existence nor do they act on anything. They consist of the ex-

tremely pragmatic, self-admitted value-neutral individuals who see the acquisition of what they call "knowledge for knowledge's sake" as their *only* goal. They are the people who have built what can be called a "false security" around their knowledge seeking. It is "false" because their knowledge is only temporary. Once presented, it simply awaits refutation, and the process begins anew. They are, in effect, valueless—they are the social scientists who refuse, on scientific grounds, to even *discuss* the concept of meaning. They are easily recognized among our ranks, for they are the "professionals" who teach seminars on social conflict[17] and then retire to do their science.

SUMMARY AND CONCLUSIONS

I began this itinerary through the literature of the absurd by commenting, in a general sense, upon what that body of literature portrayed. Essentially, I attempted to identify the theme of the absurd as it is manifested in existentialism, the theater of the absurd, and dialectical thought. I concluded that this body of ideas is useful in calling our attention *anew* to the subject-object relationship in any social analysis. Accordingly, the literature of the absurd is useful in forcing us to reexamine our basic presuppositions.

I then proceeded to identify a sociology which may be inherent in this framework. After arguing that a conscious *awareness* of the absurd was a *catalyst* to the acquisition of meaning, I proceeded to make the case that meaning may be found in *continual rebellion* in the face of absurdity. The process, it was noted, *must* be continuous in that, coincidental with the awareness mentioned above, is the realization that no synthesis—no final resolution—is ever possible. The sociology here is in conceptualizing the absurdity as an effect of institutions—what I referred to as "institutional absurdity." It remains for research to indicate the nature of this institutionalization—the social evolutionary processes involved in its creation, especially in American society. Along these lines I suggested a reorientation toward our conception of man in society; namely, that he might better be conceptualized as a dissonance seeker, while his *reaction* to the dissonance he finds is, simultaneously, his source of meaning. This reaction, in terms of rebellion, accordingly is how he transcends his institutional absurdity—how he transcends the "absurd syndrome." It is important to note that man does not *solve* the problem of his absurd existence— he only *transcends* it. In essence, meaning may be a quest for the consciously realized unattainable.[18]

Finally, I attempted to apply the absurdity framework to sociology and, as expected, found a "goodness of fit." In this context I suggested that students as well as blacks in contemporary American society have achieved the *conscious realization state* noted above. Further, I implied that they have reached that stage as a result of what we as *teachers,* or as *whites,* have passed on to them. Students and blacks, then, may be *acting* so as not to "die" — acting, that is, to acquire meaning. I then suggested we follow their lead and thus attempt to transcend our own sociological-scientific absurdity. In essence, we have failed to understand a portion of our subject matter — students and blacks — possibly because we have not yet *discovered* and, thus, have not *shared* their meaning system.

I anticipate that the major complaint against my inquiry, if the sociological establishment is true to form, will be that it is too subjective, too impressionistic to be taken seriously. Perhaps. Grant me, however, that "perhaps," and we may well have the germ of a radical sociology[19] — a sociology that must begin with an immediate reorientation or face the possibility of extinction. Refuse to grant that "perhaps" and we can comfortably return to our towers and continue to spin plausible but irrelevant theory which tries, but never succeeds, in "telling it like it really is."

NOTES

1. Thus, man's freedom does not lie only in his *choice* to act (contrary to the views of Sartre and Camus) nor in his *action alone* but, rather, in his choosing to act while realizing his action is relatively inconsequential.

2. Probably the clearest examples of theater of the absurd are the plays of Samuel Beckett. In addition to the work cited in this paper, Beckett's plays *Waiting For Godot, Endgame,* and *Krapp's Last Tape* are all indicative of the theme of the absurd. That the work of Beckett is increasingly getting more attention might be evidenced in the fact that Samuel Beckett won the 1969 Nobel Prize for Literature. Interestingly, Beckett refused both the award and the $73,000 which accompanies it.

3. As will be indicated later, it is the *theoretical perspective* offered by dialectical thought which contributes to the framework of the absurd. I am referring, of course, to the perspective that every thesis contains the seeds of its own negation and not to the specific manner in which this perspective has been applied by such classical dialecticians as Hegel and Marx.

4. It is my suspicion that any comprehensive theory of order or change or, indeed, any *social theory* at all, is *inherently* dialectical in construct. This, however, is subject matter for another paper.

5. The rejection here, of *Hegel's use* of dialectic, should be obvious.

6. As opposed to *psychological* social psychology.

7. Some concern has been expressed, via an anonymous communique, that I have failed to note the "profound impact on American sociology" of such "leading theorists" as Dewey, Mead, Cooley, Blumer, and Schutz vis-à-vis subject-object relations. That these seminal theorists concerned themselves with subject-object relations, there is certainly no argument. That they had a "profound impact on American sociology," however, is debatable. If one uses, for example, textbooks published in social psychology and/or articles in our leading professional journals (*American Sociological Review* and

American Journal of Sociology) as a criterion, the paucity of discussion devoted to the works of Dewey, Mead, Cooley, and Blumer is striking. Similarly, the work of Schutz could hardly be classified in the category of having a "profound impact on American sociology." I should mention that the recent article by Norman K. Denzin ("Symbolic Interactionism and Ethnomethodology: A Proposed Synthesis." *American Sociological Review* 34, no. 6 [December 1969]:922-34) is a refreshing exception to this.

8. Dialectical thought is once again useful along these lines. Marcuse (1968, p. viii), sounding a great deal like Max Weber, has noted that the legacy of dialectical thought is that truth can be determined *only* in the subject-object totality. Further, he states: "All facts embody the knower as well as the doer: they continuously translate the past into the present. The objects thus 'contain' subjectivity in their very structure."

9. The theme concerning existence as suffering and despair, as well as the blatant absurdities of life, are portrayed lucidly in the following passage from Beckett (1965*b*, p. 406): "They love each other, marry, in order to love each other better, more conveniently, he goes to the wars, he dies at the wars, she weeps, with emotion, at having loved him, yep, marries again, in order to love again, more conveniently again, they love each other, you love as many times as necessary, as necessary in order to be happy, he comes back, the other comes back, from the wars, he didn't die at the wars after all, she goes to the station, to meet him, he dies in the train, of emotion, at the thought of seeing her again, having her again, she weeps, weeps again, with emotion again, at having lost him again, yep, goes back to the house, he's dead, the other is dead, the mother-in-law takes him down, he hanged himself, with emotion, at the thought of losing her, she weeps, weeps louder, at having loved him, at having lost him, there's a story for you, that was to teach me the nature of emotion, that's called emotion, what emotion can do, well well, so that's emotion, that's love [*sic*]."

10. Camus's work, *The Rebel*, was a reaction to nihilism generally and Nietzsche's nihilism in particular. Along these lines, I would mention that Nietzsche's nihilism may have been traditionally misunderstood. In his *Twilight of the Idols* (1964, p. 472), Nietzsche concludes a section with the moral that "morality must be shot at." He argues, in effect, that this is the only way we can ever change existing values. His argument has a great deal of affinity to Camus's as stated in the latter's *The Rebel*. [The brackets and emphases above are mine]

11. I do not wish to get involved in the obvious semantic difficulty here concerning "dissonance," then, becoming "consonance." It would, at this point only confuse the discussion. It may only be noted in passing that other sociologists have acknowledged that nonconsonance is an integral aspect of social man. Lee (1966, p. 31), for example, has noted: "An actually 'integrated' person, in the sense of a person organized at all times in terms of one set of values, is either a fiction or a candidate for confinement in a mental hospital. On the contrary, individual inconsistency and flexibility among social roles . . . are hallmarks for what passes in society for 'maturity.' "

12. The conscious realization that our acts will never resolve anything is, as I read it, the real "message" of the absurd literature.

13. Once again, I acknowledge conversations I have had with radical students on various university campuses and a special note of acknowledgment, here, should go to the radical and black caucus members of the American Sociological Association.

14. In an interesting footnote, Rubinoff (1968, p. 223, n. 5), in commenting on studying racism phenomenologically, states: "Men do not believe in racism because it is scientifically grounded; they rather endowed it with scientific credibility *in order* to believe in it." (Emphasis in the original)

15. I am indebted to Lou Patler and Walda Fishman for their help in conceptualizing these categories of meaning. It has been argued that my "sympathy for students and blacks" and my argument "in favor of action" has led me to a selective bias portrayed in the above categorization. It should be emphasized that this typology is a result of my attempt to *understand the overt social action of students and blacks.* The fact that I agree or disagree with what I see to be their perspective is, at this point, *irrelevant.* As

I clearly wish to indicate, the main intention of this typology is to summarize the thesis of the paper.

16. The reader is reminded of my refusal to accept existential thought and ideas as definitive in developing my conception of meaning. Rather, I argued this literature is useful heuristically.

17. I have been accused, in an anonymous communication, of either choosing to neglect or of being unaware of the "conflict theorists" tradition in sociology ("e.g., Gumplowicz, Coser, Simmel, etc."). The reader is assured that the former is in fact the case. Indeed, my *awareness* of this "conflict tradition in sociology" is what dictated my choosing to *neglect it.* As any careful reading of this "school" in sociology would demonstrate, none of the "conflict theorists" address themselves specifically to the *issues raised in this paper.*

18. In other words, there may be meaning in the state of anomie (see Durkheim 1963, p. 248).

19. It would at least be refreshing for a change to entertain the term "radical sociology" as something other than a contradiction in terms!

REFERENCES

Beckett, Samuel. 1965a. "Malone Dies." In *Three Novels by Samuel Beckett.* New York: Grove.

———.1965b. "The Unnamable." In *Three Novels by Samuel Beckett.* New York: Grove.

Camus, Albert. 1946. *The Stranger.* New York: Vintage.

———.1954. *The Rebel.* New York: Knopf.

———.1961. *The Fall.* New York: Knopf.

Carruth, Hayden. 1964. "Introduction." In *Nausea,* by Jean-Paul Sartre. Translated by Lloyd Alexander. New York: New Directions.

Durkheim, Emile. 1963. *Suicide.* Glencoe, Ill.: Free Press.

Hughes, H. Stuart. 1961. *Consciousness and Society.* New York: Vintage.

Lee, Alfred McClung. 1966. *Multivalent Man.* New York: Braziller.

Madge, Charles. 1964. *Society in the Mind: Element of Social Eidos.* New York: Free Press.

Marcuse, Herbert. 1968. *Reason and Revolution: Hegel and the Rise of Social Theory.* Boston: Beacon.

Nietzsche, Friedrich. 1967. *The Will to Power.* New York: Random House.

———.1964. "Twilight of the Idols or, How One Philosophizes with a Hammer." In *The Portable Nietzsche,* by Walter Kaufmann. Translated by Walter Kaufmann. New York: Viking.

Rubinoff, Lionel. 1968. *The Pornography of Power.* Chicago: Quadrangle.

Sartre, Jean-Paul. 1956. *Being and Nothingness.* New York: Philosophical Library

———.1964. *Nausea.* New York: New Directions.

Simmel, Georg. 1963. "How Is Society Possible?" In *Philosophy of the Social Sciences. A Reader,* edited by Maurice Natanson. New York: Random House.

Steiner, Ivan D., and M. Fishbein (eds.). 1965. *Current Studies in Social Psychology.* New York: Holt, Rinehart & Winston.

Sumner, William Graham. 1959. *Folkways*. New York: Dover.
Tiryakian, Edward. 1965. "Existential Phenomenology and the Sociological Tradition." *American Sociological Review* 30 (October):674-88.

BIBLIOGRAPHY

Adler, Franz. "The Social Thought of Jean-Paul Sartre." *American Journal of Sociology* 55 (1949): 284-94.

Bain, Read. "Poetry and Social Research." *Sociology and Social Research* 12 (1927): 35-49.

Baumann, Bedřich. "George H. Mead and Luigi Pirandello: Some Parallels between the Theoretical and Artistic Presentation of the Social Role Concept." *Social Research* 34 (1967): 563-607.

Bennetton, Norman A. "Social Thought of Emile Zola." *Sociology and Social Research* 13 (1929): 366-77.

Blumberg, Paul. "Sociology and Social Literature: Work Alienation in the Plays of Arthur Miller." *American Quarterly* 21 (1969): 291-310.

Bogardus, Emory S. "Social Distance in Fiction." *Sociology and Social Research* 14 (1930): 174-80.

_____."Social Distance in Shakespeare." *Sociology and Social Research* 18 (1933): 66-73.

_____."Social Distance in Greek Drama." *Sociology and Social Research* 33 (1949): 291-95.

_____."Social Distance in Poetry." *Sociology and Social Research* 36 (1951): 40-47.

Coser, Lewis A. *Sociology through Literature*. Englewood Cliffs, N.J.: Prentice-Hall, 1963.

Daykin, Walter L. "Social Thought in Negro Novels." *Sociology and Social Research* 19 (1935): 247-52.

_____."Attitudes in Negro Novels." *Sociology and Social Research* 20 (1935): 152-60.

Dealey, James Q. "Plato's Course in Social Problems." *Sociology and Social Research* 12 (1928): 203-7.

Eberts, Paul R., and Witton, Ronald A. "Recall from Anecdote: Alexis de Tocqueville and the Morphogenesis of America." *American Sociological Review* 35 (1970): 1081-97.

Fairbanks, Arthur. "Aristophanes as a Student of Society." *American Journal of Sociology* 8 (1903): 655-66.

Fernandez, Ronald. "Dostoyevsky, Traditional Domination, and Cognitive Dissonance." *Social Forces* 49 (1970): 299-303.

Gouldner, Alvin W. *Enter Plato: Classical Greece and the Origins of Social Theory*. New York: Basic Books, 1965.

Granell, Eugenio Fernandez. "Social Perspectives of Picasso's 'Guernica.' " Doctoral dissertation, New School for Social Research, 1967.

Keim, Margaret Laton. "The Chinese as Portrayed in the Works of Bret Harte: A Study of Race Relations." *Sociology and Social Research* 25 (1941): 441-50.

Keller, Albert G. "Sociology and Homer." *American Journal of Sociology* 9 (1903): 37-45.

Leighninger, Robert D. "Scott Fitzgerald's Theory of Anomia: The Novelist as Sociological Theorist." Paper presented at the annual meeting of the American Sociological Association, August 31, 1972.

Lin, Mousheng Hsitien. "Confucius on Interpersonal Relations." *Psychiatry* 2 (1939): 475-81.

Mayer, Frederick. "Whitman's Social Philosophy." *Sociology and Social Research* 33 (1949): 275-78.

Mouillaud, Genviève. "The Sociology of Stendhal's Novels: Preliminary Research." *International Social Science Journal* 19 (1967): 581-98.

Nash, Russell W. "Stereotypes and Social Types in Ellison's *Invisible Man*." *The Sociological Quarterly* 6 (1965): 349-60.

Porterfield, Austin L. "Some Uses of Literature in Teaching Sociology." *Sociology and Social Research* 41 (1957): 421-26.

Ratcliffe, S.K. "Sociology in the English Novel." *The Sociological Review* 3 (1910): 126-36.

Riemer, Svend. "Damon Runyon—Philosopher of City Life." *Social Forces* 25 (1947): 402-5.

Schutz, Alfred. "Don Quixote and the Problem of Reality." In *Collected Papers, Vol. II: Studies in Social Theory*, edited by Arvid Brodersen. The Hague: Martinus Nijhoff, 1964, pp. 135-58.

Segal, Alan. "Portnoy's Complaint and the Sociology of Literature." *British Journal of Sociology* 22 (1971): 257-68.

Stack, George J. "Nietzsche and the Laws of Manu." *Sociology and Social Research* 51 (1966): 94-106.

Truzzi, Marcello, and Morris, Scot. "Sherlock Holmes as a Social Scientist." *Psychology Today* 5 (December 1971): 62-64, 85-86.

Tyree, Andrea, et al. "The Dickensian Occupational Structure." *Sociological Inquiry* 41 (1971): 95-105.

Weitman, Sasha Reinhard. "The Sociological Theme of Tocqueville's *The Old Regime and the Revolution*." *Social Research* 33 (1966): 389-406.

Wilson, Robert N. "Samuel Beckett: The Social Psychology of Emptiness." *Journal of Social Issues* 20 (1964): 62-70.